MW00712751

interchange

FIFTH EDITION

intro

Student's Book

Jack C. Richards

WITH ONLINE SELF-STUDY

CAMBRIDGE
UNIVERSITY PRESS

CAMBRIDGE
UNIVERSITY PRESS

University Printing House, Cambridge CB2 8BS, United Kingdom

One Liberty Plaza, 20th Floor, New York, NY 10006, USA

477 Williamstown Road, Port Melbourne, VIC 3207, Australia

314–321, 3rd Floor, Plot 3, Splendor Forum, Jasola District Centre, New Delhi – 110025, India

79 Anson Road, #06–04/06, Singapore 079906

Cambridge University Press is part of the University of Cambridge.

It furthers the University's mission by disseminating knowledge in the pursuit of education, learning and research at the highest international levels of excellence.

www.cambridge.org
Information on this title: www.cambridge.org/9781316623855

© Cambridge University Press 2006, 2017

This publication is in copyright. Subject to statutory exception and to the provisions of relevant collective licensing agreements, no reproduction of any part may take place without the written permission of Cambridge University Press.

First published 2006
Second edition 2013

20 19 18 17 16 15 14

Printed in Poland by Opolgraf

A catalogue record for this publication is available from the British Library

ISBN	9781316620113	Intro Student's Book with Online Self-Study
ISBN	9781316620120	Intro Student's Book A with Online Self-Study
ISBN	9781316620137	Intro Student's Book B with Online Self-Study
ISBN	9781316620144	Intro Student's Book with Online Self-Study and Online Workbook
ISBN	9781316620151	Intro Student's Book A with Online Self-Study and Online Workbook
ISBN	9781316620168	Intro Student's Book B with Online Self-Study and Online Workbook
ISBN	9781316622377	Intro Workbook
ISBN	9781316622391	Intro Workbook A
ISBN	9781316622407	Intro Workbook B
ISBN	9781316622414	Intro Teacher's Edition with Complete Assessment Program
ISBN	9781316622216	Intro Class Audio CDs
ISBN	9781316623855	Intro Full Contact with Online Self-Study
ISBN	9781316623862	Intro Full Contact A with Online Self-Study
ISBN	9781316623879	Intro Full Contact B with Online Self-Study
ISBN	9781108403047	Presentation Plus Intro

Additional resources for this publication at www.cambridge.org/interchange

Cambridge University Press has no responsibility for the persistence or accuracy of URLs for external or third-party internet websites referred to in this publication, and does not guarantee that any content on such websites is, or will remain, accurate or appropriate. Information regarding prices, travel timetables, and other factual information given in this work is correct at the time of first printing but Cambridge University Press does not guarantee the accuracy of such information thereafter.

Informed by teachers

Teachers from all over the world helped develop *Interchange Fifth Edition*. They looked at everything – from the color of the designs to the topics in the conversations – in order to make sure that this course will work in the classroom. We heard from 1,500 teachers in:

- Surveys
- Focus Groups
- In-Depth Reviews

We appreciate the help and input from everyone. In particular, we'd like to give the following people our special thanks:

Jader Franceschi, **Actúa Idiomas,** Bento Gonçalves, Rio Grande do Sul, Brazil

Juliana Dos Santos Voltan Costa, **Actus Idiomas,** São Paulo, Brazil

Ella Osorio, **Angelo State University,** San Angelo, TX, US

Mary Hunter, **Angelo State University,** San Angelo, TX, US

Mario César González, **Angloamericano de Monterrey, SC,** Monterrey, Mexico

Samantha Shipman, **Auburn High School,** Auburn, AL, US

Linda, **Bernick Language School,** Radford, VA, US

Dave Lowrance, **Bethesda University of California,** Yorba Linda, CA, US

Tajbakhsh Hosseini, **Bezmialem Vakif University,** Istanbul, Turkey

Dilek Gercek, **Bil English,** Izmir, Turkey

erkan kolat, **Biruni University, ELT,** Istanbul, Turkey

Nika Gutkowska, **Bluedata International,** New York, NY, US

Daniel Alcocer Gómez, **Cecati 92,** Guadalupe, Nuevo León, Mexico

Samantha Webb, **Central Middle School,** Milton-Freewater, OR, US

Verónica Salgado, **Centro Anglo Americano,** Cuernavaca, Mexico

Ana Rivadeneira Martínez and Georgia P. de Machuca, **Centro de Educación Continua – Universidad Politécnica del Ecuador,** Quito, Ecuador

Anderson Francisco Guimerães Maia, **Centro Cultural Brasil Estados Unidos,** Belém, Brazil

Rosana Mariano, **Centro Paula Souza,** São Paulo, Brazil

Carlos de la Paz Arroyo, Teresa Noemí Parra Alarcón, Gilberto Bastida Gaytan, Manuel Esquivel Román, and Rosa Cepeda Tapia, **Centro Universitario Angloamericano,** Cuernavaca, Morelos, Mexico

Antonio Almeida, **CETEC,** Morelos, Mexico

Cinthia Ferreira, **Cinthia Ferreira Languages Services,** Toronto, ON, Canada

Phil Thomas and Sérgio Sanchez, **CLS Canadian Language School,** São Paulo, Brazil

Celia Concannon, **Cochise College,** Nogales, AZ, US

Maria do Carmo Rocha and CAOP English team, **Colégio Arquidiocesano Ouro Preto – Unidade Cônego Paulo Dilascio,** Ouro Preto, Brazil

Kim Rodriguez, **College of Charleston North,** Charleston, SC, US

Jesús Leza Alvarado, **Coparmex English Institute,** Monterrey, Mexico

John Partain, **Cortazar,** Guanajuato, Mexico

Alexander Palencia Navas, **Cursos de Lenguas, Universidad del Atlántico,** Barranquilla, Colombia

Kenneth Johan Gerardo Steenhuisen Cera, Melfi Osvaldo Guzman Triana, and Carlos Alberto Algarín Jiminez, **Cursos de Lenguas Extranjeras Universidad del Atlantico,** Barranquilla, Colombia

Jane P Kerford, **East Los Angeles College,** Pasadena, CA, US

Daniela, **East Village,** Campinas, São Paulo

Rosalva Camacho Orduño, **Easy English for Groups S.A. de C.V.,** Monterrey, Nuevo León, Mexico

Adonis Gimenez Fusetti, **Easy Way Idiomas,** Ibiúna, Brazil

Eileen Thompson, **Edison Community College,** Piqua, OH, US

Ahminne Handeri O.L Froede, **Englishouse escola de idiomas,** Teófilo Otoni, Brazil

Ana Luz Delgado-Izazola, **Escuela Nacional Preparatoria 5, UNAM,** Mexico City, Mexico

Nancy Alarcón Mendoza, **Facultad de Estudios Superiores Zaragoza, UNAM,** Mexico City, Mexico

Marcilio N. Barros, **Fast English USA,** Campinas, São Paulo, Brazil

Greta Douthat, **FCI Ashland,** Ashland, KY, US

Carlos Lizárraga González, **Grupo Educativo Anglo Americano, S.C.,** Mexico City, Mexico

Hugo Fernando Alcántar Valle, **Instituto Politécnico Nacional, Escuela Superior de Comercio y Administración-Unidad Santotomás, Celex Esca Santo Tomás,** Mexico City, Mexico

Sueli Nascimento, **Instituto Superior de Educação do Rio de Janeiro,** Rio de Janeiro, Brazil

Elsa F Monteverde, **International Academic Services,** Miami, FL, US

Laura Anand, **Irvine Adult School,** Irvine, CA, US

Prof. Marli T. Fernandes (principal) and Prof. Dr. Jefferson J. Fernandes (pedagogue), **Jefferson Idiomass,** São Paulo, Brazil

Herman Bartelen, **Kanda Gaigo Gakuin,** Tokyo, Japan

Cassia Silva, **Key Languages,** Key Biscayne, FL, US

Sister Mary Hope, **Kyoto Notre Dame Joshi Gakuin,** Kyoto, Japan

Nate Freedman, **LAL Language Centres,** Boston, MA, US

Richard Janzen, **Langley Secondary School,** Abbotsford, BC, Canada

Christina Abel Gabardo, **Language House,** Campo Largo, Brazil

Ivonne Castro, **Learn English International,** Cali, Colombia

Julio Cesar Maciel Rodrigues, **Liberty Centro de Línguas,** São Paulo, Brazil

Ann Gibson, **Maynard High School,** Maynard, MA, US

Martin Darling, **Meiji Gakuin Daigaku,** Tokyo, Japan

Dax Thomas, **Meiji Gakuin Daigaku,** Yokohama, Kanagawa, Japan

Derya Budak, **Mevlana University,** Konya, Turkey

B Sullivan, **Miami Valley Career Technical Center International Program,** Dayton, OH, US

Julio Velazquez, **Milo Language Center,** Weston, FL, US

Daiane Siqueira da Silva, Luiz Carlos Buontempo, Marlete Avelina de Oliveira Cunha, Marcos Paulo Segatti, Morgana Eveline de Oliveira, Nadia Lia Gino Alo, and Paul Hyde Budgen, **New Interchange-Escola de Idiomas,** São Paulo, Brazil

Patrícia França Furtado da Costa, Juiz de Fora, Brazil Patricia Servín

Chris Pollard, **North West Regional College SK,** North Battleford, SK, Canada

Olga Amy, **Notre Dame High School,** Red Deer, Canada

Amy Garrett, **Ouachita Baptist University,** Arkadelphia, AR, US

Mervin Curry, **Palm Beach State College,** Boca Raton, FL, US

Julie Barros, **Quality English Studio,** Guarulhos, São Paulo, Brazil

Teodoro González Saldaña and Jesús Monserrrta Mata Franco, **Race Idiomas,** Mexico City, Mexico

Autumn Westphal and Noga La`or, **Rennert International,** New York, NY, US

Antonio Gallo and Javy Palau, **Rigby Idiomas,** Monterrey, Mexico Tatiane Gabriela Sperb do Nascimento, **Right Way,** Igrejinha, Brazil

Mustafa Akgül, **Selahaddin Eyyubi Universitesi,** Diyarbakır, Turkey

James Drury M. Fonseca, **Senac Idiomas Fortaleza,** Fortaleza, Ceara, Brazil

Manoel Fialho S Neto, **Senac – PE,** Recife, Brazil

Jane Imber, **Small World,** Lawrence, KS, US

Tony Torres, **South Texas College,** McAllen, TX, US

Janet Rose, **Tennessee Foreign Language Institute,** College Grove, TN, US

Todd Enslen, **Tohoku University,** Sendai, Miyagi, Japan

Daniel Murray, **Torrance Adult School,** Torrance, CA, US

Juan Manuel Pulido Mendoza, **Universidad del Atlántico,** Barranquilla, Colombia

Juan Carlos Vargas Millán, **Universidad Libre Seccional Cali,** Cali (Valle del Cauca), Colombia

Carmen Cecilia Llanos Ospina, **Universidad Libre Seccional Cali,** Cali, Colombia

Jorge Noriega Zenteno, **Universidad Politécnica del Valle de México,** Estado de México, Mexico

Aimee Natasha Holguin S., **Universidad Politécnica del Valle de México UPVM,** Tultitlàn Estado de México, Mexico

Christian Selene Bernal Barraza, **UPVM Universidad Politécnica del Valle de México,** Ecatepec, Mexico

Lizeth Ramos Acosta, **Universidad Santiago de Cali,** Cali, Colombia

Silvana Dushku, **University of Illinois Champaign,** IL, US

Deirdre McMurtry, **University of Nebraska – Omaha,** Omaha, NE, US

Jason E Mower, **University of Utah,** Salt Lake City, UT, US

Paul Chugg, **Vanguard Taylor Language Institute,** Edmonton, Alberta, Canada

Henry Mulak, **Varsity Tutors,** Los Angeles, CA, US

Shirlei Strucker Calgaro and Hugo Guilherme Karrer, **VIP Centro de Idiomas,** Panambi, Rio Grande do Sul, Brazil

Eleanor Kelly, **Waseda Daigaku Extension Centre,** Tokyo, Japan

Sherry Ashworth, **Wichita State University,** Wichita, KS, US

Laine Bourdene, **William Carey University,** Hattiesburg, MS, US

Serap Aydın, Istanbul, Turkey

Liliana Covino, Guarulhos, Brazil

Yannuarys Jiménez, Barranquilla, Colombia

Juliana Morais Pazzini, Toronto, ON, Canada

Marlon Sanches, Montreal, Canada

Additional content contributed by Kenna Bourke, Inara Couto, Nic Harris, Greg Manin, Ashleigh Martinez, Laura McKenzie, Paul McIntyre, Clara Prado, Lynne Robertson, Mari Vargo, Theo Walker, and Maria Lucia Zaorob.

Classroom Language Teacher instructions

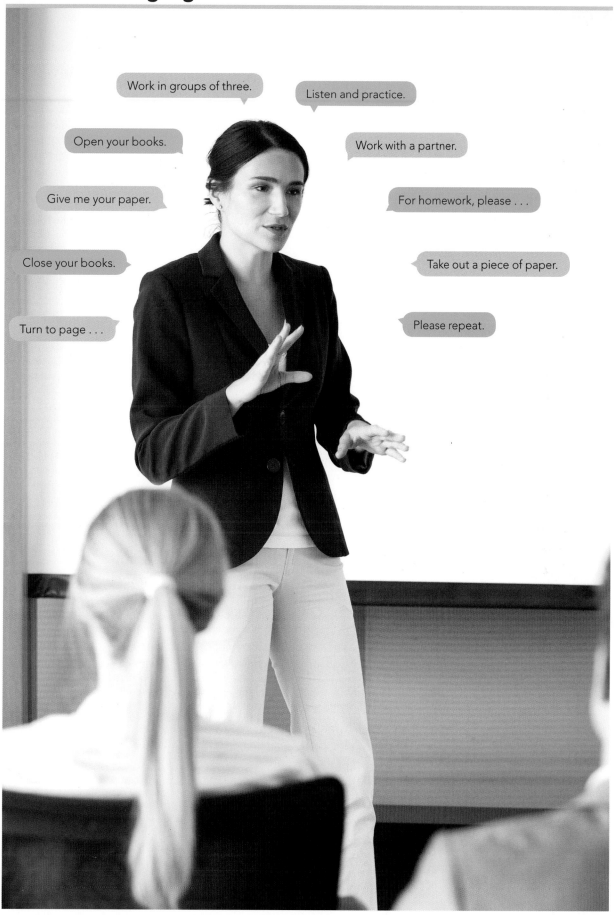

Plan of Intro Book

Titles/Topics	Speaking	Grammar
UNIT 1 PAGES 2–7		
What's your name? Alphabet; greetings and leave-takings; names and titles of address; numbers 0–10, phone numbers, and email addresses	Introducing yourself and friends; saying hello and good-bye; asking for names and phone numbers	Possessive adjectives *my*, *your*, *his*, *her*; the verb *be*; affirmative statements and contractions
UNIT 2 PAGES 8–13		
Where are my keys? Possessions, classroom objects, personal items, and locations in a room	Naming objects; asking for and giving the locations of objects	Articles *a*, *an*, and *the*; *this/these*, *it/they*; plurals; yes/no and *where* questions with *be*; prepositions of place: *in*, *in front of*, *behind*, *on*, *next to*, and *under*
PROGRESS CHECK PAGES 14–15		
UNIT 3 PAGES 16–21		
Where are you from? Cities and countries; adjectives of personality and appearance; numbers 11–103 and ages	Talking about cities and countries; asking for and giving information about place of origin, nationality, first language, and age; describing people	The verb *be*: affirmative and negative statements, yes/no questions, short answers, and Wh-questions
UNIT 4 PAGES 22–27		
Is this coat yours? Clothing; colors; weather and seasons	Asking about and describing clothing and colors; talking about the weather and seasons; finding the owners of objects	Possessives: adjectives *our* and *their*, pronouns, names, and *whose*; present continuous statements and yes/no questions; conjunctions *and*, *but*, and *so*; placement of adjectives before nouns
PROGRESS CHECK PAGES 28–29		
UNIT 5 PAGES 30–35		
What time is it? Clock time; times of the day; everyday activities	Asking for and telling time; asking about and describing current activities	Time expressions: *o'clock*, A.M., P.M., *noon*, *midnight*, *in the morning/afternoon/evening*, *at 7:00/night/midnight*; present continuous Wh-questions
UNIT 6 PAGES 36–41		
I ride my bike to school. Transportation; family relationships; daily routines; days of the week	Asking for and giving information about how people go to work or school; talking about family members; describing daily and weekly routines	Simple present statements with regular and irregular verbs; simple present yes/no and Wh-questions; time expressions: *early*, *late*, *every day*, *on Sundays/weekends/weekdays*
PROGRESS CHECK PAGES 42–43		
UNIT 7 PAGES 44–49		
Does it have a view? Houses and apartments; rooms; furniture	Asking about and describing houses and apartments; talking about the furniture in a room	Simple present short answers; *there is*, *there are*; *there's no*, *there isn't a*, *there are no*, *there aren't any*
UNIT 8 PAGES 50–55		
Where do you work? Jobs and workplaces	Asking for and giving information about work; giving opinions about jobs; describing workday routines	Simple present Wh-questions with *do* and *does*; placement of adjectives after *be* and before nouns
PROGRESS CHECK PAGES 56–57		

Pronunciation/Listening	Writing/Reading	Interchange Activity
Linked sounds Listening for the spelling of names, phone numbers, and email addresses	Writing a list of names, phone numbers, and email addresses	"Celebrity classmates": Introducing yourself to new people PAGE 114
Plural -s endings Listening for the locations of objects	Writing the locations of objects	"Find the differences": Comparing two pictures of a room PAGE 115
Syllable stress Listening for countries, cities, and languages; listening to descriptions of people	Writing questions requesting personal information	"Let's talk!": Finding out more about your classmates PAGE 118
The letters s and sh Listening for descriptions of clothing and colors	Writing questions about what people are wearing	"Celebrity fashions": Describing celebrities' clothing PAGES 116–117
Rising and falling intonation Listening for times of the day; listening to identify people's actions	Writing times of the day "Message Me!": Reading an online chat between two friends	"What's wrong with this picture?": Describing what's wrong with a picture PAGE 119
Third-person singular -s endings Listening for activities and days of the week	Writing about your weekly routine "What's Your Schedule Like?": Reading about someone's daily schedule	"Class survey": Finding out more about classmates' habits and routines PAGE 120
Words with th Listening to descriptions of homes; listening to people shop for furniture	Writing about your dream home "Unique Hotels": Reading about two interesting hotels	"Find the differences": Comparing two apartments PAGE 121
Reduction of do Listening to people describe their jobs	Writing about jobs "Dream Jobs": Reading about two unusual jobs	"The perfect job": Figuring out what job is right for you PAGE 122

Titles/Topics	Speaking	Grammar

1 What's your name?

- ▶ Say hello and make introductions
- ▶ Say good-bye and exchange contact information

1 CONVERSATION My name is Joshua Brown.

▶ **A** Listen and practice.

Joshua	Hello. My name is Joshua Brown.
Isabella	Hi. My name is Isabella Martins.
Joshua	It's nice to meet you, Isabella.
Isabella	Nice to meet you, too.
Joshua	I'm sorry. What's your last name again?
Isabella	It's Martins.

First names	Last names
↓	↓
Joshua	Brown
Isabella	Martins

B PAIR WORK Introduce yourself to your partner.

2 SNAPSHOT

▶ Listen and practice.

Names and nicknames

Nicholas (Nick)	Madison (Maddie)	Jennifer (Jen)
Emily (Em)	Joshua (Josh)	Isabella (Izzy)
Michael (Mike)	William (Will)	Elizabeth (Liz)

Nicholas Hoult

Jennifer Lawrence

What are some popular names and nicknames in your country?
Do you have a nickname? What is it?

3 GRAMMAR FOCUS

▶ My, your, his, her

What's **your** name?	**My** name's Carlos.	What**'s** = What **is**
What's **his** name?	**His** name's Joshua.	
What's **her** name?	**Her** name's Isabella.	

GRAMMAR PLUS *see page 132*

A Complete the conversations. Use *my*, *your*, *his*, or *her*.

1. A: Hello. What's _____your_____ name?
    B: Hi. _____ name is Carlos.
        What's _____ name?
    A: _____ name is Akina.

2. A: What's _____ name?
    B: _____ name is Ethan.
    A: And what's _____ name?
    B: _____ name is Caroline.

B PAIR WORK Practice the conversations with a partner.

4 SPEAKING Spelling names

▶ A Listen and practice.

A	B	C	D	E	F	G	H	I	J	K	L	M	N	O	P	Q	R	S	T	U	V	W	X	Y	Z
a	b	c	d	e	f	g	h	i	j	k	l	m	n	o	p	q	r	s	t	u	v	w	x	y	z

▶ B CLASS ACTIVITY Listen and practice. Then practice with your own names.
Make a list of your classmates' names.

A: What's your name?
B: My name is Akina Hayashi.
A: Is that A-K-I-N-A?
B: Yes, that's right.
A: How do you spell your last name? H-A-Y-A-S-H-Y?
B: No, it's H-A-Y-A-S-H-I.

> **My *classmates***
> Akina Hayashi
> Ethan Reed

5 LISTENING Your name, please?

▶ How do you spell the names? Listen and check (✓) the correct answers.

1. ☐ Kate   **2.** ☐ Erick   **3.** ☐ Sophia   **4.** ☐ Zackary
    ☐ Cate   ☐ Eric   ☐ Sofia   ☐ Zachary

6 WORD POWER Titles

▶ **A** Listen and practice.

> **Miss** Kato (single females)   **Ms.** Yong (single or married females)
> **Mrs.** Jones (married females)   **Mr.** Rodriguez (single or married males)

▶ **B** Listen and write the titles.

1. _____ Santos   **2.** _____ Wilson   **3.** _____ Park   **4.** _____ Rossi

7 SPEAKING Saying hello

▶ **A** Listen and practice.

1. Hi, Mia and Gina. How's it going?

Great, thanks! How about you, Sandra?

2. Good morning, Taylor. How are you?

I'm just fine, Mrs. Rodriguez. Thank you.

3. Good afternoon, Amanda. How are you?

Pretty good, thanks. How are you doing?

4. Good evening, Miss Roy.

Hello, Mr. Cooper. How are you?

I'm OK, thank you.

B **CLASS ACTIVITY** Go around the class. Greet your classmates formally (with titles) and informally (without titles).

8 CONVERSATION Are you Andrea Clark?

▶ **A** Listen and practice.

Daniel Excuse me. Are you Andrea Clark?

Sheila No, I'm not. She's over there.

Daniel Oh, I'm sorry.

Lena Matt? This is your book.

Matt Oh, thank you. You're in my math class, right?

Lena Yes, I am. I'm Lena Garza.

Jack Hey, Christy, this is Ben. He's in our history class.

Christy Hi, Ben.

Ben Hi, Christy. Nice to meet you.

B GROUP WORK Greet a classmate. Then introduce him or her to another classmate.

"Hey, Eduardo, this is . . ."

9 GRAMMAR FOCUS

▶ **The verb *be***

I'm Lena Garza.	**Are you** Andrea Clark?
You're in my class.	Yes, **I am**. (~~Yes, I'm.~~)
She's over there. (**Andrea is** over there.)	No, **I'm not**.
He's in our class. (**Ben is** in our class.)	
It's Garza. (**My last name is** Garza.)	How **are you**?
	I'm fine, thanks.

I'm = I am
You're = You are
He's = He is
She's = She is
It's = It is

GRAMMAR PLUS *see page 132*

A Complete the conversation with the correct words in parentheses. Then practice with a partner.

Ben Hello, Christy. How _____are_____ (are / is) you?

Christy _____ (I'm / It's) fine, thanks. _____ (I'm / It's) sorry – what's your name again?

Ben _____ (Is / It's) Ben – Ben Durant.

Christy That's right! Ben, this _____ (is / it's) Joshua Brown. _____ (He's / She's) in our history class.

Ben _____ (I'm / It's) nice to meet you.

Joshua Hi, Ben. I think _____ (I'm / you're) in my English class, too.

Ben Oh, right! Yes, I _____ (am / 'm).

B Complete the conversations. Then practice in groups.

Cara Excuse me. _____Are_____ you Alex Lane?

James No, _____ not. My name _____
James Harris. Alex _____ over there.

Cara Oh, sorry.

Cara _____ you Alex Lane?

Alex Yes, I _____.

Cara Hi. _____ Cara Ruiz.

Alex Oh, _____ in my history class, right?

Cara Yes, I _____.

Alex _____ nice to meet you, Cara.

C **CLASS ACTIVITY** Write your name on a piece of paper.
Put the papers in a bag. Then take a different paper.
Find the other student.

A: Excuse me. Are you Min-ji Cho?

B: No, I'm not. She's over there.

A: Hi. Are you Min-ji Cho?

C: Yes, I am.

10 PRONUNCIATION Linked sounds

▶ Listen and practice. Notice the linked sounds.

I'm Isabella.   She's over there.   You're in my class.

11 SPEAKING Personal information

▶ **A** Listen and practice.

0	1	2	3	4	5	6	7	8	9	10
zero (oh)	one	two	three	four	five	six	seven	eight	nine	ten

▶ **B** **PAIR WORK** Practice these phone numbers and email addresses.
Then listen and check your answers.

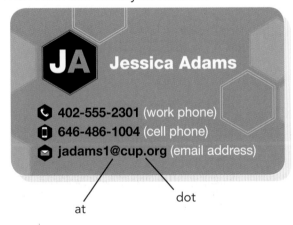

"Her name is Jessica Adams. Her work phone number is four-oh-two,
five-five-five, two-three-oh-one. Her cell . . ."

12 LISTENING Contact information

▶ **A** Isabella and Joshua are making a list of classmates' phone numbers and email addresses. Listen and complete the list.

Name	Phone Number	Email address
Ben Durant	718-555-8241	
Cara Ruiz		
Andrea Clark		
Akina Hayashi		

B CLASS ACTIVITY Make a list of your classmates' names, phone numbers, and email addresses.

A: What's your name?
B: I'm Maria Ventura.

A: And what's your phone number?
B: It's 323-555-7392.

13 INTERCHANGE 1 Celebrity classmates

Meet some "famous classmates." Go to Interchange 1 on page 114.

14 SPEAKING Saying good-bye

▶ **A** Listen and practice.

1 Bye, Robin.
See you tomorrow, Preeti.

3 See you later, Mike.
Bye-bye, Mike.

2 Good night, Jake.
Good-bye, Liz. Have a good evening!

4 Good-bye, Mr. Davis. Have a great weekend.
Thank you, Mr. Flores. You, too.

B CLASS ACTIVITY Go around the room. Say good-bye to your classmates and teacher.

2 Where are my keys?

▸ **Identify and discuss personal and classroom objects**
▸ **Discuss the location of items**

1 SNAPSHOT

▶ Listen and practice.

WHAT'S IN YOUR BAG?

☐ a laptop

☐ a cell phone

☐ a wallet

☐ an umbrella

☐ a hairbrush

☐ keys

☐ sunglasses

☐ an energy bar

Check (✓) the things in your bag.
What is one other thing in your bag?

2 ARTICLES Classroom objects

▶ **A** Listen. Complete the sentences with *a* or *an*.

articles
an + vowel sound
a + consonant sound

1. This is _____ book.

4. This is _____ notebook.

2. This is _____ English book.

5. This is _____ pen.

3. This is _____ eraser.

6. This is _____ clock.

B **PAIR WORK** Find and spell these things in your classroom.

backpack	chair	eraser	pen	notebook
board	desk	pencil	wall	wastebasket
poster	door	outlet	book	window

A: This is a chair.
B: How do you spell *chair*?
A: C-H-A-I-R.

3 CONVERSATION What are these?

▶ Listen and practice.

Brandon Excuse me. What are these?

Christina They're flash drives.

Brandon Oh, they're cool. And what's this?

Christina It's a tablet.

Brandon A tablet? Really? Wow! It's great!

Christina Yes, it is. It's a new model.

Brandon Huh . . . and what's this?

Christina It's a tablet case.

Brandon Oh. It's . . . interesting . . . and different.

4 PRONUNCIATION Plural –s endings

▶ **A** Listen and practice. Notice the pronunciation of the plural **–s** endings.

s = /z/		**s** = /s/		**(e)s** = /ɪz/	
flash drive	flash drive**s**	desk	desk**s**	tablet case	tablet case**s**
cell phone	cell phone**s**	laptop	laptop**s**	class	class**es**
pencil	pencil**s**	backpack	backpack**s**	hairbrush	hairbrush**es**

B Say the plural form of these nouns. Then complete the chart.

phone case

student ID

paper clip

newspaper

purse

tablet

television

ticket

box

/z/	/s/	/ɪz/
		phone cases

▶ **C** Listen and check your answers.

5 GRAMMAR FOCUS

This/these, it/they; plurals

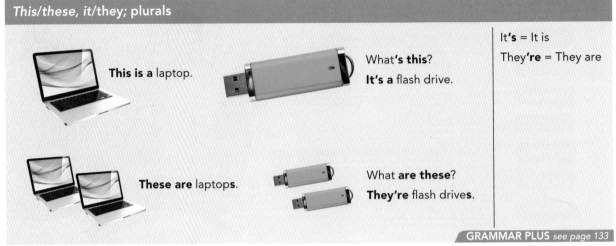

This is a laptop.

What**'s this**?
It**'s a** flash drive.

These are laptops.

What **are these**?
They**'re** flash drives.

It**'s** = It is
They**'re** = They are

GRAMMAR PLUS see page 133

Complete these conversations. Then practice with a partner.

1. **A:** What ____are these____ ?
   B: _____ .

2. **A:** What _____ ?
   B: _____ .

3. **A:** What _____ ?
   B: _____ .

4. **A:** What _____ ?
   B: _____ .

5. **A:** What _____ ?
   B: _____ .

6. **A:** What _____ ?
   B: _____ .

6 SPEAKING What's this called?

▶ **A** Listen and practice.

A: What's this called in English?
B: I don't know.
C: It's a credit card.
A: How do you spell that?
C: C-R-E-D-I-T C-A-R-D.

A: What are these called in English?
B: I think they're called headphones.
A: How do you spell that?
B: H-E-A-D-P-H-O-N-E-S.

B **GROUP WORK** Choose four things. Put them on a desk.
Then ask about the name and spelling of each thing.

▶ Listen and practice.

Lauren: Oh, no! Where are my car keys?

Matt: I don't know. Are they in your purse?

Lauren: No, they're not.

Matt: Maybe they're on the table in the restaurant.

Server: Excuse me. Are these your keys?

Lauren: Yes, they are. Thank you!

Server: You're welcome. And is this your wallet?

Lauren: Hmm. No, it's not. Where's your wallet, Matthew?

Matt: It's in my pocket. . . . Wait a minute! That *is* my wallet!

8 GRAMMAR FOCUS

▶ **Yes/No and *where* questions with *be***

Is this your wallet?	**Where's** your wallet?
Yes, **it is**. / No, **it's not**.	**It's** in my pocket.
Are these your keys?	**Where are** my keys?
Yes, **they are**. / No, **they're not**.	**They're** on the table.

GRAMMAR PLUS *see page 133*

A Complete these conversations. Then practice with a partner.

1. A: _____Is_____ this your cell phone?
 B: No, _____ not.
 A: _____ these your car keys?
 B: Yes, _____ are. Thanks!

2. A: Where _____ my glasses?
 B: Are _____ your glasses?
 A: No, they're _____.
 B: Look! _____ they in your pocket?
 A: Yes, _____. Thanks!

3. A: Where _____ your headphones?
 B: _____ on the table.
 A: No, _____ not. They're *my* headphones!
 B: You're right. My headphones _____ in my backpack.

4. A: _____ this my umbrella?
 B: No, _____ not. It's my umbrella.
 A: Sorry. _____ is my umbrella?
 B: _____ on your chair.
 A: Oh, you're right!

B **GROUP WORK** Choose one of your things and put it in a bag. Then choose something from the bag that is not your object. Find the owner of this object.

A: Is this your pen, Akiko?
B: No, it's not.

C: Are these your keys, Marcos?
D: Let me see. Yes, they are.

9 WORD POWER Prepositions; article *the*

▶ **A** Listen and practice.

Where is **the** cell phone?
The cell phone is in **the** box.

in

in front of

behind

on

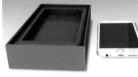

next to

under

▶ **B** Complete these sentences. Then listen and check your answers.

1. The books are _in the_ _backpack_ .

2. The flash drives are _____ _____.

3. The newspaper is _____ _____.

4. The chair is _____ _____.

5. The wallet is _____ _____.

6. The glasses are _____ _____.

C PAIR WORK Ask and answer questions about the pictures in part B.

A: Where are the books?　　　　**B:** They're in the backpack.

10 LISTENING Emily's things

▶ Listen. Where are Emily's things? Check (✓) the correct locations.

1. sunglasses	☐ on the table	☐ in her purse
2. ID	☐ in her wallet	☐ in front of the clock
3. headphones	☐ on the chair	☐ next to the television
4. tablet	☐ on the table	☐ under the table

11 SPEAKING Where are Kevin's things?

PAIR WORK Help Kevin find his things. Ask and answer questions.

| cell phone | hairbrush | laptop | umbrella | glasses | keys | tablet | credit card |

A: Where's his cell phone?
B: It's under the chair.

12 INTERCHANGE 2 Find the differences

Compare two pictures of a room. Go to Interchange 2 on page 115.

Units 1–2 Progress check

SELF-ASSESSMENT

How well can you do these things? Check (✓) the boxes.

I can . . .	Very well	OK	A little
Introduce myself and other people (Ex. 1)	☐	☐	☐
Say hello and good-bye (Ex. 1)	☐	☐	☐
Exchange contact information (Ex. 2)	☐	☐	☐
Understand names for everyday objects and possessions (Ex. 3)	☐	☐	☐
Ask and answer questions about where things are (Ex. 4, 5)	☐	☐	☐

1 SPEAKING How are you?

A Complete the conversation. Use the sentences and questions in the box.

Francisco	Hi. How are you?
Nicole	I'm fine, thanks. _____
Francisco	Pretty good, thanks. _____
Nicole	And I'm Nicole White.
Francisco	_____
Nicole	Nice to meet you, too. _____
Francisco	Yes, I am.
Nicole	_____
Francisco	See you in class.

> My name is Francisco Diaz.
> Oh, are you in my English class?
> How about you?
> ✓ Hi. How are you?
> It's nice to meet you, Nicole.
> Well, have a good day.

B **PAIR WORK** Practice the conversation from part A. Use your own information. Then introduce your partner to a classmate.

"Monica, this is my friend. His name is Kenta. . . ."

2 SPEAKING Is your phone number . . . ?

CLASS ACTIVITY Write your phone number on a piece of paper. Then put the papers in a bag. Take a different paper and find the owner. Write his or her name on the paper.

A: Kamal, is your phone number 781-555-1532?
B: No, it's not. Sorry!
A: Bruna, is your . . . ?

3 LISTENING What's this? What are these?

▶ Listen to the conversations. Number the pictures from 1 to 6.

☐　　　☐　　　☐　　　☐　　　☐　　　☐

4 SPEAKING What's wrong with this room?

A What's wrong with this room? Make a list. Find 10 things.

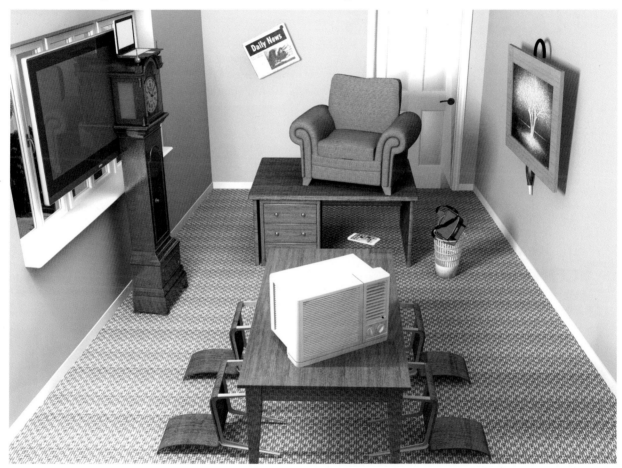

B **PAIR WORK** Ask and answer *Where* questions about the picture.

A: Where's the chair?
B: It's on the desk.

5 SPEAKING Yes or No game

Write five yes/no questions about the picture in Exercise 4. Make three questions with
"yes" answers and two questions with "no" answers. Then ask a partner the questions.

A: Is the chair behind the clock?　　　**A:** Is the clock in front of the television?
B: No, it isn't.　　　　　　　　　　　　**B:** Yes, it is.

3 Where are you from?

▸ Discuss cities, countries, nationalities, and languages
▸ Discuss people's appearances, personalities, and ages

1 SNAPSHOT

▶ Listen and practice.

THE TEN LARGEST CITIES IN THE WORLD

CITIES
1. Tokyo
2. Delhi
3. Shanghai
4. Mexico City
5. Mumbai
6. São Paulo
7. Osaka
8. Beijing
9. New York
10. Cairo

COUNTRIES
a. Brazil
b. China
c. Egypt
d. India
e. Japan
f. Mexico
g. the U.S.

(based on population)

Answers: 1.e 2.d 3.b 4.f 5.d 6.a 7.e 8.b 9.g 10.c

Match the cities with the countries. Then check your answers at the bottom of the Snapshot. What other large cities are in each country? What large cities are in your country?

2 CONVERSATION Are you from Rio?

▶ **A** Listen and practice.

Alexis Are you from Florida, Felipe?

Felipe Well, my family is in Florida now, but we're from Brazil originally.

Alexis Really? My father is Brazilian – from Rio de Janeiro!

Felipe So, is your first language Portuguese?

Alexis No, it's English. Are you from Rio?

Felipe No, we're not. We're from São Paulo.

▶ **B** Listen to Alexis and Felipe talk to Fernando, Nanami, and Sophia. Check (✓) True or False.

	True	False
1. Fernando is from Spain.	☐	☐
2. Nanami is from Japan.	☐	☐
3. Sophia's first language is French.	☐	☐

▶ **Negative statements and yes/no questions with *be***

I'm not from Rio.	**Are you** from São Paulo?		I am.		**I'm not.**
You're not late.	**Am I** early?		you are.		you're not.
She's not from Japan.	**Is she** from the U.S.?		she is.		she's not.
He's not from Chile.	**Is he** from Mexico?	Yes,	he is.	No,	he's not.
It's not English.	**Is it** French?		it is.		it's not.
We're not from China.	**Are you** from South Korea?		we are.		we're not.
You're not early.	**Are we** late?		you are.		you're not.
They're not in India.	**Are they** in Egypt?		they are.		they're not.

We**'re** = we are

GRAMMAR PLUS *see page 134*

For a list of countries, nationalities, and languages, see the appendix at the back of the book.

A Complete the conversations. Then practice with a partner.

1. A: _____Are_____ Diana and Mario from Ecuador?
   B: No, _____ not. _____ from Mexico.
   A: _____ you from Mexico, too?
   B: No, _____ not . I'm from Colombia.
   A: So, _____ your first language Spanish?
   B: Yes, it _____ .

2. A: _____ Meera from England?
   B: No, _____ not. She's from Australia.
   A: _____ she from Sydney?
   B: Yes, she _____ . But her parents are from India.
      _____ not from Australia originally.
   A: _____ Meera's first language Hindi?
   B: No, _____ not. _____ English.

3. A: Ji-hye, _____ you and Kwang-ho from South Korea?
   B: Yes, we _____ .
   A: And _____ from Seoul?
   B: No, _____ not. _____ from Busan.

Bogotá, Colombia

Busan, South Korea

B Match the questions with the answers. Then practice with a partner.

1. Are Liam and Grace from England? __d__
2. Is your first language Mandarin? _____
3. Are you Egyptian? _____
4. Is Mr. Lau from Beijing? _____
5. Is your mother from the U.K.? _____

a. No, he's not. He's from Shanghai.
b. Yes, she is. She's from London.
c. No, it's not. It's Cantonese.
d. No, they're not. They're from New Zealand.
e. Yes, we are. We're from Cairo.

C **PAIR WORK** Write five questions about your classmates. Then ask and answer your questions with a partner.

4 PRONUNCIATION Syllable stress

▶ **A** Listen and practice. Notice the syllable stress.

● •	● ●	● • •	• ● •
China	Brazil	Canada	Malaysia
Turkey	Japan	Mexico	Morocco
_____	_____	_____	_____
_____	_____	_____	_____

▶ **B** What is the syllable stress in these words? Add the words to the chart in part A. Then listen and check.

English	Spanish	Arabic	Korean
Mexican	Honduras	Chinese	Peru

C GROUP WORK Are the words in part A countries, nationalities, or languages? Make a chart and add more words.

Countries	Nationalities	Languages
Brazil	Brazilian	Portuguese
Mexico	Mexican	Spanish

5 SPEAKING Is Bruno Mars from Italy?

A Where are these people from? Check (✓) your guesses.

Bruno Mars
☐ Italy
☐ the Philippines
☐ the U.S.

Morena Baccarin
☐ Argentina
☐ Brazil
☐ the U.S.

Gael García Bernal
☐ Brazil
☐ Mexico
☐ Spain

Mao Asada
☐ China
☐ Japan
☐ South Korea

Chris Hemsworth
☐ Australia
☐ Canada
☐ England

B PAIR WORK Compare your guesses. Then check your answers at the bottom of the page.

A: Is Bruno Mars from Italy?
B: No, he's not.
A: Is he from the Philippines?

Answers: 1. the U.S. 2. Brazil 3. Mexico 4. Japan 5. Australia

6 CONVERSATION Who's that?

A Listen and practice.

 Nadia Who's that?

 Ben She's my sister.

 Nadia She's really pretty. What's her name?

 Ben Madison. We call her Maddie.

 Nadia Madison . . . that's a beautiful name. How old is she?

 Ben She's twenty-eight.

 Nadia And what's she like? Is she nice?

 Ben Well, she's shy, but she's really kind.

 Nadia And who's that little girl?

 Ben That's her daughter Mia. She's six years old.

 Nadia She's cute!

 Ben Yes, she is – and she's very smart, too.

7 SPEAKING Numbers and ages

A Listen and practice.

11 eleven	**21** twenty-one	**40** forty
12 twelve	**22** twenty-two	**50** fifty
13 thirteen	**23** twenty-three	**60** sixty
14 fourteen	**24** twenty-four	**70** seventy
15 fifteen	**25** twenty-five	**80** eighty
16 sixteen	**26** twenty-six	**90** ninety
17 seventeen	**27** twenty-seven	**100** one hundred
18 eighteen	**28** twenty-eight	**101** one hundred (and) one
19 nineteen	**29** twenty-nine	**102** one hundred (and) two
20 twenty	**30** thirty	**103** one hundred (and) three

B Listen and practice. Notice the word stress.

thirteen – thirty   fourteen – forty   fifteen – fifty   sixteen – sixty

C PAIR WORK Look at the people in Ben's family for one minute. How old are they? Close your books and tell your partner.

 A. Carol – 76    **B.** Richard – 50    **C.** Karen – 49    **D.** Amber – 17    **E.** Jay and Joe – 10

▶ **Wh-questions with *be***

What's your name?	**Who's that?**	**Who are they?**
My name is Sophia.	She's my sister.	They're my classmates.
Where are you from?	**How old is she?**	**Where are they from?**
I'm from Canada.	She's twenty-eight.	They're from San Francisco.
How are you today?	**What's she like?**	**What's San Francisco like?**
I'm fine, thanks.	She's very nice.	It's very beautiful.
	Who**'s** = Who **is**	

GRAMMAR PLUS *see page 134*

A Complete the conversations with Wh-questions. Then practice with a partner.

1. **A:** Look! <u>Who's that</u> ?
   B: Oh, she's a new student.
   A: _____ ?
   B: I think her name is Yoo-jin.
   A: Yoo-jin? _____ ?
   B: She's from South Korea.

2. **A:** Hi, Brittany. _____ ?
   B: I'm fine, thanks. My friend Leandro is here this week – from Argentina.
   A: Oh, cool. _____ ?
   B: He's really friendly.
   A: _____ ?
   B: He's twenty-five years old.

3. **A:** Azra, _____ ?
   B: I'm from Turkey. From Ankara.
   A: _____ ?
   B: Well, Ankara is the capital of Turkey. It's very old.
   A: _____ ?
   B: My last name is Ganim.

4. **A:** Good morning, Luke.
   _____ ?
   B: I'm great, thanks.
   A: Cool. _____ ?
   B: They're my friends from school.
   A: _____ ?
   B: They're from Miami, like me.

B **PAIR WORK** Write six Wh-questions about your partner and six Wh-questions about your partner's best friend. Then ask and answer the questions.

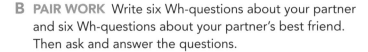

Your partner	Your partner's best friend
Where are you from?	Who's your best friend?

9 WORD POWER Describing people

▶ **A** Listen and practice.

a. pretty	**d.** talkative	**g.** funny	**j.** shy	**m.** heavy
b. handsome	**e.** friendly	**h.** quiet	**k.** short	**n.** thin
c. good-looking	**f.** kind	**i.** serious	**l.** tall	

B PAIR WORK Complete the chart with words from part A. Add two more words to each list. Then describe your personality and appearance to a partner.

Personality			Appearance		
talkative			pretty		

"I'm tall, friendly, and very talkative."

10 LISTENING Wow! Who's that?

▶ Listen to three descriptions. Check (✓) the two correct words for each description.

1. Nora is . . .	2. Taylor is . . .	3. Austin is . . .
☐ tall	☐ funny	☐ short
☐ pretty	☐ pretty	☐ serious
☐ quiet	☐ handsome	☐ talkative
☐ talkative	☐ serious	☐ tall

11 INTERCHANGE 3 Let's talk!

Talk to your classmates. Go to Interchange 3 on page 118.

4 Is this coat yours?

▸ Discuss work and free-time clothes; colors
▸ Discuss the weather and what people are wearing

1 WORD POWER Clothes

A Listen and practice.

Clothes for work

jacket
shirt
blouse
tie
suit
belt
pants
skirt
shoes
raincoat
dress
coat
high heels

Clothes for free time

hat
scarf
T-shirt
gloves
sweater
shorts
jeans
boots
socks
sneakers
pajamas
cap
swimsuits

B Complete the chart with words from part A.

Clothes for warm weather	Clothes for cold weather
86°F | 30°C	32°F | 0°C

C **PAIR WORK** Look around the classroom. What clothes do you see? Tell a partner.

"I see jeans, a sweater, boots, and . . ."

2 SPEAKING Colors

▶ **A** Listen and practice.

white	light gray	gray
dark gray	beige	light brown
brown	dark brown	black

B GROUP WORK Ask about favorite colors.

A: What are your favorite colors?
B: My favorite colors are orange and dark blue.

C GROUP WORK Describe the clothes in Exercise 1.

A: The suit is black.
B: The socks are dark blue.

3 PRONUNCIATION The letters *s* and *sh*

▶ **A** Listen and practice. Notice the pronunciation of **s** and **sh**.

suit	**s**ocks	**s**wimsuit
shirt	**sh**orts	**sh**oes

B Read the sentences. Pay attention to the pronunciation of **s** and **sh**.

1. This is Jo**sh**ua's new **s**uit.
2. These are **S**arah's purple **sh**oes!

3. Where are my **sh**oes and **s**ocks?
4. My **sh**orts and T-**sh**irts are blue!

4 CONVERSATION Whose jeans are these?

▶ Listen and practice.

Ashley — Great! Our clothes are dry.

Jessica — Hey, where is my new blouse?

Ashley — What color is your blouse? Is this yours?

Jessica — No, this blouse is blue. Mine is white. Wait! It *is* mine. My white blouse is . . . blue!

Ashley — Oh, no! Look. It's a disaster! *All* our clothes are blue . . .

Jessica — Here's the problem. It's these blue jeans. Whose jeans are these? Are they yours?

Ashley — Uh, yes, they're mine. Sorry.

5 GRAMMAR FOCUS

Possessives

Adjectives		Pronouns	Names	
my		**mine.**	**Jack's** tie.	s = /s/
your		**yours.**	**Taylor's** shoes.	s = /z/
These are **his** shoes.	These shoes are	**his.**	**Alex's** coat.	s = /ɪz/
her		**hers.**		
our		**ours.**	**Whose** tie is this? It's **Greg's.**	
their		**theirs.**	**Whose** shoes are these? They're **Taylor's.**	

GRAMMAR PLUS *see page 135*

A Complete the conversations with the correct words in parentheses. Then practice with a partner.

1. **A:** This isn't _____my_____ (my / mine) raincoat. Is it _____ (your / yours)?

   B: No, it's not _____ (my / mine). Ask Emma. Maybe it's _____ (her / hers).

2. **A:** Hey! These aren't _____ (our / ours) sneakers!

   B: You're right. _____ (Our / Ours) are over there.

3. **A:** Are these _____ (your / yours) gloves, Erin?

   B: No, they're not _____ (my / mine). Maybe they are Logan's. _____ (His / Your) gloves are gray.

4. **A:** _____ (Whose / Yours) T-shirts are these? Are they Hayley's and Brad's?

   B: No, they're not _____ (their / theirs) T-shirts. _____ (Their / Theirs) are white, not blue.

B **CLASS ACTIVITY** Put one of your things in a box. Then choose a different thing from the box. Go around the class and find the owner.

A: Laura, are these sunglasses yours?

B: No, they're not mine. Maybe they're Joon-ho's.

C: Wei, is this your pen?

D: Yes, it is.

6 LISTENING Her sneakers are purple.

A Listen to someone describe six people. Number the pictures from 1 to 6 in the order you hear them.

☐ Alicia   ☐ 1 Sarah   ☐ Andrea   ☐ Amanda   ☐ Cody   ☐ Kyle

B **PAIR WORK** Now talk about the people. What colors are their clothes?

A: What color is Alicia's jacket?

B: It's beige.

7 SNAPSHOT

▶ Listen and practice.

WEATHER AND SEASONS AROUND THE WORLD

It's spring in São Paulo, Brazil. It's warm. It's very sunny.

It's summer in Seoul, South Korea. It's raining. It's hot and humid.

It's fall in Chicago in the U.S. It's cool. It's cloudy and windy.

It's winter in Toronto, Canada. It's snowing. It's very cold.

What season is it now in your town or city? What's the weather like today?
What's your favorite season?

8 CONVERSATION Are you wearing your gloves?

▶ Listen and practice.

Ashley Oh, no!

Jessica What's the matter?

Ashley It's snowing! Wow, it's so cold and windy!

Jessica Are you wearing your gloves?

Ashley No, I'm not. They're at home.

Jessica What about your scarf?

Ashley It's at home, too.

Jessica Well, you're wearing your coat.

Ashley But my coat isn't very warm. And I'm not wearing boots!

Jessica OK. Let's take a taxi.

Ashley Good idea!

▶ **Present continuous statements; conjunctions**

I**'m**	I**'m not**	OR:	Conjunctions
You**'re**	You**'re not**	You **aren't**	It's snowing, **and** it's windy.
She**'s wearing shoes.**	She**'s not**	She **isn't wearing boots.**	It's sunny, **but** it's cold.
We**'re**	We**'re not**	We **aren't**	It's windy, **so** it's very cold.
They**'re**	They**'re not**	They **aren't**	
It**'s snowing.**	It**'s not**	It **isn't raining.**	

GRAMMAR PLUS *see page 135*

A Complete these sentences from a travel show on TV. Then compare with a partner.

My name is Dylan Jones. I _'m wearing_____
a new gray suit. I _____
new black shoes, too. It's raining, but I _____
_____ a raincoat.

It's very hot and sunny today. Michael
_____ light blue shorts and white
sneakers. He _____ a white
T-shirt, but he _____ a cap.

Adriana Fuentes is from Mexico. She
_____ a pretty yellow dress
and a brown belt. She _____
high heels and a light brown jacket, but she
_____ a coat. Wow, it's
really windy!

Hee-sun and Kun-woo are here with me today.
They're 10 years old. It's really cold, so they
_____ winter clothes. They
_____ boots, gloves, hats,
and scarves. And they _____
heavy coats!

▶ **Present continuous yes/no questions**

Are you **wearing** gloves?	Yes, I **am**.	No, I**'m not**.
Is she **wearing** boots?	Yes, she **is**.	No, she**'s not**./No, she **isn't**.
Are they **wearing** sunglasses?	Yes, they **are**.	No, they**'re not**./No, they **aren't**.

GRAMMAR PLUS *see page 135*

B PAIR WORK Ask and answer these questions about the people in part A.

1. Is Dylan wearing a gray suit?
2. Is he wearing a raincoat?
3. Is he wearing black shoes?
4. Is Michael wearing jeans?
5. Is he wearing a T-shirt?
6. Is he wearing a cap?

7. Is Adriana wearing a skirt?
8. Is she wearing a jacket?
9. Is she wearing high heels?
10. Are Hee-sun and Kun-woo wearing swimsuits?
11. Are they wearing gloves and hats?
12. Are they wearing sneakers?

A: Is Dylan wearing a gray suit?
B: Yes, he is. Is he wearing a raincoat?
A: No, he's not. OR No, he isn't.

adjective + noun

My suit is **black**.
I'm wearing **a black suit**.

C Write four more questions about the people in part A.
Then ask a partner the questions.

10 LISTENING You look great in pink.

▶ **A** Listen. What are their names? Write the
names **Brittany**, **Ryan**, **John**, **Robert**,
Kayla, and **Amber** in the correct boxes.

Kayla

B GROUP WORK Ask questions about
the people in the picture.

A: Is John wearing a brown jacket?
B: Yes, he is.
C: Is he wearing a cap?

C GROUP WORK Write five questions about
your classmates. Then ask and answer the
questions.

Are Maria and Bruno wearing jeans?

Is Bruno wearing a red shirt?

11 INTERCHANGE 4 Celebrity fashions

What are your favorite celebrities wearing? Go to Interchange 4 on pages 116–117.

Units 3–4 Progress check

SELF-ASSESSMENT

How well can you do these things? Check (✓) the boxes.

I can . . .	Very well	OK	A little
Ask and answer questions about countries of origin, nationalities, and languages (Ex. 1)	☐	☐	☐
Understand descriptions of people (Ex. 2)	☐	☐	☐
Ask and answer questions about people's appearance and personality (Ex. 2, 5)	☐	☐	☐
Ask and answer questions about people's possessions (Ex. 3)	☐	☐	☐
Talk and write about my and other people's favorite things (Ex. 4)	☐	☐	☐
Ask and answer questions about what people are wearing (Ex. 5)	☐	☐	☐

1 SPEAKING Interview with my classmates

Match the questions with the answers. Then ask and answer the questions with a partner. Answer with your own information.

1. Are you from Argentina? __h__
2. Where are you and your family from? _____
3. What is your hometown like? _____
4. Is English your first language? _____
5. Who is your best friend? _____
6. How old is your best friend? _____
7. Is our teacher from the U.S.? _____
8. Are our classmates friendly? _____

a. It's very beautiful.
b. Yes, she is.
c. We're from Montevideo.
d. My best friend is Takuya.
e. Yes, they are.
f. No, it's not. It's Spanish.
g. He's nineteen.
h. No, I'm not. I'm from Uruguay.

2 LISTENING Where's your friend Jacob?

▶ **A** Listen to four conversations. Check (✓) the correct description for each person. You will check more than one adjective.

1. Jacob
- ☐ tall
- ☐ short
- ☐ funny
- ☐ serious
- ☐ nice
- ☐ shy

2. Monica
- ☐ tall
- ☐ talkative
- ☐ pretty
- ☐ shy
- ☐ nice
- ☐ friendly

3. Hannah
- ☐ thin
- ☐ short
- ☐ quiet
- ☐ shy
- ☐ serious
- ☐ funny

4. Ki-nam
- ☐ tall
- ☐ short
- ☐ funny
- ☐ friendly
- ☐ talkative
- ☐ quiet

B Write five yes/no questions about the people in part A. Then ask a partner the questions.

Is Jacob tall?
Is Monica thin?

3 SPEAKING Are these your clothes?

CLASS ACTIVITY Draw three pictures of clothes on different pieces of paper.
Then put the papers in a bag. Take three different papers, go around
the class, and find the owners.

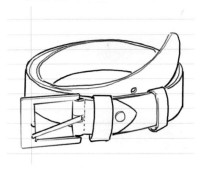  

A: Anna, is this your belt?

B: No, it's not mine. Maybe it's Miki's.

A: Ji-hun, are these your sneakers?

C: Yes, they're mine. Thanks!

4 SPEAKING Similar or different?

A Write your favorite things in the chart. Then ask a partner about his or her
favorite things. Write them in the chart.

Favorite	Me	My partner
1. season		
2. color		
3. clothes		

B Compare answers. What's the same? What's different? Write sentences.

Spring is my favorite season, and it's Mariana's favorite season. That's the same.

My favorite color is green, but Mariana's favorite color is red, so that's different.

5 SPEAKING I'm thinking of . . .

GROUP WORK Think of a student in the class. Your classmates
ask yes/no questions to guess the student.

A: I'm thinking of a student in this class.

B: Is it a woman?

A: Yes, it is.

C: Is she short?

A: No, she isn't.

D: Is she wearing blue jeans?

WHAT'S NEXT?

Look at your Self-assessment again. Do you need to review anything?

5 What time is it?

▶ Discuss cities and time zones
▶ Discuss people's activities

1 SNAPSHOT

▶ Listen and practice.

Time Zones

Mexico City 10:00 A.M.	New York 11:00 A.M.	Dubai 7:00 P.M.	Seoul 12:00 A.M.

Is your city or town in the same time zone as one of these cities?
What other events or shows are on television in different time zones?

2 CONVERSATION It's two o'clock in the morning!

▶ **A** Listen and practice.

2:00 A.M. ▼

Amar Hello?

Brian Hi, Amar! This is Brian. I'm calling from New York.

Amar Brian? Wait. . . . Where are you?

Brian I'm home on vacation, remember? I'm calling about the soccer game. Great game!

Amar Oh, that's good. But what time is it there?

Brian It's 2:00 P.M. And it's two o'clock in Australia, too. Right?

Amar That's right – it's two o'clock in the morning!

Brian 2:00 A.M.? Oh, of course! I'm really sorry.

Amar That's OK. Congratulations on the game!

2:00 P.M. ▲

3 GRAMMAR FOCUS

▶ What time is it?

 It's two **o'clock**.

 It's two-oh-five.
It's five **after** two.

 It's two-fifteen.
It's **a quarter after** two.

 It's two-thirty.

 It's two-forty.
It's twenty **to** three.

 It's two forty-five.
It's **a quarter to** three.

GRAMMAR PLUS *see page 136*

A PAIR WORK Look at these clocks. What time is it?

A: What time is it?
B: It's ten after ten. OR It's ten-ten.

▶ Is it A.M. or P.M.?

It's six (o'clock) **in the morning**.
It's 6:00 A.M.

It's twelve (o'clock).
It's 12:00 P.M.
It's **noon**.

It's four (o'clock) **in the afternoon**.
It's 4:00 P.M.

It's six (o'clock) **in the evening**.
It's 6:00 P.M.

It's nine (o'clock) **at night**.
It's 9:00 P.M.

It's twelve (o'clock) **at night**.
It's 12:00 A.M.
It's midnight.

GRAMMAR PLUS *see page 136*

B PAIR WORK Say each time a different way.

1. It's eight o'clock in the morning. *"It's 8:00 A.M."*
2. It's three o'clock in the afternoon.
3. It's six o'clock in the evening.
4. It's twelve o'clock at night.
5. It's 10:00 A.M.
6. It's 4:00 P.M.
7. It's 7:00 P.M.
8. It's 12:00 P.M.

4 LISTENING What time is it in Tokyo?

A Lauren and John are calling friends in different parts of the world.
Listen. What time is it in these cities?

City	Time
Vancouver	4:00 P.M.
Bangkok	
London	
Tokyo	
São Paulo	

B Listen again. Check (✓) the correct answers.

1. Tanawat is . . . ☐ getting married. ☐ in São Paulo. ☐ sleeping.

2. Richard is . . . ☐ in London. ☐ in Bangkok. ☐ late.

3. Misaki is . . . ☐ in Tokyo. ☐ in Vancouver. ☐ watching TV.

5 CONVERSATION What are you doing?

Listen and practice.

JAY Hey, Kate!

KATE What are you doing?

JAY I'm cooking.

KATE I know, but why are you cooking now?
It's three o'clock in the morning!

JAY I'm sorry, but I'm really hungry.

KATE Hmm . . . What are you making?

JAY Spaghetti.

KATE With tomato sauce?

JAY With tomato sauce and cheese.

KATE I love spaghetti! Uh . . . I'm getting hungry, too.

JAY Good. Let's eat!

6 PRONUNCIATION Rising and falling intonation

A Listen and practice. Notice the intonation of the yes/no and Wh-questions.

Is he cooking? ⤴   What's he making? ⤵
Are they sleeping?   What are they doing?

B Listen to the questions. Draw a rising arrow (⤴) for rising intonation
and a falling arrow (⤵) for falling intonation.

1. ___⤴___   **2.** _____   **3.** _____   **4.** _____   **5.** _____   **6.** _____

Present continuous Wh-questions

San Diego   4:00 A.M.

What's Daniel **doing**?
He**'s sleeping** right now.

Guadalajara   6:00 A.M.

What's Leticia **doing**?
It's 6:00 A.M., so she**'s getting up**.

Washington, D.C.   7:00 A.M.

What are Lya and Erin **doing**?
They're having breakfast.

Brasilia   9:00 A.M.

What's Tiago **doing**?
He**'s going** to work.

Edinburgh   noon

What are Kim and Paul **doing**?
It's noon, so they**'re eating** lunch.

Cairo   3:00 P.M.

What's Amina **doing**?
She**'s working**.

Jakarta   7:00 P.M.

What's Tamara **doing**?
She**'s eating** dinner right now.

Osaka   9:00 P.M.

What's Kento **doing**?
He**'s checking** his messages.

Your city   00:00

What are you **doing**?
It's . . . I**'m** . . .

GRAMMAR PLUS *see page 136*

A **PAIR WORK** Ask and answer the questions about the pictures.

1. Who's having breakfast?
2. Who's eating dinner?
3. Where's Amina working?
4. Where's Kento checking his messages?
5. What's Daniel doing?
6. What's Tiago wearing?
7. Why is Leticia getting up?
8. Why are Kim and Paul having lunch?

spelling
sleep ⟶ sleep**ing**
get ⟶ get**ting** (+ *t*)
have ⟶ hav**ing** (− *e*)

B **GROUP WORK** Write five more questions about the pictures.
Then ask and answer your questions in groups.

8 WORD POWER What are they doing?

▶ **A** Listen and practice. *"They're dancing."*

dance

drive

listen to music

play basketball

read

ride a bike

run

shop

study

swim

take a walk

watch a movie

B PAIR WORK Ask and answer questions about the pictures in part A.

A: Are they running?
B: No, they're not.

A: What are they doing?
B: They're dancing.

C GROUP WORK Make two teams. Write an activity on a piece of paper. Give the paper to the other team. Two members act out each activity. Their team guesses. Can they guess the activity?

A: Are you running?
B: No, we're not.

C: Are you riding bikes?
D: Yes, we are!

riding bikes

9 INTERCHANGE 5 What's wrong with this picture?

What's wrong with this picture? Go to Interchange 5 on page 119.

A Skim the conversation. Write the name of the correct person on each picture.

MESSAGE ME!

Eva and Pam are friends. They message on social media every day. Pam lives in Atlanta, in the United States. Eva is visiting friends in Puebla, Mexico.

| Profile | Photos | Share | Find Friends |

Eva35   Hey! How are you today, Pam?

PamL   Hi, Eva! I'm fine, thanks. What are you doing?

Eva35   I'm sitting on the couch watching a movie. It's great!

PamL   Lucky you! I'm writing a report. It's for my job.

Eva35   Oh, really? Are you at your office?

PamL   Yeah. My friend Lety is making me coffee. She's helping me with the report.

Eva35   Cool. I'm . . . Oh, wait. My cell phone is ringing. Be right back. Sorry. It's my friend, Paul. He's making lunch.

PamL   Right. I have to go, Eva. Sorry. My boss is calling me.

Eva35   OK. Good luck with the report! Have a good evening!

PamL   Thanks, Eva. Enjoy your movie!

B Read the conversation. Who is doing these things? Choose the correct answers.

1. Pam   Eva   . . . is watching a movie.
2. Eva   Pam   . . . is visiting friends.
3. Pam   Eva   . . . is working in an office.
4. Lety   Paul   . . . is making coffee.
5. Paul   Pam   . . . is calling Eva on her cell phone.
6. Eva   Pam's boss   . . . is calling Pam.

C PAIR WORK Think about online conversations you have with friends. What do you say? What do you ask about? Write a short conversation.

6 I ride my bike to school.

▸ Discuss transportation and family
▸ Discuss daily and weekly routines

1 SNAPSHOT

▶ Listen and practice.

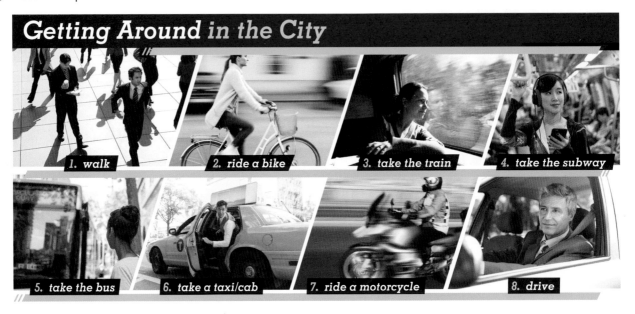

Getting Around in the City

1. walk
2. ride a bike
3. take the train
4. take the subway
5. take the bus
6. take a taxi/cab
7. ride a motorcycle
8. drive

Check (✓) the kinds of transportation you use.
What are some other kinds of transportation?

2 CONVERSATION They use public transportation.

▶ Listen and practice.

Yuto: Nice car, Austin! Is it yours?

Austin: No, it's my sister's. She has a new job and she drives to work.

Yuto: Is her job here in the suburbs?

Austin: No, it's downtown.

Yuto: My parents work downtown, but they don't drive to work. They use public transportation.

Austin: The bus or the train?

Yuto: The bus doesn't stop near our house, so they take the train.

3 WORD POWER Family members

▶ A PAIR WORK Complete the sentences about the Mitchell family. Then listen and check your answers.

1. Lisa is Tom's _____wife_____.
2. Megan and Austin are their _____.
3. Tom is Lisa's _____.
4. Austin is Lisa's _____.
5. Megan is Tom's _____.
6. Austin is Megan's _____.
7. Megan is Austin's _____.
8. Tom and Lisa are Austin's _____.

> kids = children
> mom = mother
> dad = father

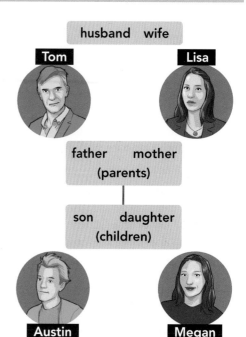

husband   wife

Tom   Lisa

father   mother
(parents)

son   daughter
(children)

Austin   Megan

brother   sister

B PAIR WORK Who are the people in your family? What are their names?

"My father's name is Arthur. My sisters' names are Emilia and Sabrina."

4 GRAMMAR FOCUS

▶ Simple present statements

I	**walk**	to school.	I	**don't live**	far from here.	**don't** = do not
You	**ride**	your bike to school.	You	**don't live**	near here.	**doesn't** = does not
He	**works**	near here.	He	**doesn't work**	downtown.	
She	**takes**	the bus to work.	She	**doesn't drive**	to work.	
We	**live**	with our parents.	We	**don't live**	alone.	
They	**use**	public transportation.	They	**don't need**	a car.	

GRAMMAR PLUS *see page 137*

A Tom Mitchell is talking about his family. Complete the sentences with the correct verb forms. Then compare with a partner.

1. My family and I _____live_____ (live / lives) in the suburbs. My wife and I _____ (work / works) near here, so we _____ (walk / walks) to work. Our daughter Megan _____ (work / works) downtown, so she _____ (drive / drives) to work. Our son _____ (don't / doesn't) drive. He _____ (ride / rides) his bike to school.

2. My parents _____ (live / lives) in the city. My mother _____ (take / takes) the subway to work. My father is retired, so he _____ (don't / doesn't) work now. He also _____ (use / uses) public transportation, so they _____ (don't / doesn't) need a car.

> **verb endings:** *he, she, it*
>
> walk → walk**s**
> ride → ride**s**
> study → stud**ies**
> watch → watch**es**

> **Simple present statements with irregular verbs**

I/you/we/they	*he/she/it*
I **have** a bike.	My mother **has** a car.
We **do** our homework every day.	My father **does** a lot of work at home.
My parents **go** to work by train.	The train **goes** downtown.

GRAMMAR PLUS *see page 137*

B Yuto is talking about his family and his friend Austin. Complete the sentences. Then compare with a partner.

1. My parents _____have_____ (have / has) a house in the suburbs. My mom and dad _____ (go / goes) downtown to work. My parents are very busy, so I _____ (do / does) a lot of work at home.

2. My brother doesn't live with us. He _____ (have / has) an apartment in the city. He _____ (go / goes) to school all day, and he _____ (do / does) his homework at night.

3. I _____ (have / has) a new friend. His name is Austin. We _____ (go / goes) to the same school, and sometimes we _____ (do / does) our homework together.

C PAIR WORK Tell your partner about your family.

"I have one brother and two sisters. My brother is a teacher. He has a car, so he drives to work."

---

5 PRONUNCIATION Third-person singular –s endings

Listen and practice. Notice the pronunciation of the **–s** endings.

s = /s/	**s = /z/**	**(e)s = /ɪz/**	*irregular*
take tak**es**	drive driv**es**	dance danc**es**	do do**es**
sleep sleep**s**	study studi**es**	watch watch**es**	have ha**s**

---

6 CONVERSATION What time do you get up?

Listen and practice.

Paige Let's go to the park Sunday morning.

Adam Good idea, but let's go in the afternoon. I sleep late on weekends.

Paige What time do you get up?

Adam I get up at noon.

Paige Really? That's late. Do you eat breakfast at noon?

Adam Yeah. What time do *you* get up?

Paige At ten o'clock.

Adam Oh, that's early for a Sunday.

Paige Hey, I have an idea! Let's eat at Park Café. They serve breakfast all day!

▶ **Simple present questions**

Do you **get up** early on Sundays?	**What time do** you **get up**?
No, I **get up** late.	At noon.
Does he **eat** breakfast at seven o'clock?	**What time does** she have dinner?
No, he **eats** breakfast at seven-thirty.	At eight o'clock.
Do they **take** a taxi to class?	**When do** they **take** the subway?
No, they **take** the bus.	On Mondays and Wednesdays.

GRAMMAR PLUS *see page 137*

A Complete the questions with *do* or *does*.

1. _____Do_____ you get up late on Sundays?
2. _____ you have lunch at home every day?
3. What time _____ your father leave work on Fridays?
4. _____ your mother cook on weekdays?
5. _____ your father shop on Saturdays?
6. _____ you take a walk in the evening?
7. When _____ you listen to music?
8. What time _____ you check your email?
9. What time _____ your parents have dinner?
10. When _____ you study English?
11. _____ your best friend ride a bike on weekends?
12. _____ your father drive to work every morning?

time expressions	
early	**in** the morning
late	**in** the afternoon
every day	**in** the evening
at 9:00	**on** Sundays
at noon/midnight	**on** weekdays
at night	**on** weekends

B **PAIR WORK** Ask and answer the questions from part A. Use time expressions from the box.

A: Do you get up late on Sundays?
B: No, I don't. I get up at eight o'clock. I play basketball on Sunday mornings.

C Unscramble the questions to complete the conversations. Then ask a partner the questions. Answer with your own information.

1. **A:** _What time do you eat dinner_____ ?
   you / what time / dinner / do / eat
   B: At 7:00 P.M.

2. **A:** _____ ?
   you / every morning / check your messages / do
   B: Yes, I check my messages on the bus every morning.

3. **A:** _____ ?
   at / start / does / seven o'clock / this class
   B: No, this class starts at eight o'clock.

4. **A:** _____ ?
   listen to music / you / do / when
   B: I listen to music in the evening.

5. **A:** _____ ?
   on weekends / you and your friends / do / play sports
   B: Yes, we play volleyball on Saturdays.

8 LISTENING Kayla's weekly routine

Listen to Kayla talk about her weekly routine. Check (✓) the days she does each thing.

	Monday	Tuesday	Wednesday	Thursday	Friday	Saturday	Sunday
get up early	☐	☐	☐	☐	☐	☐	☐
go to work	☐	☐	☐	☐	☐	☐	☐
play tennis	☐	☐	☐	☐	☐	☐	☐
go shopping	☐	☐	☐	☐	☐	☐	☐
see friends	☐	☐	☐	☐	☐	☐	☐
dinner with family	☐	☐	☐	☐	☐	☐	☐
study	☐	☐	☐	☐	☐	☐	☐

9 SPEAKING My weekly routine

A What do you do every week? Write your routine in the chart.

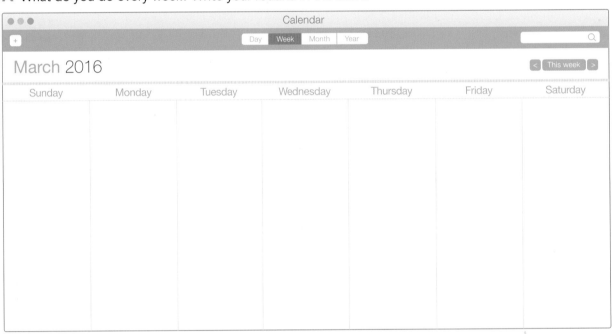

● ● ●	Calendar					
		Day **Week** Month Year				🔍
March 2016						< This week >
Sunday	Monday	Tuesday	Wednesday	Thursday	Friday	Saturday

B GROUP WORK Discuss your weekly routines.
Ask and answer questions.

A: I play tennis on Sunday mornings.

B: What do you do on Sunday afternoons?

A: I see my friends. We watch movies or play games. What about you?

C: On Sundays, I have lunch with my parents. In the afternoon, we talk or take a walk.

10 INTERCHANGE 6 Class survey

Find out more about your classmates.
Go to Interchange 6 on page 120.

A Scan the interview. What's unusual about Mike's job?

What's your
schedule like?

Every week, we interview someone with an unusual schedule. In this week's interview, we meet Mike Watts, a professional "sleeper." Yes, that's correct. Mike's job pays him to sleep! Here, Mike talks to us about his schedule.

News Now: Hi Mike, thanks for talking to us. What's your schedule like?

Mike: Hi there! My schedule's strange, but I love it. I go to bed at 10:00 P.M. in a different hotel room every night.

News Now: Wow! That's cool! Do you get up early?

Mike: Yes, I get up at 6:00 A.M. I'm an early bird! I like the morning. At 8:00 A.M., I have a big breakfast in the hotel restaurant.

News Now: So, who pays you to do that?

Mike: I work for a travel blog. They pay me to stay in different hotels and write about them. People read the blog and go to the hotels. Right now, I'm at a hotel in Finland, Hotel Finn.

News Now: And what do you do before you go to bed?

Mike: Every afternoon, from 2:00 P.M. to 4:00 P.M., I write about each room. I talk about the bed, the lights, the noise . . .

News Now: Who reads the blog?

Mike: Lots of different people read it. Business people, tourists, travel agencies . . . people who want to know about hotels, really!

News Now: What do you do in the evening?

Mike: At 7:00 P.M., I talk to the hotel manager. Then I go to my new room and go to bed.

News Now: Do you like sleeping?

Mike: Yes, I do! I'm very good at it!

B Read the article. Number the activities in Mike's schedule from 1 to 5. Then answer the questions. Write the times.

_____ **a.** Mike writes about each room.   _____ **d.** He goes to his new room.

__1__ **b.** He gets up.   _____ **e.** He has a big breakfast.

_____ **c.** He talks to the hotel manager.

1. What time does Mike write about each room? _____
2. What time does he get up? _____
3. What time does he talk to the hotel manager? _____
4. What time does he go to bed? _____
5. What time does he have breakfast? _____

C Are you an "early bird," like Mike? Or are you a "night owl"? Write five sentences about your schedule. Compare with a partner.

early bird

night owl

SELF-ASSESSMENT

How well can you do these things? Check (✓) the boxes.

I can . . .	Very well	OK	A little
Understand times and descriptions of activities (Ex. 1)	☐	☐	☐
Ask and answer questions about present activities (Ex. 2)	☐	☐	☐
Talk about personal routines (Ex. 3)	☐	☐	☐
Ask and answer questions about routines (Ex. 4)	☐	☐	☐
Ask and answer questions about celebrities' appearances and activities (Ex. 5)	☐	☐	☐

1 LISTENING I'm calling from Los Angeles.

▶ It's 9:00 A.M. in Los Angeles. Stephanie is calling friends around the world.
Listen to the conversations and complete the chart.

	1. Chelsea	2. Carlos	3. Nicholas
City	New York		
Time			
Activity			

2 SPEAKING We're on vacation!

Student A: Imagine your classmates are on vacation. Student B calls you. Ask questions about your classmates.

Student B: Imagine you are on vacation with your classmates. Call Student A. Answer Student A's questions about your classmates.

A: Hello?
B: Hi, it's . . . . I'm on vacation in . . .
A: In . . . ? Wow! What are you doing?
B: . . .
A: Who are you with?
B: . . .
A: What's he/she doing?
B: . . .
A: Well, have fun. Bye!

3 SPEAKING One day in my week

A Choose one day of the week and write it in the blank.
What do you do on this day? Complete the chart.

	Day:
In the morning	
In the afternoon	
In the evening	
At night	

B PAIR WORK Tell your partner about your routine on the day from part A.

A: On Saturdays, I exercise in the morning. I run in the park with my friends.
B: What time do you run?
A: We run at 9:00.

4 SPEAKING Lifestyle survey

A Answer the questions in the chart. Check (✓) Yes or No.

	Yes	No	Name
1. Do you live with your parents?	☐	☐	
2. Do both your parents work?	☐	☐	
3. Do you play video games at night?	☐	☐	
4. Do you eat dinner with your family?	☐	☐	
5. Do you stay at home on weekends?	☐	☐	
6. Do you work on Saturdays?	☐	☐	

B CLASS ACTIVITY Go around the class and find classmates with the same answers.
Write their names in the chart. Try to write a different name on each line.

5 SPEAKING Guess who!

GROUP WORK Think of a famous person. Your classmates ask
yes/no questions to guess the person.

Is it a man? a woman?   Does he/she speak English?
Does he/she live in . . . ?   Does he/she play soccer? basketball?
Is he/she a singer? an actor?   Does he/she wear glasses?

WHAT'S NEXT?

Look at your Self-assessment again. Do you need to review anything?

7 Does it have a view?

▶ Describe houses and apartments
▶ Discuss furniture and dream homes

1 SNAPSHOT

▶ Listen and practice.

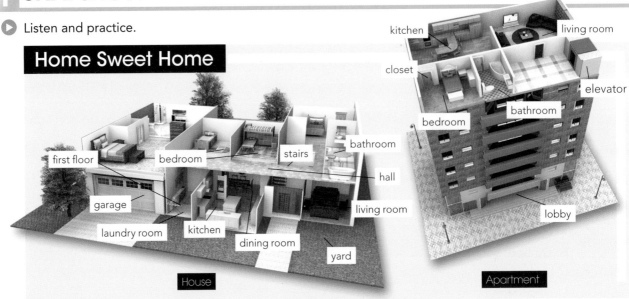

Home Sweet Home

first floor · bedroom · stairs · bathroom · hall · living room · garage · kitchen · dining room · yard · laundry room

House

kitchen · living room · closet · elevator · bedroom · bathroom · lobby

Apartment

What rooms are in houses in your country? What rooms are in apartments?
What rooms are in your house or apartment? What is your favorite room?

2 CONVERSATION Do you live downtown?

▶ Listen and practice.

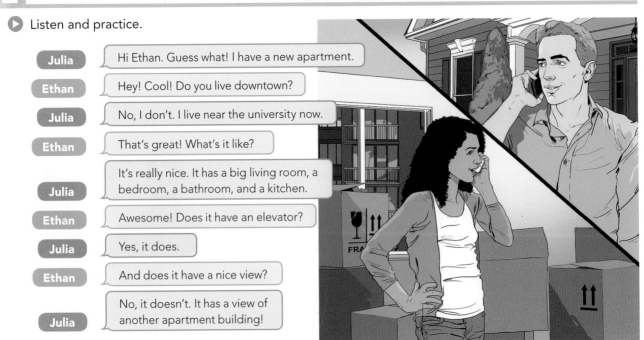

Julia Hi Ethan. Guess what! I have a new apartment.

Ethan Hey! Cool! Do you live downtown?

Julia No, I don't. I live near the university now.

Ethan That's great! What's it like?

Julia It's really nice. It has a big living room, a bedroom, a bathroom, and a kitchen.

Ethan Awesome! Does it have an elevator?

Julia Yes, it does.

Ethan And does it have a nice view?

Julia No, it doesn't. It has a view of another apartment building!

3 GRAMMAR FOCUS

Simple present short answers

Do you **live** in an apartment?	**Does** Ethan **live** in a house?
Yes, I **do**. / No, I **don't**.	Yes, he **does**. / No, he **doesn't**.
Do the bedrooms **have** closets?	**Does** the house **have** a yard?
Yes, they **do**. / No, they **don't**.	Yes, it **does**. / No, it **doesn't**.

GRAMMAR PLUS *see page 138*

A Complete the conversation. Then practice with a partner.

Julia _____Do_____ you _____live_____ in an apartment?

Ethan No, I _____. I _____ in a house.

Julia _____ it _____ a yard?

Ethan Yes, it _____.

Julia That sounds nice. _____ you _____ alone?

Ethan No, I _____. I _____ with my family.

Julia _____ you _____ any brothers or sisters?

Ethan Yes, I _____. I _____ four sisters.

Julia Really? _____ your house _____ many bedrooms?

Ethan Yes, it _____. It _____ four.

Julia _____ you _____ your own bedroom?

Ethan Yes, I _____. I'm really lucky.

B **PAIR WORK** Read the conversation in part A again. Ask and answer these questions about Ethan.

1. Does he live in an apartment?
2. Does his house have a yard?
3. Does he live alone?
4. Does he have his own room?

C **PAIR WORK** Write five questions to ask your partner about his or her home. Then ask and answer the questions.

4 LISTENING We have a nice yard.

Listen to four people describe their homes. Number the pictures from 1 to 4.

5

WORD POWER Furniture and appliances

▶ **A** Listen and practice.

an armchair   a stove   curtains   pictures

a bed   a table   a coffee table

a microwave   lamps   a sofa

a desk   a refrigerator   a coffee maker   a dresser   chairs

a mirror   a bookcase   a rug   cupboards

B Which rooms have the things in part A? Complete the chart.

A kitchen has . . .	a table a stove
A dining room has . . .	a table
A living room has . . .	
A bedroom has . . .	

C **GROUP WORK** What furniture is in your house or apartment? Tell your classmates.

"My living room has a sofa, a bookcase, and a rug . . ."

6 CONVERSATION I really need some furniture.

▶ Listen and practice.

Eric This apartment is great, Lara.

Lara Thanks. I love it, but I really need some furniture.

Eric What do you need?

Lara Oh, lots of things. For example, there are some chairs in the kitchen, but there isn't a table.

Eric That's true. And there's no sofa in the living room.

Lara And there aren't any armchairs, there isn't a rug . . . There's only this lamp!

Eric So let's go shopping next weekend!

7 GRAMMAR FOCUS

▶
There is, there are

There's a bed in the bedroom.	**There are some** chairs in the kitchen.	There**'s** = There is
There's no sofa in the bedroom.	**There are no** chairs in the living room.	
There isn't a table in the kitchen.	**There aren't any** chairs in the living room.	

GRAMMAR PLUS *see page 138*

A Look at the picture of Ann's apartment. Complete the sentences. Then practice with a partner.

1. _____There's no_____ dresser in the bedroom.
2. _____ chairs in the kitchen.
3. _____ lamp in the living room.
4. _____ refrigerator.
5. _____ rugs on the floor.
6. _____ curtains on the windows.
7. _____ armchair in the bedroom.
8. _____ books in the bookcase.

B Write five sentences about things you have or don't have in your home. Then compare with a partner.

> There are two sofas in my living room.

8 INTERCHANGE 7 Find the differences

Compare two apartments. Go to Interchange 7 on page 121.

9 PRONUNCIATION Words with *th*

A Listen and practice. Notice the pronunciation of /θ/ and /ð/.

/ð/ /θ/   /ð/   /ð/   /θ/ /θ/

There are **th**irteen rooms in **th**is house. **The** house has **th**ree ba**th**rooms.

B **PAIR WORK** List other words with /θ/ and /ð/. Then use them to write two sentences. Read them aloud.

There are thirty-three books on their bookcase.

10 LISTENING A furniture website

Listen to Jacob and Courtney talk about furniture on a website. What does Courtney like? What doesn't she like? Choose ☺ (likes) or ☹ (doesn't like).

☺ ☹	armchairs	☺ ☹	a sofa
☺ ☹	a rug	☺ ☹	lamps
☺ ☹	a bookcase	☺ ☹	a mirror
☺ ☹	a coffee table	☺ ☹	curtains

11 SPEAKING My dream home

A Write a description of your dream home.

What is your dream home?
Where is it?
What rooms does it have?
What things are in the rooms?
Does it have a view?

My dream home is a loft in a big city. There is one large living room with a lot of windows. There are two bedrooms and . . .

B **PAIR WORK** Ask your partner about his or her dream home.

A: What is your dream home?
B: My dream home is a loft in a big city.
A: What rooms does it have?
B: Well, there is a big living room, a small kitchen . . .

a beach house

a loft in a big city

a country villa

a cabin in the mountains

12 READING ▶

A Scan the article. Which hotel has a room that looks like a dessert?

🧳 TRAVELNEWS   Home   Posts   Archives   🔍

Unique Hotels

Which do you like – the world of science or the world of fiction?
In this week's vacation post, we discover a hotel made for fans of
nature and another hotel for fans of stories.

Bubble Hotel, Allauch, France   4 new 💬

Just imagine sleeping in a giant, clear bubble in a
forest. That's exactly what happens here. At night,
hotel guests lie in bed and watch the stars and
moon. Each bubble has a comfortable bed and a
nice bathroom with a shower. There's also an
air-conditioner to keep the room cool in summer
and a heater to keep it warm when it's cold outside.

Each bubble room is different. Guests choose the
"Zen" bubble if they want to feel relaxed. Or they
stay in the "Love Nature" bubble for a beautiful view.
Sometimes there are rabbits and squirrels playing
outside. Is there anything missing? Well, yes, there
isn't a TV because no one needs a TV in a bubble!

The Roxbury, New York, the United States   4 new 💬

In the mountains near New York City, there's a very unusual
hotel. Its name is the Roxbury. It has many rooms, but every
single room is different. There's the Wizard's Emeralds room,
for example. It has a yellow "road" in the middle – just like in
The Wizard of Oz. There's a green shower in the bathroom
with big red flowers on the walls.

Do you like sweet things?

Maryann's Coconut
Cream Pie room looks
just like a dessert –
good enough to eat! The
bed is round like a pie,
and the ceiling looks like
whipped cream.

How about space?

When you walk into George's
Spacepad, you see an enormous
red bathtub. It glows in the dark!
There isn't a shower, but there are
silver curtains, crazy lights, and
two cozy sofas. It's really out of
this world!

B Read the article. What's in each hotel? Complete the sentences.

sofas	animals	moon	round bed	✓ yellow road
stars	bathtub	TV	shower	air-conditioner

At The Roxbury

1. In the Wizard's Emeralds room, there is a _____ *yellow road* _____.

2. There is a _____ in Maryann's Coconut Cream Pie room.

3. In George's Spacepad, there are two _____. There is a red
_____, but there isn't a _____.

At the Bubble Hotel

4. There is a view of the _____ and the _____.

5. There is an _____ to keep the room cool.

6. There are sometimes _____ playing outside.

7. There isn't a _____.

C **GROUP WORK** Talk about these questions.

1. Which hotel do you like? Why?

2. Imagine you have a hotel. What do you do to make it interesting?

8 Where do you work?

▶ Discuss jobs and workplaces using simple present Wh-questions
▶ Discuss opinions about jobs using *be* + adjective and adjective + noun

1 WORD POWER Jobs

A Match the jobs with the pictures. Then listen and practice.

a. accountant	e. doctor	i. office manager	m. security guard
b. bellhop	f. front desk clerk	✓ j. police officer	n. server
c. cashier	g. host	k. receptionist	o. taxi driver
d. chef	h. nurse	l. salesperson	p. vendor

1.   j   2.   3.
4.   5.   6.
7.   8.   9.
10.   11.
12.   13.
14.   15.   16.

B **PAIR WORK** Ask questions about the people in part A. What are their jobs?

A: What does she do?
B: She's a police officer.

2 SPEAKING Workplaces

A PAIR WORK Who works in these places? Complete the chart with jobs from Exercise 1. Add one more job to each list.

A: A doctor works in a hospital.　　　**B:** A nurse works in a hospital, too.

IN A HOSPITAL	IN AN OFFICE	IN A STORE	IN A HOTEL
a doctor			
a nurse			

B CLASS ACTIVITY Ask and answer *Who* questions about jobs. Use these words.

wears a uniform	sits all day	stands all day	works with a team
talks to people	works hard	works at night	makes a lot of money

A: Who wears a uniform?
B: A police officer wears a uniform.
C: A security guard wears a uniform, too.

3 CONVERSATION What does he do?

▶ Listen and practice.

 JORDAN Where does your brother work?

 ALICIA In a hotel.

JORDAN Oh, really? My brother works in a hotel, too. He's an accountant.

ALICIA How does he like it?

JORDAN He hates it. He doesn't like the manager.

ALICIA That's too bad. What hotel does he work for?

JORDAN The Plaza.

ALICIA That's funny. My brother works there, too.

 JORDAN Oh, that's interesting. What does he do?

 ALICIA Actually, he's the manager!

Where do you work? **51**

> **Simple present Wh-questions**

Where do you **work**?	**Where does** he **work**?	**Where do** they **work**?
In a hospital.	In a hotel.	In an office.
What do you **do**?	**What does** he **do**?	**What do** they **do**?
I'm a doctor.	He's a manager.	They're accountants.
How do you **like** it?	**How does** he **like** it?	**How do** they **like** it?
I really like it.	It's OK.	They hate it.

GRAMMAR PLUS *see page 139*

A Complete these conversations. Then practice with a partner.

1. A: _____What_____ does your sister _____do_____?

    B: My sister? She's a teacher.

    A: _____ does she _____ it?

    B: It's difficult, but she loves it.

2. A: _____ does your brother _____?

    B: In an office. He's an accountant.

    A: Oh? _____ does he _____ it?

    B: He doesn't really like it.

3. A: _____ do your parents _____ their jobs?

    B: Oh, I guess they like them.

    A: I don't remember. _____ do they _____?

    B: In a big hospital. They're doctors.

4. A: _____ do you _____?

    B: I'm a student.

    A: I see. _____ do you _____ your classes?

    B: They're great. I like them a lot.

B **PAIR WORK** Ask questions about these people. Where do they work? What do they do? How do they like it?

Jeff

Jodie

Chad and Tracy

    A: Where does Chad work?

    B: He works in . . .

5 PRONUNCIATION Reduction of *do*

Listen and practice. Notice the reduction of **do**.

Where **do you** work?   Where **do they** work?

What **do you** do?   What **do they** do?

6

SNAPSHOT

▶ Listen and practice.

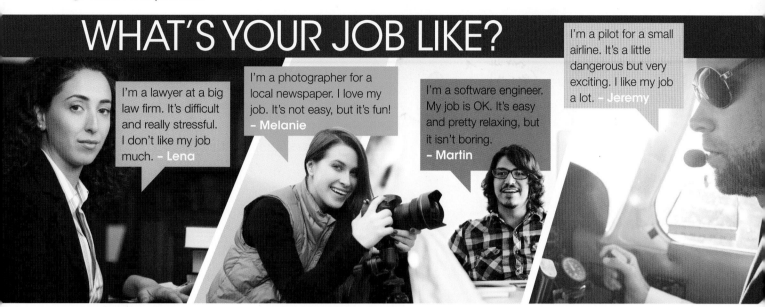

WHAT'S YOUR JOB LIKE?

I'm a lawyer at a big law firm. It's difficult and really stressful. I don't like my job much. – Lena

I'm a photographer for a local newspaper. I love my job. It's not easy, but it's fun! – Melanie

I'm a software engineer. My job is OK. It's easy and pretty relaxing, but it isn't boring. – Martin

I'm a pilot for a small airline. It's a little dangerous but very exciting. I like my job a lot. – Jeremy

Who likes his or her job? Who doesn't? Why? Why not?
What jobs do you think are interesting? What jobs are not very interesting?

7 **CONVERSATION** It's a dangerous job.

▶ Listen and practice.

JACK	Hey, Paula. I hear you have a new job.
PAULA	Yes. I'm teaching math at Lincoln High School.
JACK	How do you like it?
PAULA	It's difficult, but the students are terrific. How are things with you?
JACK	Not bad. Guess what! I'm a firefighter now.
PAULA	Really? Wow! How do you like it?
JACK	It's a dangerous job, but it's really interesting. I love it!
PAULA	OK, but please be careful!

8 **LISTENING** Is your job interesting?

▶ Listen to four people talk about their jobs. Complete the chart with the correct jobs and adjectives.

	What do they do?	What's it like?
1. Yasmin		
2. Kana		
3. Luke		
4. Brandon		

9 GRAMMAR FOCUS

▶ **Placement of adjectives**

be + adjective	adjective + noun
A doctor's job **is stressful**.	A doctor has **a stressful job**.
A firefighter's job **is dangerous**.	A firefighter has **a dangerous job**.

GRAMMAR PLUS *see page 139*

A Write each sentence a different way. Then compare with a partner.

1. A photographer's job is interesting. _A photographer has an interesting job._
2. A pilot's job is exciting. _____
3. A teacher's job is stressful. _____
4. A cashier has a boring job. _____
5. An accountant has a difficult job. _____
6. A receptionist has an easy job. _____

B GROUP WORK Write one job for each adjective. Do your classmates agree?

1. easy	_actor_	4. boring	_____
2. difficult	_____	5. exciting	_____
3. dangerous	_____	6. relaxing	_____

A: A graphic designer has an easy job.
B: I don't agree. A graphic designer's job is difficult.
C: I think . . .

graphic designer

10 INTERCHANGE 8 The perfect job

What do you want in a job? Go to Interchange 8 on page 122.

11 SPEAKING Workday routines

GROUP WORK Ask three classmates about their jobs (or their friends' or family members' jobs). Then tell the class.

Ask about a classmate	Ask about a classmate's friend or family member
Do you have a job?	Tell me about your . . .
Where do you work?	Where does he/she work?
What do you do, exactly?	What does he/she do, exactly?
Is your job interesting?	Is his/her job difficult?
What time do you start work?	What time does he/she start work?
When do you finish work?	When does he/she finish work?
Do you like your job?	Does he/she like his/her job?
What do you do after work?	What does he/she do after work?

A Do you think all jobs are boring? Think again! Look at the photos. What do these people do?

Dream Jobs

Crocodile Researcher ♡ 💬

I have a great job. I study crocodiles! It's an important job. Let me explain why. Here in Australia, we have a lot of crocodiles, but sometimes the crocodiles are sick. I want to know why. I study the food the crocodiles eat. I also learn how fast they grow and where they live. How do I do this? Well, in the morning, I take my camera, and I watch the crocodiles in the river. I take photos. Sometimes the crocodiles eat toads. Some toads make them sick and they die. I want to help the crocodiles.

Ice Cream Flavor Expert ♡ 💬

Believe it or not, I taste ice cream for my job. Yes, it's a dream job, but it's also difficult! I work at a big ice cream company. Every day, I taste lots of different flavors three times each. Why is that? Well, I taste a little of the ice cream we make in the morning, afternoon, and at night. That way, I know that all the ice cream is good. I use my eyes first: Does the ice cream look nice? Then I taste the ice cream with a spoon: Does it taste fresh and sweet? Then I spit it out. Yes, I really spit it out!

Subscribe to our site

enter email   **Sign up**

B Read the article. Check (✓) True or False.

	True	False
1. Both people have jobs they do outside.	☐	☐
2. The crocodile researcher studies what crocodiles eat.	☐	☐
3. The crocodile researcher watches the crocodiles at night.	☐	☐
4. The ice cream flavor expert tastes each flavor three times.	☐	☐
5. Ice cream flavor experts don't look at the ice cream.	☐	☐

C What's your dream job? Why? Write a short description. Compare with a partner.

Units 7–8 Progress check

SELF-ASSESSMENT

How well can you do these things? Check (✓) the boxes.

I can . . .	Very well	OK	A little
Ask and answer questions about living spaces (Ex. 1)	☐	☐	☐
Talk about rooms and furniture (Ex. 1)	☐	☐	☐
Ask and answer questions about work (Ex. 2)	☐	☐	☐
Understand descriptions of jobs (Ex. 3)	☐	☐	☐
Give and respond to opinions about jobs (Ex. 4)	☐	☐	☐

1 SPEAKING A new apartment

A Imagine you are moving into this apartment. What things are in the rooms?
Draw pictures. Use the furniture in the box and your own ideas.

> bed   chairs   desk   dresser   lamp   mirror   sofa   table

B **PAIR WORK** Ask questions about your partner's apartment.

A: I'm moving into a new apartment!
B: That's great! Where is it?
A: . . .
B: What's it like? Does it have many rooms?
A: Well, it has . . .

B: Does the . . . have . . . ?
A: . . .
B: Do you have a lot of furniture?
A: Well, there's . . . in the . . .
There are some . . . in the . . .
B: Do you have everything you need for the apartment?
A: No, I don't. There's no . . .
There isn't any . . .
There aren't any . . .
B: OK. Let's go shopping this weekend!

2 SPEAKING What does he do?

A Complete the conversations with Wh-questions.

1. **A:** <u>Where does your father work</u> ?
   B: My father? He works in a store.
   A: _____ ?
   B: He's a salesperson.
   A: _____ ?
   B: He likes his job a lot!

2. **A:** _____ ?
   B: I'm an accountant.
   A: _____ ?
   B: I work in an office.
   A: _____ ?
   B: It's OK. I guess I like it.

B **PAIR WORK** Your partner asks the questions in part A.
Answer with your own information.

3 LISTENING How do you like your job?

▶ Listen to Rachel, Daniel, and Mai talk about their jobs.
Check (✓) the correct answers.

	Where do they work?		**What do they do?**	
1. Rachel	☐ office	☐ store	☐ receptionist	☐ doctor
2. Daniel	☐ hospital	☐ school	☐ nurse	☐ teacher
3. Mai	☐ hotel	☐ office	☐ manager	☐ front desk clerk

4 SPEAKING Boring or interesting?

GROUP WORK What do you think of these jobs? Give your opinions.

veterinarian

dentist

architect

hairstylist

A: I think a veterinarian has a stressful job.
B: I don't really agree. I think a veterinarian's job is relaxing.
C: Well, I think a veterinarian's job is difficult. . . .

WHAT'S NEXT?

Look at your Self-assessment again. Do you need to review anything?

I always eat breakfast.

▸ Discuss food
▸ Describe eating habits

1 WORD POWER Foods

▶ **A** Listen and practice.

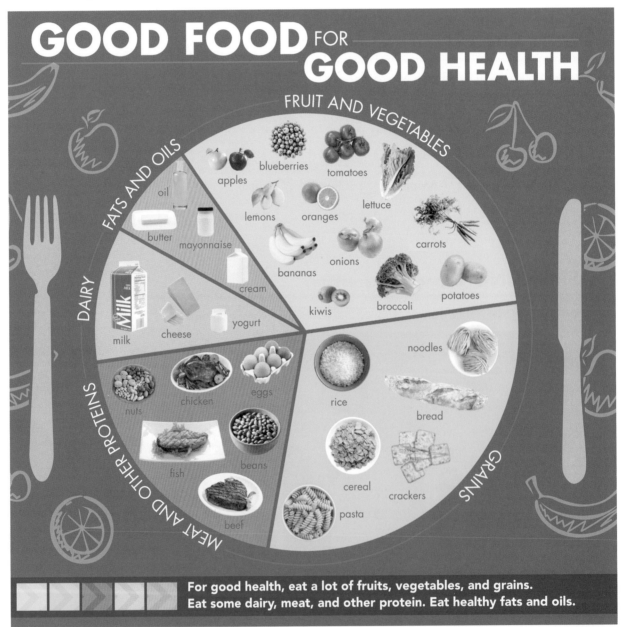

GOOD FOOD FOR GOOD HEALTH

FATS AND OILS
oil
butter
mayonnaise

FRUIT AND VEGETABLES
apples
blueberries
tomatoes
lemons
oranges
lettuce
cream
bananas
onions
carrots
kiwis
broccoli
potatoes

DAIRY
milk
cheese
yogurt

MEAT AND OTHER PROTEINS
nuts
chicken
eggs
fish
beans
beef

GRAINS
rice
noodles
bread
cereal
crackers
pasta

For good health, eat a lot of fruits, vegetables, and grains.
Eat some dairy, meat, and other protein. Eat healthy fats and oils.

B PAIR WORK What foods do you like? What don't you like?
Make a list. Then tell a partner.

A: I like chicken, potatoes, and apples. I don't like beef, broccoli, or onions.

B: I like . . .

I like	I don't like
chicken	beef
potatoes	broccoli
apples	onions

2 CONVERSATION Let's get some lettuce and some tomatoes.

▶ Listen and practice.

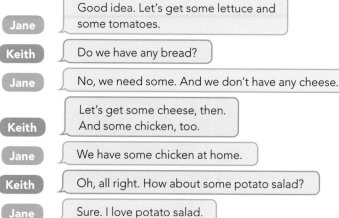

Keith Do we need any lettuce for the sandwiches?

Jane Good idea. Let's get some lettuce and some tomatoes.

Keith Do we have any bread?

Jane No, we need some. And we don't have any cheese.

Keith Let's get some cheese, then. And some chicken, too.

Jane We have some chicken at home.

Keith Oh, all right. How about some potato salad?

Jane Sure. I love potato salad.

Keith Great! Let's buy some.

3 GRAMMAR FOCUS

▶

Count and noncount nouns; *some* and *any*

Count nouns	Noncount nouns
an egg → egg**s**	bread
a potato → potato**es**	lettuce
Do we need **any** potatoes?	Do we need **any** lettuce?
Yes. Let's get **some** (potatoes).	Yes. Let's get **some** (lettuce).
No. We don't need **any** (potatoes).	No. We don't need **any** (lettuce).

GRAMMAR PLUS *see page 140*

A Complete the conversation with *some* or *any*.

Keith Oh, they don't have _____any_____ potato salad.

Jane But we have lots of potatoes at home. Let's make _____.

Keith Great. Do we have _____ mayonnaise?

Jane No. We need to buy _____. And we need _____ onions.

Keith Oh, no, I don't want _____ onions in the salad.

Jane OK, don't worry. Let's get _____ celery, then.

Keith No, I don't want _____ celery. I have an idea.
Let's put _____ apples in it.

Jane Are you serious? Apples in potato salad? Well, OK . . .

B Complete the chart with foods from Exercise 1. Then compare with a partner.

Count			Noncount		
crackers			bread		

4 PRONUNCIATION Sentence stress

▶ **A** Listen and practice. Notice the stressed words.

A: Do we need any beans?

B: Yes. We need some beans.

A: Do we need any rice?

B: No. We don't need any rice.

B PAIR WORK Ask *Do we need . . . ?* questions about the food in the picture.
Then look at the shopping list and answer.

A: Do we need any apples?
B: Yes. We need some apples. Do we need any bananas?
A: Let's see . . . No, we don't need any bananas.

Shopping basket 60%
- apples ☐
- broccoli ☐
- celery ☐
- oranges ☐
- lettuce ☐
- onions ☐
- potatoes ☐
- tomatoes ☐

5 SNAPSHOT

▶ Listen and practice.

BREAKFAST AROUND THE WORLD

THE UNITED STATES
- ☐ cereal with milk
- ☐ fresh fruit
- ☐ orange juice
- ☐ coffee
- ☐ pastries

JAPAN
- ☐ fish
- ☐ rice
- ☐ soup
- ☐ pickles
- ☐ green tea

COSTA RICA
- ☐ rice and beans
- ☐ eggs
- ☐ red peppers
- ☐ bananas
- ☐ coffee with milk

What do you have for breakfast? Check (✓) the foods and drinks.
What else do you have for breakfast?

6 CONVERSATION We always have green tea.

▶ Listen and practice.

Eva: What is a typical Japanese breakfast, Kaito?

Kaito: Well, we usually have fish, rice, and soup.

Eva: Fish for breakfast? That's interesting.

Kaito: Oh, it's really good. Sometimes we have a salad, too. But we never have coffee.

Eva: Really? What do you have?

Kaito: We always have green tea.

Eva: I love green tea!

Kaito: Listen, my family usually has a Japanese-style breakfast on weekends. Why don't you come to my house on Sunday?

Eva: That's very nice of you. Thanks!

7 GRAMMAR FOCUS

▶ **Adverbs of frequency**

always	Do you **ever** have fish for breakfast?	100%	always
usually	Yes, I **always** do.		usually
often	**Sometime**s I do.		often
I **sometimes** eat breakfast.	No, I **never** do.		sometimes
hardly ever			hardly ever
never		0%	never
Sometimes I eat breakfast.			

GRAMMAR PLUS *see page 140*

A Put the adverbs in the correct places. Then practice with a partner.

       usually
A: Do you ʌhave a big breakfast? (usually)
B: Well, on Sunday I have a big breakfast with my friends. (always)
A: Do you eat breakfast at work on weekdays? (ever)
B: Yes, I have breakfast at the office restaurant. (sometimes)
A: Do you eat breakfast at your desk? (often)
B: No, I eat breakfast at my desk. (hardly ever)

B Unscramble the sentences.

1. I / have / hardly ever / beef / for lunch   <u>I hardly ever have beef for lunch.</u>
2. when I watch TV / I / snacks / eat / never   _____
3. eat / for / eggs / breakfast / sometimes / I   _____
4. have / I / dinner / with / usually / family / my   _____

C Rewrite the sentences from part B with your own information. Then compare with a partner.

A: I usually have beef or chicken for lunch.
B: I never have beef. I don't like it. I often have fish and a salad for lunch.

8 LISTENING Carrots are my favorite!

A Devon and Victoria are talking about food.
How often does Victoria eat these foods?
Listen and check (✓) Often, Sometimes, or Never.

	OFTEN	SOMETIMES	NEVER
noodles	✓		
chicken			
fish			
eggs			
carrots			

B GROUP WORK Do you ever eat the foods in part A? Tell your classmates.

A: I often eat noodles.
B: Really? I never eat noodles.
C: Well, I . . .

9 SPEAKING Mealtime survey

A Add two questions about mealtime habits to the chart. Then ask two people the questions.
Write their names and complete the chart.

		Name:	Name:
1.	Do you always have a big breakfast?		
2.	What time do you usually have lunch?		
3.	What do you usually have for lunch?		
4.	Do you often have snacks in the afternoon?		
5.	Do you ever go to a restaurant for dinner?		
6.	What's something you never eat for dinner?		
7.	_____ ?		
8.	_____ ?		

A: Pedro, do you always have a big breakfast?
B: No, I hardly ever do. I have coffee and milk. Sometimes I eat bread or crackers.

B CLASS ACTIVITY Tell your classmates about your partners' mealtime habits.

"Pedro hardly ever has a big breakfast. But he always eats lunch and dinner . . . "

10 INTERCHANGE 9 Planning a party

Decide what food and drinks to serve at a party. Go to Interchange 9 on page 123.

A Look at the pictures. Which foods do you like?

IT'S A FOOD Festival!

LA TOMATINA

People usually eat tomatoes. But once a year, in Buñol, Spain, people just throw them! Yes, that's correct. The whole town of Buñol has a giant tomato fight! It's very messy. By the end of the day, there are squashed tomatoes all over town. In fact, there are 120 tons of squashed tomatoes!

GARLIC FESTIVAL

All over the world, people use garlic in their cooking. Some people in California, in the U.S., really like garlic. They like it so much that every year they celebrate it with a garlic festival. You can taste garlic in everything you can think of. There's even garlic ice cream and garlic popcorn.

MONKEY BUFFET FESTIVAL

There's something very interesting about this food festival. It's not for people, it's for monkeys! In Lopburi, Thailand, people bring all kinds of different fruits and leave them out for the monkeys to eat. They bring pineapples, apples, mangoes . . . and bananas, of course. It's the people's way of saying thank you to the monkeys. That's because tourists come to see the monkeys, and that helps the people's businesses. Isn't that cool?

BREAD FOR THE DAY OF THE DEAD

The Day of the Dead is a very important day in Mexico. Many people celebrate their family members and friends by baking special bread. They make bread in the shape of humans, flowers, bones, and animals. The bread is sweet, and sometimes it has anise seeds or orange in it.

B Read the article. Then correct these sentences.

1. There's a big tomato fight in ~~Mexico~~ Spain once a year.
2. People in California don't like garlic.
3. Some people in the U.S. use tomatoes to make ice cream and popcorn.
4. The Monkey Buffet Festival happens in Spain.
5. In Thailand, people give fruit to the tourists.
6. Some Mexicans make bread in the shape of houses and other buildings.

C **GROUP WORK** Do you eat any special food at celebrations in your country? What do you celebrate and which foods do you eat? Tell your classmates.

10 What sports do you like?

▸ Discuss sports to watch and play
▸ Discuss skills, abilities, and talents

1 SNAPSHOT

▶ Listen and practice.

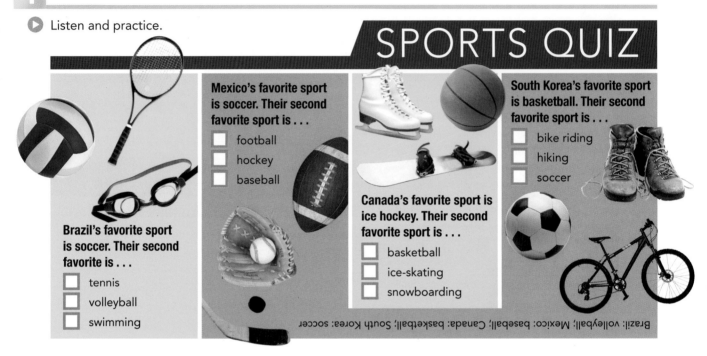

SPORTS QUIZ

Mexico's favorite sport is soccer. Their second favorite sport is . . .
- [ ] football
- [ ] hockey
- [ ] baseball

South Korea's favorite sport is basketball. Their second favorite sport is . . .
- [ ] bike riding
- [ ] hiking
- [ ] soccer

Canada's favorite sport is ice hockey. Their second favorite sport is . . .
- [ ] basketball
- [ ] ice-skating
- [ ] snowboarding

Brazil's favorite sport is soccer. Their second favorite is . . .
- [ ] tennis
- [ ] volleyball
- [ ] swimming

Brazil: volleyball; Mexico: baseball; Canada: basketball; South Korea: soccer

Can you guess what sports are the second favorite in each country? Check (✓) the sports.
Do you like sports? What sports are popular in your country?

2 CONVERSATION When do you play all these sports?

▶ Listen and practice.

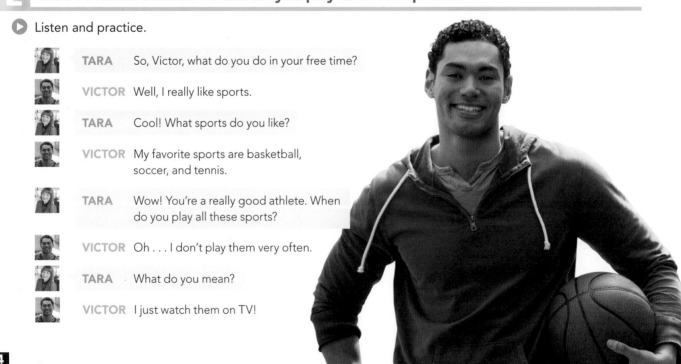

TARA So, Victor, what do you do in your free time?

VICTOR Well, I really like sports.

TARA Cool! What sports do you like?

VICTOR My favorite sports are basketball, soccer, and tennis.

TARA Wow! You're a really good athlete. When do you play all these sports?

VICTOR Oh . . . I don't play them very often.

TARA What do you mean?

VICTOR I just watch them on TV!

GRAMMAR FOCUS

Simple present Wh-questions

What sports do you play?	I play **soccer and basketball**.
Who do you play basketball **with**?	I play **with some friends from work**.
Where do you play?	We play **at a gym near the office**.
How often do you practice?	We practice **twice a week**.
When do you practice?	We practice **on Tuesdays and Thursdays**.
What time do you start?	We start **at six in the evening**.

GRAMMAR PLUS *see page 141*

A Complete the conversations with the correct Wh-question words. Then practice with a partner.

1. **A:** _____How often_____ do you go bike riding?
   B: Oh, about once or twice a week.
   A: I love to go bike riding. I go every Sunday.
   B: Really? _____ do you go?
   A: Usually at about ten in the morning.
   B: Oh, yeah? _____ do you go with?
   A: A group of friends. Come with us next time!

2. **A:** I watch sports on TV every weekend.
   B: Really? _____ do you like to watch?
   A: Soccer. It's my favorite!
   B: _____ do you usually watch soccer?
   A: In the evening or on weekends.
   B: And _____ do you usually watch it?
   At home?
   A: No, at my brother's house. He has a home theater!

B Complete the conversation with Wh-questions. Then compare with a partner.

A: _What sports do you like_____?
B: I like a lot of sports, but I really love volleyball!
A: _____?
B: I usually play with my sister and some friends.
A: _____?
B: We practice on Saturdays.
A: _____?
B: We start at about noon.
A: _____?
B: We usually play at a sports club, but sometimes we play on the beach.

C **PAIR WORK** Ask your partner five questions about sports or other activities. Then tell the class.

A: What sports do you like?
B: I don't like sports very much.
A: Oh? What do you like to do in your free time?

What sports do you like? **65**

4 LISTENING What do you think of sports?

▶ Listen to the conversations about sports. Complete the chart.

	Favorite sport	Do they play or watch it?	
		Play	**Watch**
1. James	_football_	☑	☐
2. Brianna	_____	☐	☐
3. Matthew	_____	☐	☐
4. Nicole	_____	☐	☐

5 SPEAKING Free-time activities

A Add one more question about free-time activities to the chart. Then ask two people the questions. Write their names and complete the chart.

	Name:	Name:
1. What sports do you like to watch or play?		
2. What do you do on the weekends?		
3. What do you like to do when the weather is nice?		
4. What do you like to do when it's raining?		
5. How often do you play video games?		
6. _____?		

A: Soo-hyun, what sports do you like?
B: I like a lot of sports. My favorites are soccer and baseball.

B CLASS ACTIVITY Tell your classmates about your partners' free-time activities.

6 CONVERSATION What can I do?

▶ Listen and practice.

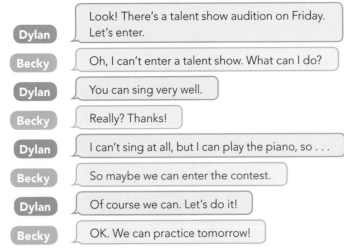

Dylan Look! There's a talent show audition on Friday. Let's enter.

Becky Oh, I can't enter a talent show. What can I do?

Dylan You can sing very well.

Becky Really? Thanks!

Dylan I can't sing at all, but I can play the piano, so . . .

Becky So maybe we can enter the contest.

Dylan Of course we can. Let's do it!

Becky OK. We can practice tomorrow!

7 GRAMMAR FOCUS

Can for ability

I			you		I	What **can** I do?
You			I		you	You **can** sing.
She	**can**	sing very well.	**Can** she sing?	Yes, she	**can**.	
He	**can't**	sing at all.	he	No, he	**can't**.	Who **can** sing?
We			we		we	Becky **can**.
They			they		they	

GRAMMAR PLUS *see page 141*

A Six people are talking about things they can and can't do. Complete these sentences.

Ben

1. I _____can_____ swim.

Sara

2. I _____ fix cars.

Diane

3. I _____ sing.

Jeff

4. I _____ ice-skate.

Lisa

5. I _____ play the piano.

Megan

6. I _____ cook.

B **PAIR WORK** Ask and answer questions about the pictures in part A.

A: Can Ben swim?
B: Yes, he can.

C **GROUP WORK** Can your classmates do the things in part A? Ask and answer questions.

"Can you swim, Diego?"

8 PRONUNCIATION *Can and can't*

A Listen and practice. Notice the pronunciation of **can** and **can't**.

/kən/   /kænt/
I **can** play the piano.   I **can't** sing at all.

B **PAIR WORK** Your partner reads a sentence for each number. Check (✓) the sentence you hear.

1. ☐ I can cook.   **2.** ☐ I can drive.   **3.** ☐ I can swim.   **4.** ☐ I can dance.
    ☐ I can't cook.   ☐ I can't drive.   ☐ I can't swim.   ☐ I can't dance.

9 LISTENING Are you good at sports?

▶ Listen to three people talk about their abilities. Write J (Joshua), M (Monica), or A (Anthony) on the things they can do well.

   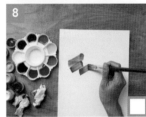

10 WORD POWER Talents and abilities

▶ **A** Complete the word map with talents and abilities from the list. Then listen and practice.

✓ bake cookies
build a robot
design a website
do math in your head
edit a video
fix a computer
make electronic music
play chess
ride a horse
run a marathon
skateboard
take good photos
tell good jokes

MUSICAL OR ARTISTIC
_____
_____
_____
_____

ATHLETIC
_____
_____
_____

TALENTS AND ABILITIES

TECHNICAL
_____
_____
_____

OTHER
bake cookies
_____
_____

B GROUP WORK Who can do the things in part A?
Make a list of guesses about your classmates.

A: Who can bake cookies?
B: I think Melanie can.
C: Who can design . . . ?

bake cookies - Melanie

design a website

C CLASS ACTIVITY Go around the room and check your guesses.

A: Melanie, can you bake cookies?
B: Yes, I can.

11 INTERCHANGE 10 Hidden talents and abilities

Learn more about your classmates' hidden talents and abilities. Go to Interchange 10 on page 124.

A Some people like to set world records. Why do you think they like to do that?

Awesome Sports Records

base jumping

Base jumping is a dangerous sport.
People jump off buildings, bridges, and other high places. The Burj Khalifa tower in Dubai, United Arab Emirates, is 824 meters (2,717 feet) tall. That's a very scary jump. But Fred Fugen and Vince Reffet of France can jump it! They also enjoy skydiving and parachuting.

Do you know what a unicycle is?
It's a bicycle with just one wheel. David Weichenberger of Austria has the world record for longest jump on a unicycle. He can jump 2.95 meters (about 10 feet).

Kalamandalam Hemalatha of India
has an amazing marathon record, but it's not for running. She can dance, and dance, and dance! In fact, Kalamandalam can dance for 123 hours and 15 minutes. That's the longest dance marathon on record. Kalamandalam's special dance is from India. It's called the Mohiniyattam dance.

Mohiniyattam dance

Otto the skateboarding dog

Do you know about Otto?
Otto likes surfing, skateboarding, and playing soccer. Otto is a champion skateboarder, but he's a dog from Lima, Peru! Otto has the record for skateboarding through the legs of 30 people!

Can you squash an apple?
Can you squash it using just the muscles in your arms? One woman can! Her name is Linsey Lindberg. Linsey is from Texas, in the U.S. In one minute, she can squash 10 apples. That's one apple every six seconds.

B Read the records. Then check (✓) the correct answers to the questions.

1. What's special about a unicycle?
   ☐ **a.** It has no wheels.   ☐ **b.** It has one wheel, not two.
2. Who likes base jumping?
   ☐ **a.** David Weichenberger   ☐ **b.** Fred Fugen
3. What sort of marathon can Kalamandalam do?
   ☐ **a.** a dance marathon   ☐ **b.** a running marathon
4. How does Linsey Lindberg squash apples?
   ☐ **a.** with her hands   ☐ **b.** with her arm muscles
5. What is one sport that Otto plays?
   ☐ **a.** basketball   ☐ **b.** soccer

C **GROUP WORK** Do you think it's fun to set world records? Why or why not? What other world records do you know about? Tell your classmates.

Units 9–10 Progress check

SELF-ASSESSMENT

How well can you do these things? Check (✓) the boxes.

I can . . .	Very well	OK	A little
Make and respond to suggestions (Ex. 1)	☐	☐	☐
Talk about food and drink (Ex. 1, 2)	☐	☐	☐
Ask and answer questions about eating habits (Ex. 2)	☐	☐	☐
Understand descriptions of sporting activities (Ex. 3)	☐	☐	☐
Ask and answer questions about likes and dislikes (Ex. 4)	☐	☐	☐
Talk about job abilities (Ex. 5)	☐	☐	☐

1 SPEAKING Planning a class party

A GROUP WORK Plan a class party. Choose two main dishes, two salads, two drinks, and two desserts. Then tell the class.

Main dishes		
Salads		
Drinks		
Desserts		

useful expressions

Do we want any . . . ?
Let's get/make some . . .
I don't want/like . . .
Everybody likes . . .

2 SPEAKING Movie snacks

PAIR WORK Does your partner ever have these snacks at the movies? Add one more snack to the chart. Ask questions and complete the survey.

	Always	Usually	Sometimes	Hardly ever	Never
1. candy	☐	☐	☐	☐	☐
2. coffee	☐	☐	☐	☐	☐
3. pizza	☐	☐	☐	☐	☐
4. popcorn	☐	☐	☐	☐	☐
5. soda	☐	☐	☐	☐	☐
6. _____	☐	☐	☐	☐	☐

A: Do you ever have candy at the movies?
B: Yes, I sometimes have candy.

3 LISTENING Do you play any sports?

▶ Listen to Stephanie ask Raymond about sports. Check (✓) Raymond's answers.

1. ☐ I play football.
   ☐ I play soccer.

2. ☐ Some friends from school.
   ☐ Some friends from work.

3. ☐ At 6:00 A.M.
   ☐ At 6:00 P.M.

4. ☐ Every day.
   ☐ Every week.

5. ☐ On the weekends.
   ☐ In the afternoons.

6. ☐ At the park.
   ☐ In the yard.

4 SPEAKING My favorite things

A Complete the chart with things you love, like, and don't like.

	I love . . .	I like . . .	I don't like . . .
Sports			
Other activities			
Foods			
Clothes			

B PAIR WORK Find out what your partner loves, likes, and doesn't like.
Then ask more questions with *who*, *where*, *how often*, or *when*.

A: What sports do you love?
B: I love bike riding.

A: Who do you usually go bike riding with?
B: I usually go with my brother and sister.

5 SPEAKING Talents and abilities

GROUP WORK What can these people do well? Make a list.
Use the abilities in the box and your own ideas. Then tell the class.

chef

mechanic

artist

musician

A: A chef can cook very well.
B: A chef can also bake things, like cakes and cookies.
A: Also, a chef can . . .

bake	fix a motorcycle
cook	paint
draw	play the guitar
fix a car	read music

WHAT'S NEXT?

Look at your Self-assessment again. Do you need to review anything?

11 I'm going to have a party.

▸ **Discuss evening, weekend, and birthday plans**
▸ **Discuss plans to celebrate holidays, special occasions, and festivals**

1 WORD POWER Months and dates

A Listen and practice the months of the year.

Months					
January	February	March	April	May	June
July	August	September	October	November	December

B Complete the dates. Then listen and practice.

Dates							
1st	first	11th	eleventh	21st	twenty-first		
2nd	second		twelfth		twenty-second		
	third	13th	thirteenth	23rd	twenty-third		
4th	fourth	14th	fourteenth		twenty-fourth		
5th	fifth		fifteenth	25th	twenty-fifth		
	sixth	16th	sixteenth		twenty-sixth		
7th	seventh	17th	seventeenth	27th	twenty-seventh		
8th	eighth	18th	eighteenth		twenty-eighth		
9th	ninth		nineteenth	29th	twenty-ninth		
	tenth	20th	twentieth		thirtieth		
					thirty-first		

C CLASS ACTIVITY Go around the room. Ask for your classmates' birthdays.

A: When's your birthday?   **B:** It's November eighteenth. When's yours?

2 CONVERSATION Is she going to bake a cake?

Listen and practice.

 AVA   Are you going to do anything exciting this weekend?

 MARTIN Well, I'm going to celebrate my birthday.

 AVA   Oh, happy birthday! When is it, exactly?

 MARTIN It's April twenty-first – Sunday.

 AVA   So what are your plans?

 MARTIN I'm going to go to my friend Rosa's house.
She's going to cook a special dinner for me.

 AVA   Nice! Is Rosa going to bake a birthday cake for you, too?

 MARTIN A cake for me? Mmm . . . I hope so!

3 GRAMMAR FOCUS

GRAMMAR PLUS *see page 142*

The future with *be going to*

Are you **going to do** anything this weekend?	Yes, I am. I**'m going to celebrate** my birthday.
	No, I'm not. I**'m going to stay** home.
Is Rosa **going to cook** dinner for you?	Yes, she is. She**'s going to cook** a special dinner.
	No, she's not. She**'s going to order** takeout.
Are your friends **going to be** there?	Yes, they are. They**'re going to stop** by after dinner.
	No, they're not. They**'re going to be** away all weekend.

A What are these people going to do this weekend? Write sentences.
Then compare with a partner.

1.   *He's going to go biking.*

B PAIR WORK Is your partner going to do the things in part A this weekend?
Ask and answer questions.

"Are you going to go biking this weekend?"

4 PRONUNCIATION Reduction of *going to*

A Listen and practice. Notice the reduction of **going to** to /gənə/.

A: Are you **going to** go to the game?
B: No. I'm **going to** study for a test.

A: Are you **going to** go to a restaurant?
B: Yes. We're **going to** go to Nick's Café.

B PAIR WORK Ask your partner about his or her evening plans.
Try to reduce **going to**.

5 LISTENING Holiday plans

A What are these people's plans for a Monday holiday? Write your guesses in the chart.

B Listen to the interview. What are the people really going to do on Monday? Complete the chart.

Morgan   Isaac   Brian   Lauren

	Your guess	What they're really going to do
Morgan	Morgan is going to go to the gym.	
Isaac		
Brian		
Lauren		

6 INTERCHANGE 11 Take a guess

Make guesses about your classmates' plans. Go to Interchange 11 on page 125.

7 SNAPSHOT

Listen and practice.

Celebrating Holidays in the U.S.

New Year's Eve   Valentine's Day   Independence Day   Halloween   Thanksgiving   Christmas

Do you celebrate any of these holidays? Do any of your friends celebrate them?
What are some holidays in your country? What's your favorite holiday?

8 CONVERSATION We're going to go dancing.

▶ Listen and practice.

ALLIE So, Jim, do you have any plans for Valentine's Day?

JIM I sure do. I'm going to take Marissa out for dinner.

ALLIE Oh, really? Where are you going to eat?

JIM At the Red Rose. They have great desserts.

ALLIE Wow! That sounds really nice!

JIM Yeah! How about you? What are you and Matt going to do?

ALLIE Well, we're not going to go to a fancy restaurant. We're going to go dancing.

JIM Sounds like fun, too.

9 GRAMMAR FOCUS

GRAMMAR PLUS *see page 142*

Wh-questions with *be going to*	
What are you **going to do** for Valentine's Day?	I**'m going to go** to a dance club.
	I**'m not going to go** to a restaurant.
How is Allie **going to get** to the dance club?	She**'s going to drive**.
	She**'s not going to take** the bus.
Where are Jim and his girlfriend **going to eat**?	They**'re going to eat** at the Red Rose.
	They**'re not going to eat** at Nick's Café.

A Complete these conversations with the correct form of *be going to*. Then practice with a partner.

1. **A:** Where _____*are*_____ you _____*going to spend*_____ (spend) Thanksgiving?
   B: My parents and I _____ (visit) my grandparents.

2. **A:** Who _____ you _____ (invite) to your Independence Day picnic?
   B: I _____ (ask) my family and some good friends.

3. **A:** What _____ you _____ (do) for New Year's Day?
   B: I don't know. I _____ (not do) anything special.

4. **A:** How _____ your children _____ (celebrate) Halloween?
   B: They _____ (go) to their school's party.

5. **A:** What _____ your sister _____ (do) for Valentine's Day?
   B: Her boyfriend _____ (take) her out to dinner.

B **GROUP WORK** Ask your classmates about their plans. Use the names of holidays and the time expressions in the box.

A: What are you going to do tonight?
B: I'm going to go to a party.
C: Oh, really? Who's going to be there?
B: Well, Chris and Sam are going to come. . . .

time expressions	
tonight	next week
tomorrow	next month
tomorrow afternoon	next summer
tomorrow night	next year

10 WORD POWER Let's celebrate!

▶ **A** Listen and practice.

wear special clothes

eat special food

decorate

give gifts

play music

go to a parade

go on a picnic

watch fireworks

B **PAIR WORK** Are you going to celebrate a special day this year? Are you (or is someone you know) going to do any of the things in part A?

A: I'm going to go to a wedding next month. I'm going to wear special clothes.

B: Is it a family member's wedding?

11 SPEAKING Holidays and festivals

A **PAIR WORK** Choose any holiday or festival. Then ask and answer these questions.

What is the holiday or festival?

When is it?

What are you going to do?

Where are you going to go?

Who's going to be there?

When are you going to go?

How are you going to get there?

A: What is the holiday or festival?

B: It's my city's Cherry Blossom Festival.

A: When is it?

B: It's on March twenty-third.

A: What are you going to do?

B: I'm going to go to the park. . . .

B **CLASS ACTIVITY** Tell the class about your partner's plans.

Carnival, Brazil

Cherry Blossom Festival, Japan

A Scan the blog post. Who sends a letter when people are 100 years old?

Home   Posts   Archives   Follow

HAPPY BIRTHDAY TO YOU!

In this week's blog, we look at some birthday customs around the world.

Harry Baker, Perth, Australia

It's my birthday next Wednesday. I'm going to be 10 years old. In my country, we always eat fairy bread on our birthdays. My mom's going to make me a huge plate of fairy bread. It's a snack. We make it with bread, butter, and colorful sugar called "hundreds and thousands."

Jim Dixon, Montego Bay, Jamaica

I love birthdays! They're a lot of fun. Here in Jamaica, we have an old custom. We like to surprise people on their birthday. Guess what we do? We throw flour at our friends! It's my best friend's birthday tomorrow. I'm going to go to the store soon. I'm going to buy a lot of flour to throw at him.

Victoria Smith, London, UK

My grandmother is going to be 100 years old in June. She's very excited because she's going to get a special letter from the Queen. The Queen sends a letter to every person who reaches 100. It's a tradition that makes people very happy.

Jiang Li, Beijing, China

In my country, we celebrate birthdays with a special type of food. Noodles are a sign of long life for us. This year, I'm going to make some "long life noodles" for all my friends. We're going to eat them together and have a great evening!

B Read the questions. Write short answers.

1. Which two countries celebrate birthdays with food? _____
2. Why is Jim going to the store? _____
3. What three things do you need to make fairy bread? _____
4. What do noodles mean in China? _____

C GROUP WORK How do people usually celebrate birthdays in your country? Do you have plans for your next birthday? How about the birthday of a friend or a family member? What are you going to do? Tell your classmates.

12 How do you feel?

▸ **Discuss the body and common ailments**
▸ **Discuss common remedies and give health advice**

1 WORD POWER Parts of the body

▶ **A** Listen and practice.

B GROUP WORK Say a sentence with a body part. Take turns repeating the sentence and keep adding body parts. The group with the last student to say a correct sentence wins.

A: I have one head.

B: I have one head and two eyes.

C: I have one head, two eyes, and one nose.

D: I have one head, two eyes, one nose, and . . .

2 CONVERSATION Do you want some tea?

▶ Listen and practice.

Craig: Hi, Nathan. How's it going?

Nathan: Oh, hi, Craig. Not so well, actually. I don't feel well.

Craig: Yeah, you don't look so good. What's wrong?

Nathan: I don't know. I have a stomachache.

Craig: That's too bad. Do you have the flu?

Nathan: No, I just feel really sick.

Craig: Well, can I get you anything? Do you want some tea?

Nathan: No, but thanks anyway.

Craig: Well, I'm going to have some pizza. Is that OK? Call me if you need me.

3 GRAMMAR FOCUS

▶ *Have* + noun; *feel* + adjective

		Negative adjectives	Positive adjectives
What's the matter?	How are you?	horrible	fine
What's wrong?	How do you feel?	awful	great
I have a stomachache.	**I feel sick.**	terrible	terrific
I have a headache.	**I feel better.**	miserable	fantastic
I have the flu.	**I don't feel well.**		

GRAMMAR PLUS *see page 143*

▶ **A** Listen and practice. *"He has a backache."*

a backache

an earache

a headache

a stomachache

a toothache

a cold

a cough

a fever

the flu

a sore throat

B CLASS ACTIVITY Imagine you don't feel well today. Go around the class. Find out what's wrong with your classmates.

A: How are you today, Paul?
B: I feel terrible. I have a backache.

A: I'm sorry to hear that.
B: How do *you* feel?

useful expressions

That's good.
I'm glad to hear that.
That's too bad.
I'm sorry to hear that.

4 LISTENING Are you OK?

A Where do these people hurt? Guess. Write down the parts of the body.

1. Amber _____

2. David _____

3. Alyssa _____

4. Nicholas _____

B Listen to the conversations. Check your guesses.

5 SNAPSHOT

Listen and practice.

Common Remedies

chamomile tea | cough syrup | chicken soup | cold medicine

eye drops | aspirin | antacid | nasal spray | ice pack

What medications or home remedies do you use when you're sick?
What remedies are good, in your opinion? What remedies aren't good?

6 CONVERSATION Try to relax.

▶ Listen and practice.

Dr. Yun	Hello, Ms. Lake. How are you today?
Ms. Lake	Not so good.
Dr. Yun	What's wrong, exactly?
Ms. Lake	I'm exhausted!
Dr. Yun	Hmm. Why are you so tired?
Ms. Lake	I don't know. I just can't sleep at night.
Dr. Yun	OK. Let's take a look at you.

A few minutes later . . .

Dr. Yun	I'm going to give you some pills. Take one pill every evening after dinner.
Ms. Lake	OK.
Dr. Yun	And don't drink coffee, tea, or soda.
Ms. Lake	Anything else?
Dr. Yun	Yes. Try to relax.
Ms. Lake	All right. Thanks, Dr. Yun.

7 LISTENING I think I have a cold.

▶ Listen to Dr. Yun talk to four other patients. What does she give them? Check (✓) the correct medications.

	Cough syrup	Aspirin	Cold medicine	Eye drops	Nasal spray	Ice packs
1. Roberto	☐	☐	☐	☐	☐	☐
2. Courtney	☐	☐	☐	☐	☐	☐
3. Ryan	☐	☐	☐	☐	☐	☐
4. Samantha	☐	☐	☐	☐	☐	☐

8 PRONUNCIATION Sentence intonation

▶ **A** Listen and practice. Notice the intonation in these sentences.

Take these pills.   Don't take cough syrup.

Drink some tea.   Don't drink coffee.

Try to relax.   Don't work too hard.

B PAIRWORK Practice the conversation in Exercise 6 again. Pay attention to the sentence intonation.

How do you feel? 81

9 GRAMMAR FOCUS

▶ **Imperatives**

Get some rest.	**Don't stay** up late.
Drink lots of juice.	**Don't drink** soda.
Take one pill every evening.	**Don't work** too hard.

GRAMMAR PLUS *see page 143*

Complete these sentences. Use the correct forms of the words in the box.

✓call	stay	not go	not drink
see	take	✓not worry	not eat

1. _____Call_____ a dentist.
2. ___Don't worry___ too much.
3. _____ a hot bath.
4. _____ to school.

5. _____ in bed.
6. _____ a doctor.
7. _____ coffee.
8. _____ any candy.

10 SPEAKING Good advice?

A Write two pieces of advice for each problem.

"My feet hurt."

"I have a sore wrist."

"My eyes are dry."

"I can't sleep at night."

1. _____
_____
_____
_____

2. _____
_____
_____
_____

3. _____
_____
_____
_____

4. _____
_____
_____
_____

B GROUP WORK Act out the problems from part A. Your classmates give advice.

A: I don't feel well.
B: What's the matter?

A: My feet hurt.
B: I have an idea. Take a hot bath. And don't . . .

11 INTERCHANGE 12 Problems, problems

Give advice for common problems. Go to Interchange 12 on page 126.

A What does your body do to keep you alive? Take the quiz to find out!

DO YOU KNOW

YOUR BODY?

1 The human heart beats about 200 times a minute.
☐ True   ☐ False

2 Your body loses about 40,000 tiny pieces of skin an hour.
☐ True   ☐ False

3 Your brain sends billions of signals every minute.
☐ True   ☐ False

4 Your brain stops working when you're asleep.
☐ True   ☐ False

5 140 million cells in your eyes help to tell you what you can see.
☐ True   ☐ False

6 Brain cells do not live in the stomach.
☐ True   ☐ False

7 Women's hearts beat faster than men's hearts.
☐ True   ☐ False

8 Your brain makes electricity.
☐ True   ☐ False

9 Your natural smell changes as you age.
☐ True   ☐ False

10 Some bacteria (small living things) in your body help you live.
☐ True   ☐ False

1.False   2.True   3.True   4.False   5.True   6.False   7.True   8.True   9.True   10.True

B Read and answer the quiz. Check your answers. Then answer the questions.

1. What does your body lose every hour? _____
2. What part of the body sends signals and makes electricity? _____
3. What is one thing that changes as you age? _____
4. What cells live in the stomach? _____
5. What's another name for small living things? _____

C GROUP WORK What information in the quiz is most surprising? What else do you know about the human body? Tell your classmates.

Units 11–12 Progress check

SELF-ASSESSMENT

How well can you do these things? Check (✓) the boxes.

I can . . .	Very well	OK	A little
Talk about ways to celebrate holidays (Ex. 1)	☐	☐	☐
Use future time expressions (Ex. 1, 2)	☐	☐	☐
Understand conversations about problems (Ex. 3)	☐	☐	☐
Talk about problems (Ex. 4)	☐	☐	☐
Ask how people are and give advice (Ex. 4)	☐	☐	☐

1 SPEAKING Holiday customs

A Complete the questions with names of different holidays.

Are you going to . . . ?	Name
eat special food on	
give gifts on	
have a party on	
play music on	
wear special clothes on	

B CLASS ACTIVITY Are your classmates going to do the things in part A? Go around the class and find out. Try to write a different person's name on each line.

2 SPEAKING Future plans

Complete these questions with different time expressions. Add one more question.
Then ask a partner the questions.

1. How are you going to get home ___tonight___?
2. What time are you going to go to bed _____?
3. Where are you going to go _____?
4. What are you going to do _____?
5. Who are you going to eat dinner with _____?
6. _____?

3 LISTENING Everyone has problems.

▶ Listen to six conversations. Number the pictures from 1 to 6.

☐ This person can't dance very well.

☐ This person has the flu.

☐ This person needs some ketchup.

☐ This person has a backache.

☐ This person doesn't want to go to the dentist.

☐1 This person feels sad.

4 SPEAKING Thanks for the advice!

A Write a problem on a piece of paper. Then write advice for the problem on a different piece of paper.

> I have a toothache.

> Call your dentist.

B **CLASS ACTIVITY** Put the papers with problems and the papers with advice in two different boxes. Then take a new paper from each box. Go around the class and find the right advice for your problem.

A: I feel terrible.
B: What's the matter?
A: I have a toothache.
B: I can help. Drink some tea.
A: Er . . . I don't know. But thanks, anyway.

A: I feel awful.
C: Why? What's wrong?
A: I have a toothache.
C: I know! Call your dentist.
A: That's great advice. Thanks!

WHAT'S NEXT?

Look at your Self-assessment again. Do you need to review anything?

1 WORD POWER Places to go, things to buy

▶ **A** Where can you get these things? Match the things with the places. Then listen and practice.

"You can buy a backpack at a department store."

a. a post office

b. a drugstore

c. a gas station

1. a backpack   _d_
2. cold medicine   ____
3. a debit card   ____
4. eggs   ____
5. an espresso   ____
6. gasoline   ____
7. a magazine   ____
8. stamps   ____

d. a department store

e. a bank

f. a bookstore

g. a coffee shop

h. a supermarket

B **PAIR WORK** What else can you get or do in the places in part A?

A: You can send packages at a post office.

B: And you get cereal and milk at a supermarket.

2 LISTENING I can't find my cell phone.

▶ **A** Vanessa is looking for her cell phone with her friend Tom. What does Tom need?
Where is he going to get the things? Complete the chart.

	What does Tom need?	Where is he going to get it?
1.		
2.		
3.		
4.		

B **PAIR WORK** What do you need? Where are you going to get it? Tell your partner.

"I need some gas, so I'm going to go to the gas station. . . ."

3 CONVERSATION Excuse me. Can you help me?

▶ Listen and practice.

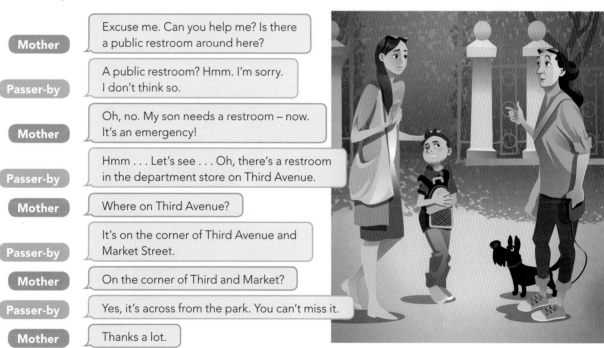

Mother Excuse me. Can you help me? Is there a public restroom around here?

Passer-by A public restroom? Hmm. I'm sorry. I don't think so.

Mother Oh, no. My son needs a restroom – now. It's an emergency!

Passer-by Hmm . . . Let's see . . . Oh, there's a restroom in the department store on Third Avenue.

Mother Where on Third Avenue?

Passer-by It's on the corner of Third Avenue and Market Street.

Mother On the corner of Third and Market?

Passer-by Yes, it's across from the park. You can't miss it.

Mother Thanks a lot.

4 PRONUNCIATION Compound nouns

▶ **A** Listen and practice. Notice the stress in these compound nouns.

•	•	•	•
bookstore	department store	gas station	post office
•	•	•	•
coffee shop	drugstore	restroom	supermarket

B **PAIR WORK** Practice these sentences. Pay attention to the stress in the compound nouns.

There's a bookstore in the gas station.   There isn't a post office in the supermarket.
There's a coffee shop in the supermarket.   There aren't restrooms in the drugstore.

Prepositions of place

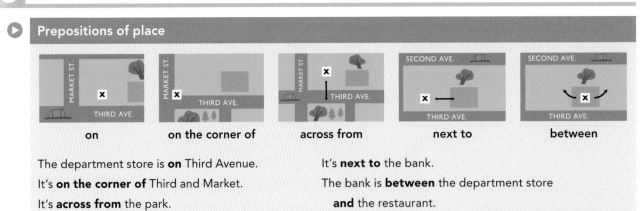

| on | on the corner of | across from | next to | between |

The department store is **on** Third Avenue.

It's **on the corner of** Third and Market.

It's **across from** the park.

It's **next to** the bank.

The bank is **between** the department store

and the restaurant.

GRAMMAR PLUS *see page 144*

A Look at the map and complete the sentences. Then compare with a partner.

1. The coffee shop is _____on_____ Main Street. It's _____ the shoe store.
2. The movie theater is _____ Park and Third. It's _____ the park.
3. The gas station is _____ the parking lot. It's _____ Second and Market.
4. The post office is _____ Main and Second. It's _____ the hospital.
5. The bank is _____ the restaurant and the department store.
   It's _____ Third Avenue.

B **PAIR WORK** Where are these places on the map? Ask and answer questions.

> the park   the drugstore   the bookstore   the hospital   the shoe store

A: Where is the park?
B: It's between Park and Market, across from the department store.

6 LISTENING I think it's on Main Street.

▶ Look at the map in Exercise 5. Listen to four conversations. Where are the people going? Number the places from 1 to 4.

☐ the hospital   ☐ the bank   ☐ the gas station   ☐ the coffee shop

7 SNAPSHOT

▶ Listen and practice.

NEW YORK CITY'S Tourist Attractions ▼

The Empire State Building

Brooklyn Bridge

Central Park

Times Square

Rockefeller Center

The Statue of Liberty

What do you know about these places? What makes them popular?
What are some popular tourist attractions in your country? What are your top five attractions?

8 CONVERSATION How do I get to Rockefeller Center?

▶ Listen and practice.

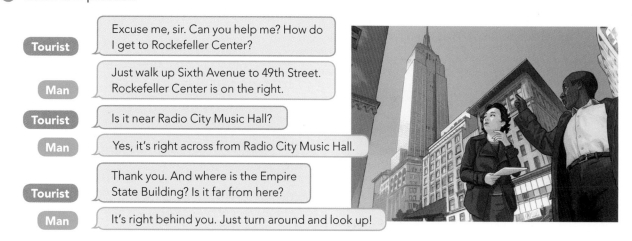

Tourist Excuse me, sir. Can you help me? How do I get to Rockefeller Center?

Man Just walk up Sixth Avenue to 49th Street. Rockefeller Center is on the right.

Tourist Is it near Radio City Music Hall?

Man Yes, it's right across from Radio City Music Hall.

Tourist Thank you. And where is the Empire State Building? Is it far from here?

Man It's right behind you. Just turn around and look up!

9 GRAMMAR FOCUS

▶ **Directions**

How do I get to Rockefeller Center?

Walk up/Go up Fifth Avenue.

Turn left on 49th Street.

It's **on the right**.

How can I get to the New York Public Library?

Walk down/Go down Fifth Avenue.

Turn right on 42nd Street.

It's **on the left**.

GRAMMAR PLUS *see page 144*

A **PAIR WORK** Imagine you are tourists at Grand Central Terminal.
Ask for directions. Follow the arrows.

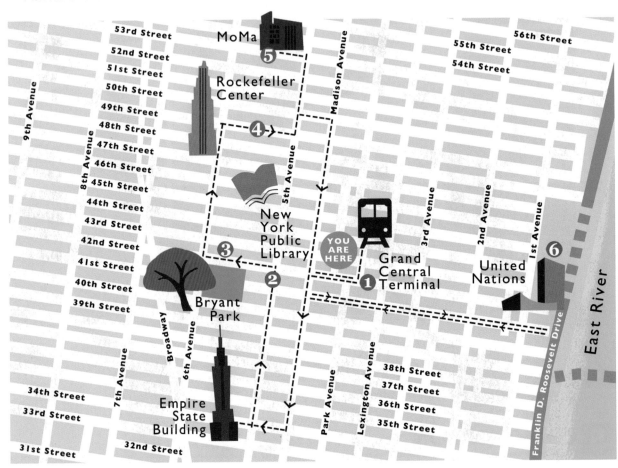

A: Excuse me. How do I get to the Empire State Building?

B: Walk up 42nd Street. Turn left on . . .

B **PAIR WORK** Ask for directions to places near your school.

A: How do I get to the bus stop?

B: Walk . . .

10 INTERCHANGE 13 Giving directions

Student A, go to Interchange 13A on page 127; Student B, go to Interchange 13B on page 128.

A Skim the guide. Where can you have some tea?

A Tour of **Palermo, Buenos Aires**

The art museum

Why not start at MALBA, the art museum on Avenida Figuero Alcorta? There are some fantastic sculptures and paintings there.

Japanese Gardens

Next, walk up to the park, turn left, and get a taste of Japan in Argentina. You can visit the Japanese Gardens and see about 150 different types of plants from Japan. Don't forget to taste some Japanese tea before you leave.

Galileo Galilei planetarium

Then turn right on Avenida Sarmiento and head over to the Galileo Galilei planetarium. There, you can see a piece of rock from the moon. There's a telescope you can look at the sky through, too.

The Spanish Monument

Across the park from the planetarium, you can see the Spanish Monument. It's a huge statue. It's a gift from the Spanish people to the Argentinian people.

PALERMO

AV. SANTA FE
AV. LAS HERAS
AV. DEL LIBERTADOR
AV. FIGUERO ALCORTA
AV. SARMIENTO

Statue of Domingo Faustino Sarmiento

Turn right to see another big statue. That's the statue of Domingo Faustino Sarmiento. He was a writer and a president of Argentina. Auguste Rodin, a famous French artist, made the statue.

Campo Argentino del Polo

End your tour at the Campo Argentino del Polo. That's where people play a sport named polo, on horseback. The biggest polo competition in the world takes place there!

B Read the information in the guide. Where can you . . . ?

1. see horses _____

2. look at the sky _____

3. see many types of plants _____

4. find a statue of a writer _____

5. see some art _____

C **PAIR WORK** Think of a place you both know and like. Plan a guide to tell visitors where things are.

14 I had a good time.

▸ Discuss past weekend activities
▸ Discuss past vacation activities

1 SNAPSHOT

▶ Listen and practice.

THINGS TO DO ON THE WEEKEND >>>

☐ answer email

☐ clean the house

☐ do the laundry

☐ exercise

☐ go grocery shopping

☐ visit relatives

☐ wash the car

☐ work or study

Check (✓) the activities you usually do on weekends. Do you like doing them? Why or why not?
What other activities do you do on the weekends?

2 CONVERSATION Did you have a good weekend?

▶ Listen and practice.

Shaun Hi, Yuna. Did you have a good weekend?

Yuna Well, I had a busy weekend, so I'm a little tired.

Shaun Really? Why?

Yuna Well, on Saturday, I exercised in the morning. Then I cleaned the apartment, did the laundry, and went shopping. And in the evening, I visited my parents.

Shaun And what did you do on Sunday?

Yuna I studied for our test all day.

Shaun Oh, no! I didn't study for the test! I just watched TV shows all weekend!

GRAMMAR FOCUS

Simple past statements; regular verbs

						Spelling		
I	**stayed**	home.	I	**didn't stay**	home.	stay	→	stay**ed**
You	**watched**	a TV show.	You	**didn't watch**	a game.	watch	→	watch**ed**
She	**exercised**	on Saturday.	She	**didn't exercise**	on Sunday.	exercise	→	exercise**d**
We	**studied**	English.	We	**didn't study**	math.	study	→	stud**ied**
They	**shopped**	for groceries.	They	**didn't shop**	for clothes.	shop	→	shop**ped**
				did**n't** = did **not**				

GRAMMAR PLUS *see page 145*

A Ray is talking about his weekend. Complete the sentences. Then compare with a partner.

On Friday night, I ___wanted___ (want) to go out, but my friends _____ (not call). I _____ (decide) to stay home, and I _____ (play) video games. On Saturday, I _____ (visit) my friend Pablo. We _____ (talk) and _____ (listen) to music. In the evening, he _____ (invite) some friends over, and we _____ (cook) a great meal. I _____ (not work) very hard on Sunday. I _____ (not study) at all. I just _____ (walk) to the mall and _____ (shop).

B Complete the sentences. Use your own information. Then compare with a partner.

1. Yesterday, I _____ (watch) a basketball game.
2. Last night, I _____ (stay) home.
3. Last week, I _____ (clean) the house.
4. Last month, I _____ (shop) for clothes.
5. Last year, I _____ (visit) a different country.

4 PRONUNCIATION Simple past –ed endings.

A Listen and practice. Notice the pronunciation of –**ed**.

/t/	/d/	/ɪd/
worked	cleaned	wanted
watched	stayed	visited

B Listen and write these verbs under the correct sounds.

cooked	decided	exercised	invited	listened	shopped

GRAMMAR FOCUS

Simple past statements: irregular verbs

I **did** my homework.
I **didn't do** the laundry.

You **got up** at noon.
You **didn't get up** at 8:00.

She **went** to the bookstore.
She **didn't go** to the library.

We **met** our classmates.
We **didn't meet** our teacher.

You **came** home late.
You **didn't come** home early.

They **had** a barbecue.
They **didn't have** a picnic.

GRAMMAR PLUS *see page 145*

A Complete the chart. Then listen and check.

Present	Past	Present	Past	Present	Past
_____	bought	_____	made	_____	saw
_____	ate	_____	read /rɛd/	_____	sat
_____	felt	_____	rode	_____	took

B PAIR WORK Did you do the things in the pictures yesterday? Tell your partner.

"Yesterday, I didn't do my homework. But I did the laundry. . . ."

6 SPEAKING Last weekend

A Write five things you did and five things you didn't do last weekend.

B GROUP WORK Tell your classmates about your weekend.

A: I went to a party last weekend.
B: I didn't go to a party. But I met my friends.
C: I met my friends, too! We went . . .

Things I did	Things I didn't do
I went to a party.	I didn't clean the house.
I danced a lot.	I didn't see a movie.
I . . .	I didn't . . .

7 CONVERSATION Did you have fun?

Listen and practice.

 KIM Hi, Martin! Welcome back! So, did you go to Montreal?

 MARTIN No, I didn't. I went to Sydney with my sister.

 KIM Really? Did you like it?

 MARTIN Yeah, we loved it! We visited the Opera House and went to Bondi Beach.

 KIM Did you go surfing?

 MARTIN No, we didn't. Actually, we went swimming in the Ocean Pool. And one day we climbed Sydney Harbor Bridge.

 KIM Wow! Did you have fun?

 MARTIN Yes, I did. But my sister didn't like climbing very much. She got really tired.

8 GRAMMAR FOCUS

Simple past yes/no questions

Did you **have** a good summer?
Yes, I **did**. I **had** a great summer.

Did you **go** surfing?
No, I **didn't**. I **went** swimming.

Did Martin **like** his vacation?
Yes, he **did**. He **liked** it a lot.

Did Martin and his sister **go** to Montreal?
No, they **didn't**. They **went** to Sydney.

GRAMMAR PLUS *see page 145*

A Complete the conversations. Then practice with a partner.

1. A: _____Did_____ you _____have_____ (have) a good summer?
   B: Yes, I _____ . I _____ (have) a great summer.
   I _____ (go) out with my friends a lot.

2. A: _____ you _____ (go) anywhere last summer?
   B: No, I _____ . I _____ (stay) here.
   I _____ (get) a part-time job, so I _____ (make)
   some extra money.

3. A: _____ you _____ (take) any classes last summer?
   B: Yes, I _____ . I _____ (take) tennis lessons, and
   I _____ (play) tennis every day!

4. A: _____ you _____ (speak) English last summer?
   B: No, I _____ . But I _____ (read) blogs
   in English, and I _____ (watch) English movies.

B **PAIR WORK** Ask the questions from part A.
Answer with your own information.

A: Did you have a good summer?
B: Yes, I did. I went to the beach every day.

9 LISTENING Did you have a good summer?

▶ Listen to Fernando, Olivia, Cameron, and Abigail. What did they do last summer? Check (✓) the correct answers.

Fernando	Olivia	Cameron	Abigail
☐ stayed home	☐ watched videos	☐ went bike riding	☐ worked in the yard
☐ visited his brother	☐ read books	☐ went swimming	☐ got a job
☐ went to the beach	☐ watched TV	☐ played baseball	☐ painted the house

10 WORD POWER Summer activities

▶ **A** Find two words from the list that go with each verb in the chart. Then listen and check.

a barbecue   a picnic
beach volleyball   soccer
camping   a summer class
✓ a new bike   swimming
new people   a trip
old friends   ✓ up late

get	_a new bike_	_up late_
go		
have		
meet		
play		
take		

B PAIR WORK Add two activities to the list. Check (✓) six things to ask your partner. Then ask and answer questions.

Did you . . . last summer?

☐ do anything interesting   ☐ play any games
☐ eat any new foods   ☐ read any books
☐ see any museum exhibits   ☐ see any movies
☐ meet any interesting people   ☐ take any classes
☐ play any sports   ☐ take any trips
☐ _____   ☐ _____

A: Did you do anything interesting last summer?
B: Yes, I did. I went white-water rafting.

C CLASS ACTIVITY Tell the class about your partner's summer.

"Last summer, Alma went white-water rafting with some friends. They had a lot of fun."

11 INTERCHANGE 14 Past activities

Did you and your partner do similar things when you were children?
Go to Interchange 14 on page 129.

12 READING ◉

A Scan the social media posts. Who had a busy weekend? Who saw old friends on the weekend? Who had fun learning something new? Who had a terrible weekend?

● ● ●

| SOCIAL | Find friends 🔍 | 👤 💬 🌐 |

DID YOU HAVE A GOOD WEEKEND?

Nick Bond
I just had the worst weekend ever! It was my best friend Pete's wedding and my car broke down on the drive. I was on a quiet road and suddenly there was a bang. Then the car just didn't move! I missed the wedding and came home on the back of a truck. ☹

♡ like   💬 comment   ▷ Share post

Jessie Taylor
Hey guys! Guess what? I just got back from my first ever parasailing class! It was amazing! I traveled to a town by the ocean and met my instructor. We went high up above the ocean where people jump off the rocks. It was kind of scary but so exciting. Here's a picture of me. See? That's me!

♡ like   💬 comment   ▷ Share post

Armando Torres
So . . . on Saturday morning I did chores at home. You know, laundry and stuff. Then I went grocery shopping because . . . well, because there was no food in the house! Sunday morning, I fixed my bike, walked the dog, called my mom, and made lunch. Then I wrote a report for work, cleaned the house, and went to bed.

♡ like   💬 comment   ▷ Share post

Juliette Blum
Wow. What an awesome weekend. I went running in the park on Saturday evening, and I met someone I knew from school 10 years ago. It was so cool. Her name is Marie and we always hung out together when we were kids. She's married now and has a baby!

♡ like   💬 comment   ▷ Share post

B Read the social media posts. Then correct these sentences.

1. Nick got married.   _Nick's best friend got married._
2. On the way to the wedding, Nick's truck broke down. _____
3. Jessie's parasailing class was terrible. _____
4. It was Jessie's second parasailing class. _____
5. Armando watched TV on Saturday morning. _____
6. Armando fixed his car and walked his dog. _____
7. Juliette went running on Sunday morning. _____
8. Juliette is married and has a baby.   _____

C PAIR WORK How was your weekend? Did you have fun? Why? Why not? Tell your partner.

Units 13–14 Progress check

SELF-ASSESSMENT

How well can you do these things? Check (✓) the boxes.

I can . . .	Very well	OK	A little
Understand conversations about where to get things in a town (Ex. 1)	☐	☐	☐
Ask and answer questions about where places are (Ex. 2)	☐	☐	☐
Ask for and give directions (Ex. 2)	☐	☐	☐
Talk about past activities (Ex. 3, 4)	☐	☐	☐
Ask and answer questions about past activities (Ex. 4)	☐	☐	☐

1 LISTENING What are you looking for?

▶ Listen to the conversations. What do the people need?
Where can they get or find it? Complete the chart.

	What?	Where?
1.		
2.		
3.		
4.		

2 SPEAKING Is there a . . . near here?

A **PAIR WORK** Are these places near your school? Where are they?
Ask and answer questions.

bank	coffee shop	hospital	post office
bookstore	department store	park	supermarket

A: Is there a bank near here?
B: Yes, there's a bank on Second Avenue. It's across from the Korean restaurant.

B **PAIR WORK** Give directions from your school to the places in part A.
Your partner guesses the place.

A: Go out of the school and turn left. Walk for about three minutes.
It's on the right, next to the drugstore.
B: It's the coffee shop.
A: That's right!

3 SPEAKING On my last vacation . . .

A Write four statements about your last vacation. Two are true and two are false.

B **PAIR WORK** Read your statements. Your partner says, "I think it's true," OR "I think it's false." Who has more correct guesses?

> I went to New Zealand.
>
> It rained all day, every day.
>
> I didn't go to the beach.
>
> I read two books.

A: On my last vacation, I went to New Zealand.
B: I think it's false.
A: That's right. It's false. OR Sorry. It's true.

4 SPEAKING Did you . . . last weekend?

A Check (✓) the things you did last weekend. Then add two more things you did.

Last weekend, I . . .

- [ ] ate at a restaurant
- [ ] cleaned the house
- [ ] did homework
- [ ] did the laundry
- [ ] downloaded movies
- [ ] exercised
- [ ] played video games
- [ ] rode my bicycle
- [ ] visited relatives
- [ ] washed the car
- [ ] watched a game on TV
- [ ] uploaded photos
- [ ] went shopping
- [ ] went out with friends
- [ ] _____
- [ ] _____

B **PAIR WORK** Ask your partner about his or her weekend.

A: Did you eat at a restaurant last weekend, Narumi?
B: Yes, I did. I ate at a very good Italian restaurant. What about you? Did you eat at a restaurant?
A: No, I didn't. . . .

C **GROUP WORK** Join another pair. Tell them about your partner's weekend.

"Narumi ate at a very good Italian restaurant."

WHAT'S NEXT?

Look at your Self-assessment again. Do you need to review anything?

15 Where were you born?

▸ Discuss family and personal history
▸ Discuss school experiences and memories

1 SNAPSHOT

▶ Listen and practice.

Where Were They Born?

Esperanza Spalding
musician

John Oliver
comedian

Lupita Nyong'o
actress

Shin-Soo Choo
baseball player

Shigeru Miyamoto
game designer

a. Japan

b. Mexico

c. South Korea

d. the U.K.

e. the U.S.

1. _____ 2. _____ 3. _____ 4. _____ 5. _____

Answers: 1. e   2. d   3. b   4. c   5. a

Match the people with the countries where they were born. Then check your answers.
What famous people were born in your country? What do they do?

2 CONVERSATION I was born in Brazil.

▶ Listen and practice.

Mario: Bianca. That's a nice name. Where were you born?

Bianca: I was born in Brazil.

Mario: Oh! So you weren't born in the U.S. Your English is really good.

Bianca: Thanks. I studied English for many years.

Mario: Did you study English in Brazil?

Bianca: Yeah, I started when I was seven.

Mario: You were pretty young.

Bianca: Yes, I went to a bilingual school. I had classes in English and in Portuguese.

Mario: You were lucky to learn another language so well.

Bianca: Do you speak a second language, too?

Mario: Well, I speak a little Italian. My parents were born in Milan.

3 GRAMMAR FOCUS

Past of *be*

I	**was**	born here.	I	**wasn't**	born in Italy.	
You	**were**	pretty young.	You	**weren't**	very old.	
She	**was**	seven.	She	**wasn't**	in college.	
We	**were**	at the hair salon.	We	**weren't**	at the café.	
They	**were**	born in Milan.	They	**weren't**	born in Rome.	

Were you in class yesterday?
Yes, I **was**. / No, I **wasn't**.
Was your first teacher American?
Yes, she **was**. / No, she **wasn't**.
Were your parents born in the U.S.?
Yes, they **were**. / No, they **weren't**.

weren't = were **not**   wasn't = was **not**

GRAMMAR PLUS see page 146

A Bianca is talking about her family. Choose the correct verb forms.
Then compare with a partner.

My family and I _____were_____ (was / were) all born in Brazil –
we _____ (wasn't / weren't) born in the U.S. I _____ (was / were)
born in the city of Recife, and my brother _____ (was / were) born
there, too. My parents _____ (wasn't / weren't) born in Recife.
They _____ (was / were) born in Rio de Janeiro. In Rio, my father
_____ (was / were) a teacher and my mother _____ (was / were)
an engineer. They have their own business in Recife now.

B **PAIR WORK** Look at the picture below. Ask and answer these questions.

1. Was Tessa on time for class yesterday?
2. Was it English class?
3. Was it a sunny day?
4. Was it 10:00?

5. Was Mr. Walker very angry?
6. Were Alyssa and Jacob late to class?
7. Were they at the board?
8. Were the windows open?

A: Was Tessa on time for class yesterday?
B: No, she wasn't. She was late. Was it English class?

4 PRONUNCIATION Negative contractions

▶ **A** Listen and practice.

one syllable		two syllables	
aren't	don't	isn't	doesn't
weren't	can't	wasn't	didn't

▶ **B** Listen and practice.

They **didn't** like the comedy because it **wasn't** funny.
I **don't** like coffee, and she **doesn't** like tea.
This **isn't** my book. I **can't** read French.
They **weren't** in class yesterday, and they **aren't** in class today.

C Write four sentences with negative contractions.
Then read them to a partner.

I didn't go to the party because
my friends weren't there.

5 CONVERSATION I grew up in New York.

▶ Listen and practice.

Bianca So, Mario, where did you grow up?

Mario I grew up in New York.

Bianca Were you born there?

Mario Yeah. I was born in Brooklyn.

Bianca And when did you come to Los Angeles?

Mario In 2008.

Bianca How old were you then?

Mario I was eighteen. I went to college here.

Bianca Oh. What was your major?

Mario Photography. I was a photographer for five years after college.

Bianca Really? Why did you become a hairstylist?

Mario Because I needed the money. And I love it. So, what do you think?

Bianca Well, uh . . .

6 GRAMMAR FOCUS

Wh-questions with *did*, *was*, and *were*

Where **did** you **grow up**?	I **grew up** in New York.
What **did** your father **do** there?	He **worked** in a department store.
When **did** you **come** to Los Angeles?	I **came** to Los Angeles in 2008.
Why **did** you **become** a hairstylist?	Because I **needed** the money.
Where **were** you **born**?	I **was born** in Brooklyn.
When **were** you **born**?	I **was born** in 1990.
How old **were** you in 2008?	I **was** eighteen.
What **was** your major in college?	Photography. I **was** a photographer for five years.

GRAMMAR PLUS *see page 146*

A Match the questions with the answers. Then compare with a partner.

1. Where were you born? _e_
2. Where did you grow up? _____
3. How was your first day of school? _____
4. Who was your best friend in school? _____
5. What was he like? _____
6. Why did you take this class? _____

a. His name was Akio.
b. He was really friendly.
c. I wanted to improve my English.
d. I grew up in Tokyo.
e. In Kyoto, Japan.
f. It was a little scary.

B PAIR WORK Ask and answer the questions in part A. Use your own information and make the necessary changes.

C GROUP WORK Ask the questions. Use a year in your answers.

1. When were you born?
2. When was your father born?
3. When was your mother born?
4. When did you turn 13?
5. When did you start high school?
6. When did you begin to study English?

saying years
1900 = nineteen hundred
1906 = nineteen oh six
1995 = nineteen ninety-five
2000 = two thousand
2007 = two thousand (and) seven
2015 = two thousand (and) fifteen OR twenty-fifteen

7 LISTENING I wasn't born here.

A Listen. What year were these people born? Complete the sentences.

1. Melissa was born in _____.
2. Colin was born in _____.
3. Kumiko was born in _____.
4. Omar was born in _____.

B Listen again. Where did these people grow up? Complete the sentences.

1. Melissa grew up in _____.
2. Colin grew up in _____.
3. Kumiko grew up in _____.
4. Omar grew up in _____.

8 WORD POWER School days

A Complete the word map with words from the list. Then listen and check.

✓ auditorium
cafeteria
college
computer lab
elementary school
geography
high school
history
library
middle school
physical education
science

CLASSES
_____
_____
_____

SCHOOL DAYS

TYPES OF SCHOOLS
_____
_____
_____

PLACES
_____ auditorium
_____
_____

B **PAIR WORK** Find out about your partner's elementary, middle, or high school days. Ask these questions. Then tell the class.

What classes did you take?	Who was your favorite teacher? Why?
What was your favorite class? Why?	Where did you spend your free time? Why?
What classes didn't you like? Why not?	What was a typical day of school like?
Who was your best friend?	What didn't you like about school?

"In high school, Julian's favorite class was physical education because he liked to play sports . . ."

9 SPEAKING Can you remember . . . ?

A **GROUP WORK** How often do you have English class? What do you remember from your last class? Ask and answer these questions.

1. Who was in class? Who wasn't there?
2. Who was late that day?
3. Who was very tired?
4. What color were your teacher's shoes?
5. What were your teacher's first words?
6. Did all the students bring their books?
7. What did you learn?
8. What did you do after class?

B **CLASS ACTIVITY** What does your group remember? Tell the class.

10 INTERCHANGE 15 This is your life.

Did you and your partner do similar things when you were children? Go to Interchange 15 on page 130.

A Scan the article. What is a "third culture kid?" Do you know anyone who moved to another country?

THE STORY OF A THIRD CULTURE KID

SRI LANKA

Tommy was born in Colombo, the largest city in the island country of Sri Lanka. The streets of Colombo were busy, and Tommy loved the colors, sights, and smells. He played on sandy beaches with his friends. He spoke Sinhalese with his friends and family and learned English at school. He loved visiting the neighborhood markets with his family to buy fresh fruits and vegetables. Typical Sri Lankan dishes made with coconuts and rice were some of his favorite foods.

When he was six, Tommy moved with his parents to a small town near New York City. His parents both had new jobs there. For Tommy, life in his new town was a big surprise. Everything was different! The streets were quieter and less colorful. The grocery stores sold so many different types of fruits, vegetables, cheeses, and cereals. There were so many restaurants in his new town – he tried Italian food, Chinese food, Greek food, and Mexican food. The weather was different, too. Tommy saw snow for the very first time!

Looking back, Tommy remembers learning that the culture in the United States was different from the culture in Sri Lanka. Not better, not worse, just different. Tommy learned new things every day. He learned Spanish in school. He also learned ways that people in the U.S. communicate with each other. Tommy remembers everyone saying "How are you doing?" but it wasn't a question. It was like saying "Hi!"

Tommy was a "third culture kid." That means he was raised in a different country than his parents. Many third culture kids believe that they are lucky. They know and understand more than one culture, and they often speak more than one language. Tommy went to college in Los Angeles and studied languages. Now he works for a big charity that helps children around the world get a good education.

Sometimes it's hard to learn a whole new way of life, but Tommy says it's the best thing that ever happened. He calls Sri Lanka "home" and the U.S. "home," too!

B Read the article. Check (✓) True or False.

	True	False
1. Tommy lived in Sri Lanka most of his life.	☐	☐
2. He was born in Sri Lanka.	☐	☐
3. Tommy liked traditional Sri Lankan food.	☐	☐
4. He didn't learn any new languages in the U.S.	☐	☐
5. In the U.S., Tommy ate mostly at Sri Lankan restaurants.	☐	☐
6. Tommy is happy to be a third culture kid.	☐	☐

C Number these events in Tommy's life from 1 (first) to 8 (last).

____ **a.** Tommy saw snow for the first time.

____ **b.** Tommy went to college.

____ **c.** Tommy moved to the U.S.

____ **d.** As a small boy, Tommy played on the beach.

____ **e.** He learned a new language in the U.S.

_1_ **f.** Tommy was born on an island.

____ **g.** In Sri Lanka, Tommy studied English in school.

____ **h.** He works for a charity in the U.S.

D **GROUP WORK** Tommy thinks living in another culture is a good thing. Why do you think he says that? Do you agree? Tell your classmates.

16 Can I take a message?

▸ Make phone calls and leave messages
▸ Make, accept, and decline invitations

1 CONVERSATION Please ask her to call me.

▶ Listen and practice.

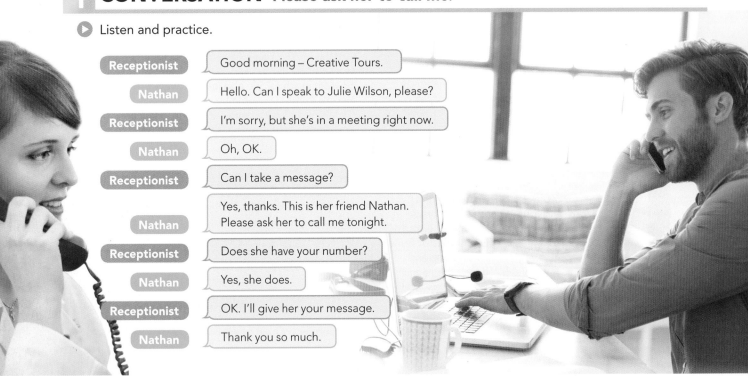

Receptionist: Good morning – Creative Tours.

Nathan: Hello. Can I speak to Julie Wilson, please?

Receptionist: I'm sorry, but she's in a meeting right now.

Nathan: Oh, OK.

Receptionist: Can I take a message?

Nathan: Yes, thanks. This is her friend Nathan. Please ask her to call me tonight.

Receptionist: Does she have your number?

Nathan: Yes, she does.

Receptionist: OK. I'll give her your message.

Nathan: Thank you so much.

2 WORD POWER Prepositional phrases

▶ A Listen and practice.

at home	**at** the mall	**in** bed	**in** the shower	**on** vacation
at work	**at** the library	**in** class	**in** the hospital	**on** a trip
at school	**at** the beach	**in** Mexico	**in** a meeting	**on** his/her break

at work

on vacation

in a meeting

B PAIR WORK Make a list of five friends and family members. Give it to your partner. Where are these people right now? Ask and answer questions.

A: Where's your brother right now?
B: He's on vacation. He's in India.

LISTENING Sorry I missed your call.

▶ **A** Listen to Nathan return three phone calls. Why did he miss each call? Check (✓) the correct answers.

1. He was . . . ☐ shopping.   ☐ in the shower.   ☐ at a party.
2. He was . . . ☐ studying.   ☐ at the mall.   ☐ sick.
3. He was . . . ☐ in class.   ☐ sleeping.   ☐ at work.

▶ **B** Listen again. Why did they call Nathan? Correct the sentences.

1. Hannah called Nathan because he is having a party.
2. Andrea called Nathan because she needs to see Nathan's textbook.
3. Alexis called Nathan because Sam can come in to work on Saturday.

4 GRAMMAR FOCUS

▶ **Subject and object pronouns**

Subjects		Objects
I		me
You		you
He		him
She got Nathan's message.	Nathan left **her** a message.	
We		us
They		them

GRAMMAR PLUS *see page 147*

A Complete the phone conversations with the correct pronouns. Then practice with a partner.

1. **A:** Can _____I_____ speak with Ms. Murphy, please?
   B: _____'s not here. But maybe _____ can help you.
   A: Please give _____ my new cell number. It's 555-2981.

2. **A:** Hi, this is Colin Shaw. Is Mr. Kerr there?
   B: _____'m sorry, but _____'s not here right now. Do you want to leave a message?
   A: Yes. Please tell _____ to call me at work.

3. **A:** Hello, this is Carol's Café. Are Lauren and Matt in?
   B: No, _____'re not. I'm their son. Can I help _____?
   A: _____ found their keys. _____ left _____ on the table.
   B: Just bring _____ the keys. I can give _____ to my parents.
   A: I'm sorry, but _____ can't. Can your mom or dad call _____?
   B: OK.

B PAIR WORK Role-play this phone conversation.

Student A: "Call" your business partner Robert White's office. You want a meeting on Monday at 4:00 P.M.

Student B: You are Robert White's assistant. Answer the phone. Mr. White is not in. Take a message.

C PAIR WORK Change roles. This time you want a meeting on Tuesday at 2:00 P.M.

5 SNAPSHOT

▶ Listen and practice.

Popular Activities in the U.S.

- ☐ go camping
- ☐ go to an amusement park
- ☐ go to a street fair
- ☐ go to a concert
- ☐ have a barbecue
- ☐ see a play or musical

Check (✓) the activities that are popular in your country.
What other activities are popular in your country?
What are your favorite activities? Are there any activities you don't like? Why?

6 CONVERSATION Do you want to see a movie?

▶ Listen and practice.

NATHAN Hello?

JULIE Hi, Nathan. I got your message.

NATHAN Hi. Thanks for calling me back. Sorry I called you at work.

JULIE Oh, that's OK. I was in a meeting, so I turned my cell phone off. What's up?

NATHAN Well, do you want to see a movie with me tonight?

JULIE Tonight? I'm sorry, but I can't. I have to work late tonight.

NATHAN Oh, that's too bad. How about tomorrow night?

JULIE Sure, I'd love to. What time do you want to meet?

NATHAN How about around seven o'clock at the Astoria on Pratt Avenue?

JULIE Terrific! Text me when you leave your office, OK?

▶ **A** Listen and practice. Notice the reduction of **want to** and **have to**.

/wanə/

A: Do you **want to** go to dinner with me tonight?

/hæftə/

B: I'm sorry, but I can't. I **have to** study for a test.

B PAIR WORK Practice the conversation in Exercise 6 again. Try to reduce **want to** and **have to**.

8 **GRAMMAR FOCUS**

▶ **Invitations; verb + *to***

Do you want to see a play with me tonight?

Sure. I**'d** really **like to** see a good play.

I**'d like to** (see a play), but I **have to** work late.

I**'d** = I would

Would you like to go to an amusement park?

Yes, I**'d love to** (go to an amusement park)!

I**'d like to** (go), but I **need to** study.

GRAMMAR PLUS *see page 147*

A Complete the invitations. Then match them with the responses.

Invitations

1. Would you ____like to____ go to an art festival this weekend? __d__

2. Do you _____ go to a volleyball game tomorrow night? _____

3. Would you _____ see a comedy tonight? _____

4. Do you _____ go swimming on Saturday? _____

5. Do you _____ play soccer after school today? _____

6. Would you _____ go to a hip-hop concert on Saturday night? _____

Responses

a. I'd like to, but I don't have a swimsuit!

b. I'm sorry, but I have to talk to the teacher after school.

c. I don't really like volleyball. Do you want to do something else?

d. I'd like to, but I can't. I'm going to go on a trip this weekend.

e. Yes, I'd love to. It's my favorite type of music.

f. Tonight? I can't. I need to help my parents.

B PAIR WORK Practice the invitations from part A. Respond with your own information.

A: Would you like to go to an art festival this weekend?

B: I'd like to, but I can't. I have to . . .

9 SPEAKING What is your excuse?

A Do you ever use these excuses? Check (✓) Often, Sometimes, or Never. Add your own excuse, and then compare with a partner.

	Often	Sometimes	Never
I have to work late.	☐	☐	☐
I have a headache.	☐	☐	☐
I have to babysit.	☐	☐	☐
I have a class.	☐	☐	☐
I need to do the laundry.	☐	☐	☐
I need to go to bed early.	☐	☐	☐
I need to study for a test.	☐	☐	☐
I want to visit my family.	☐	☐	☐
I'm not feeling well.	☐	☐	☐
I already have plans.	☐	☐	☐
_____	☐	☐	☐

B Write down three things you want to do this weekend.

> I want to go to the street fair on Saturday.

C CLASS ACTIVITY Go around the class and invite your classmates to do the things from part B. Your classmates respond with excuses.

A: Would you like to go to a concert tonight?
B: I'm sorry, but I can't. I have to work late tonight.

10 LISTENING I'll see you then!

A These four people need to change their plans. Listen to their phone calls. Who will be late? Who can't come? Check (✓) the correct answers.

	Will be late	Can't come
1. Jason	☐	☐
2. Jessica	☐	☐
3. Christian	☐	☐
4. Danielle	☐	☐

B Listen again. Who can't come? Write their first names and their excuses.

First name	Excuse
_____	_____
_____	_____

11 INTERCHANGE 16 The perfect weekend

Make plans with your classmates. Go to Interchange 16 on page 131.

12 READING ▶

A Look at the guide. What type of festival is Austin City Limits?

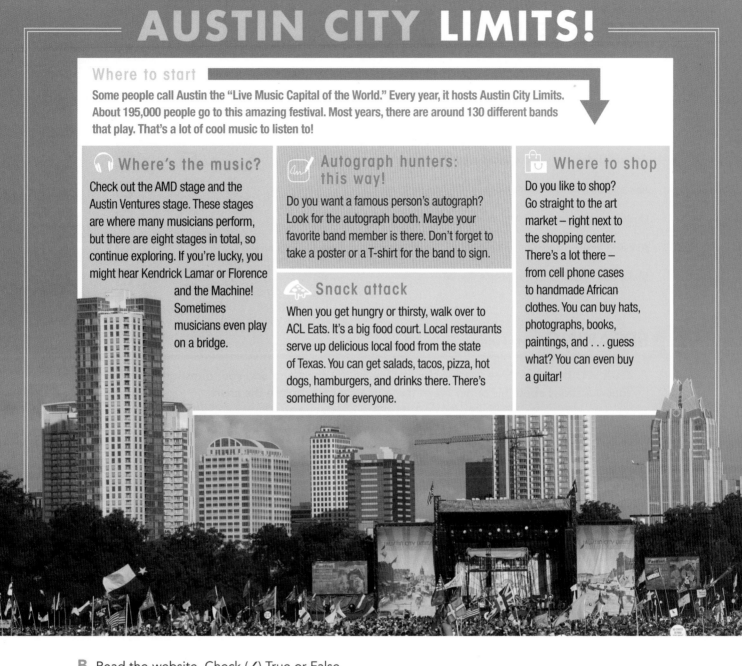

AUSTIN CITY LIMITS!

Where to start

Some people call Austin the "Live Music Capital of the World." Every year, it hosts Austin City Limits. About 195,000 people go to this amazing festival. Most years, there are around 130 different bands that play. That's a lot of cool music to listen to!

🎧 Where's the music?

Check out the AMD stage and the Austin Ventures stage. These stages are where many musicians perform, but there are eight stages in total, so continue exploring. If you're lucky, you might hear Kendrick Lamar or Florence and the Machine! Sometimes musicians even play on a bridge.

✍ Autograph hunters: this way!

Do you want a famous person's autograph? Look for the autograph booth. Maybe your favorite band member is there. Don't forget to take a poster or a T-shirt for the band to sign.

🍕 Snack attack

When you get hungry or thirsty, walk over to ACL Eats. It's a big food court. Local restaurants serve up delicious local food from the state of Texas. You can get salads, tacos, pizza, hot dogs, hamburgers, and drinks there. There's something for everyone.

🛍 Where to shop

Do you like to shop? Go straight to the art market – right next to the shopping center. There's a lot there – from cell phone cases to handmade African clothes. You can buy hats, photographs, books, paintings, and . . . guess what? You can even buy a guitar!

B Read the website. Check (✓) True or False.

	True	False
1. About 130,000 people go to enjoy the festival.	☐	☐
2. There are eight stages for musicians.	☐	☐
3. You can buy food at the festival, but you can't buy clothes.	☐	☐
4. ACL Eats is the name of a stage.	☐	☐
5. The art market is near the shopping center.	☐	☐
6. It's possible to get an autograph at the festival.	☐	☐

C GROUP WORK What events do you like to go to? Is there a special event in your city or town? Tell your classmates.

SELF-ASSESSMENT

How well can you do these things? Check (✓) the boxes.

I can . . .	Very well	OK	A little
Talk about my past (Ex. 1)	☐	☐	☐
Ask about famous people using simple past yes/no questions (Ex. 2)	☐	☐	☐
Ask and answer questions about someone's past (Ex. 2)	☐	☐	☐
Understand phone calls and leave or pass on messages (Ex. 3)	☐	☐	☐
Ask and answer questions about things I want, need, and have to do (Ex. 4)	☐	☐	☐
Make and respond to invitations (Ex. 5)	☐	☐	☐

 SPEAKING Interview

A **PAIR WORK** Write three years in the first line of the chart and add your question. Ask your partner four questions about his or her life in these years and complete the chart.

	20 _____	20 _____	20 _____
How old were you in . . .?			
Who was your best friend in . . .?			
What were you like in . . .?			
_____ were / was _____ in . . .?			

B **CLASS ACTIVITY** Tell the class about your partner's life.

"In 2001, Leo was two. He . . ."

2 SPEAKING Who were they?

GROUP WORK Think of a famous person from the past. Your classmates ask yes/no questions to guess the person.

Was he/she born in . . . ?
Was he/she a singer? an actor? a politician?
Was he/she tall? heavy? good-looking?

A: I'm thinking of a famous man from the past.
B: Was he born in the U.S.?
A: No, he wasn't.
C: Was he . . . ?

Audrey Hepburn

Nelson Mandela

Paul Walker

3 LISTENING Give me a call!

▶ Listen and check (✓) the best response.

1. ☐ Yes. Please tell her to call me.
   ☐ Yes. Please tell him to call me.
2. ☐ Sure. Does he have your number?
   ☐ No, sorry. He's not here right now.
3. ☐ Yes, you do.
   ☐ No, I don't.

4. ☐ I have to babysit.
   ☐ I had a terrible headache.
5. ☐ I'd love to, but I can't.
   ☐ No, I didn't go. I was at work.
6. ☐ I'm sorry. He's not here right now.
   ☐ No, Amanda is at work right now.

4 SPEAKING Find someone who . . .

A CLASS ACTIVITY Go around the class. Ask questions to complete
the chart. Try to write a different name on each line.

Find someone who . . .	Name
has to babysit this weekend	
needs to do the laundry tomorrow	
wants to go home early	
wants to go shopping on Saturday	
wants to see a movie tonight	
has to go to the doctor this week	
needs to work this weekend	
doesn't want to do homework tonight	

A: Ayumi, do you have to babysit this weekend?
B: Yes, I do. I have to babysit my little sister.

B PAIR WORK Share your answers with a partner.

5 SPEAKING Would you like to . . . ?

A Make a list of five things you want to do this weekend.

B CLASS ACTIVITY Go around the class. Invite your classmates to do the things
from part A. Your classmates accept or refuse the invitations.

A: Would you like to go to the Natural History Museum this weekend?
B: I'm sorry, but I can't. I have to . . .
C: Do you want to go to a soccer match on Sunday?
D: Sure, I'd love to! When would you like to . . . ?

WHAT'S NEXT?

Look at your Self-assessment again. Do you need to review anything?

Interchange activities

INTERCHANGE 1 Celebrity classmates

A Imagine you are a celebrity. Write your name, phone number, and email address on the screens.

B **CLASS ACTIVITY** Go around the class. Introduce yourself to three "celebrities." Ask and answer questions to complete the screens.

A: Hi. My name is Emma Watson.

B: I'm Usain Bolt. Nice to meet you, Emma.

A: Usain, what's your email address?

B: It's U-S-A-I-N-B-O-L-T underscore eight-seven at C-U-P dot O-R-G.

A: I'm sorry. Can you repeat that?

useful expressions

I'm sorry.
Can you repeat that?
How do you spell that?

Emma Watson

Usain Bolt

Find the differences

PAIR WORK How are the two pictures different? Ask questions to find the differences.

A: Where are the sunglasses?
B: In picture 1, they're on the bicycle.
A: In picture 2, they're on the table.

GROUP WORK Describe the people in the pictures. Don't say the person's name. Your classmates guess the person.

A: He's wearing blue jeans, a beige shirt, and a black jacket. Who is it?

B: Is it John Cho?

A: No, it isn't.

B: Is it Liam Hemsworth?

A: That's right.

Bradley Cooper

Rashida Jones

Neymar

Cristiano Ronaldo

Idris Elba

Scarlett Johansson

Ariana Grande

John Cho

Ang Lee

Kate Middleton

Zoe Saldana

Liam Hemsworth

A CLASS ACTIVITY Talk to your classmates. Ask two different classmates each question. Write their names and answers.

Question	Name:	Name:
What's your last name?		
Where are you from?		
What is your parents' first language?		
How do you spell your best friend's name?		
What's your best friend like?		
What is your email address?		
What is your phone number?		

B CLASS ACTIVITY Tell the class two things about your partners.

"Yumi's last name is Suzuki. Francisco is from Guatemala."

What's wrong with this picture?

GROUP WORK What's wrong with this picture? Tell your classmates.

"Mia and Karen are playing basketball, but they're wearing dresses!"

A CLASS ACTIVITY Go around the class and find this information.
Try to write a different name on each line.

Find **someone** who ...

	Name ✎
gets up at 5:00 A.M. on weekdays	
gets up at noon on Saturdays	
does homework on Sunday night	
works at night	
works on weekends	
has a pet	
dances on Friday night	
lives alone	
takes a bus to class	
rides a motorcycle to class	
cooks on weekends	
plays the drums	
has two brothers	
writes emails every day	
speaks three languages	
doesn't eat breakfast	

work at night

cook on the weekends

play the drums

A: Do you get up at 5:00 A.M. on weekdays, Kun-woo?
B: No, I get up at six-thirty.
A: Do you get up at 5:00 A.M. on weekdays, Yasmin?
C: Yes, I get up at 5:00 A.M. every day.

B GROUP WORK Compare your answers.

A: Kun-woo gets up at six-thirty on weekdays.
B: Yasmin gets up at 5:00 on weekdays.
C: Lucas gets up at . . .

A PAIR WORK Find the differences between Tony's apartment and Nicole's apartment.

Tony's apartment

Nicole's apartment

A: There are four chairs in Tony's kitchen, but there are three chairs in Nicole's kitchen.
B: There is a sofa in Tony's living room, but there is no sofa in Nicole's living room.

B GROUP WORK Compare your answers.

The perfect job

A PAIR WORK Imagine you're looking for a job. What do you want to do? First, check (✓) your answers to the questions. Then ask your partner the same questions.

	Me		My partner	
Do you want to . . . ?	Yes	No	Yes	No
work from 9 to 5	☐	☐	☐	☐
work in an office	☐	☐	☐	☐
work outdoors	☐	☐	☐	☐
work at home	☐	☐	☐	☐
work with a team	☐	☐	☐	☐
use a computer	☐	☐	☐	☐
use English	☐	☐	☐	☐
travel	☐	☐	☐	☐
talk to people	☐	☐	☐	☐
help people	☐	☐	☐	☐
wear a suit	☐	☐	☐	☐
perform in front of people	☐	☐	☐	☐

work from 9 to 5

perform in front of people

work outdoors

work with a team

Positive

It's easy. / It's an easy job.

It's exciting. / It's an exciting job.

It's terrific. / It's a terrific job.

It's pretty relaxing. / It's a pretty relaxing job.

Negative

It's difficult. / It's a difficult job.

It's boring. / It's a boring job.

It's very stressful. / It's a very stressful job.

It's really dangerous. / It's a really dangerous job.

B PAIR WORK Think of a good job for your partner. Go to pages 50 and 53 for ideas.

A: You want to travel and use English. Do you want to be a pilot?

B: No, a pilot's job is very stressful.

A: OK, do you want to be . . . ?

Planning a party

A You're planning a small party. Choose two sweet and two salty snacks you want to serve.

almonds   vegetables and dip   cake   candy

chocolates   cookies   corn chips   grapes

hot dogs   ice cream   peanuts   pineapple

pizza   popcorn   potato chips   watermelon

B **PAIR WORK** Get together with a partner. Compare your choices and decide on
only two sweet and two salty snacks for your party.

A: Let's have pizza, popcorn, chocolates, and candy.

B: Oh, I never eat pizza and popcorn together. And I hardly ever eat chocolates or candy.
Let's have pizza, hot dogs, grapes, and watermelon.

A: Well, I like grapes, but I don't like watermelon. Let's have . . .

C **GROUP WORK** Present your choices to the other pairs. Can you decide on
only four snacks for the class?

A CLASS ACTIVITY Add two more activities to the list. Then go around the class. Find someone who can and someone who can't do each thing. Try to write a different name on each line.

Can you . . . ?	Can	Can't
do a handstand		
do yoga		
juggle three balls		
make your own clothes		
play two musical instruments		
raise one eyebrow		
say the alphabet backward		
say "hello" in three languages		
swim underwater		
whistle a song		

do a handstand

make your own clothes

raise one eyebrow

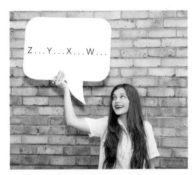
say the alphabet backward

whistle a song

juggle balls

A: Can you do a handstand?
B: Yes, I can. OR No, I can't.

B CLASS ACTIVITY Share your answers with the class.

"Nick can't do a handstand, but Sylvia can. And Yan-mei can do yoga."

C Do you have any other hidden talents or abilities?

A PAIR WORK Add one more activity to the list. Is your partner going to do any of these things? Check (✓) your guesses.

Is your partner going to . . . ?	My guesses Yes	No	My partner's answers Yes	No
1. play video games tonight	☐	☐	☐	☐
2. eat special food this month	☐	☐	☐	☐
3. buy some cheese this week	☐	☐	☐	☐
4. wear a suit this month	☐	☐	☐	☐
5. wake up early tomorrow	☐	☐	☐	☐
6. have a big breakfast on Saturday	☐	☐	☐	☐
7. study for a test tomorrow night	☐	☐	☐	☐
8. drive a car over the weekend	☐	☐	☐	☐
9. get a new apartment next year	☐	☐	☐	☐
10. watch a soccer game on Sunday	☐	☐	☐	☐
11. _____	☐	☐	☐	☐

B PAIR WORK Ask and answer questions to check your guesses.

A: Are you going to play video games tonight?
B: Yes, I am. I'm going to play my favorite video game.

C CLASS ACTIVITY How many of your guesses are correct? Who has the most correct guesses?

A PAIR WORK Imagine you have these problems. Your partner gives advice.

I really want to buy a car, but I can't save any money. I spend every single penny I have.

I can never get up on time in the morning. I'm always late for school.

I'm new in town, and I don't know any people here. How can I make some friends?

I have a big test tomorrow. My family is very noisy, so I can't study!

My job is very stressful. I usually work 10 hours a day.

It's my best friend's birthday, and I don't have a gift for her. All the stores are closed!

A: I really want to buy a car, but . . .
B: Save some money every month. Don't . . .

B CLASS ACTIVITY Think of a problem you have.
Then tell the class. Your classmates give advice.

A: I don't understand some vocabulary in this unit.
B: Review the unit and do your homework.
C: Don't worry. Ask the teacher.

Student A

A **PAIR WORK** Look at the map. You are outside the Windsor Hotel on Oak Street between Second and Third Avenues. Ask your partner for directions to the three places below. Your map does not have names on these buildings, but your partner's map does. Listen to your partner, find the places on the map, and write their names.

> garage   supermarket   flower shop

A: Excuse me. How do I get to the garage?
B: Walk down Maple Street to First Avenue. Turn . . .

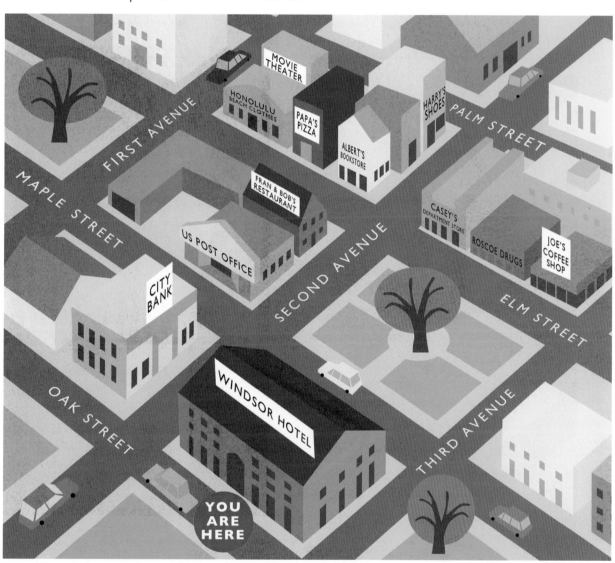

B **PAIR WORK** Your partner asks you for directions to three places. Your partner's map does not have names on these buildings, but your map does. Use the expressions in the box to give directions.

Go up/Go down . . .	It's on the corner of . . . Street	It's next to . . .
Walk up/Walk down . . .	and . . . Avenue.	It's behind . . .
Turn right/Turn left . . .	It's between . . . and . . .	It's in front of . . .
It's across from . . .		

Student B

A PAIR WORK Look at the map. You are outside the Windsor Hotel on Oak Street between Second and Third Avenues. Your partner asks you for directions to three places. Your partner's map does not have names on these buildings, but your map does. Use the expressions in the box to give directions.

A: Excuse me. How do I get to the garage?

B: Walk down Oak Street to First Avenue. Turn . . .

Go up/Go down . . .	It's on the corner of . . . Street	It's next to . . .
Walk up/Walk down . . .	and . . . Avenue.	It's behind . . .
Turn right/Turn left . . .	It's between . . . and . . .	It's in front of . . .
It's across from . . .		

B PAIR WORK Ask your partner for directions to the three places below. Your map does not have names on these buildings, but your partner's map does. Listen to your partner, find the places on the map and write their names.

coffee shop   shoe store   bookstore

A **PAIR WORK** What did you do when you were a child? First, check (✓) your answers to the questions. Then ask your partner the same questions. Check (✓) your partner's answers.

A: Did you argue with your friends as a child?

B: Yes, I did. OR No, I didn't.

A: Did you clean your room?

B: Yes, I did. OR No, I didn't.

Did you . . . as a child?	Me		My partner	
	Yes	No	Yes	No
argue with your friends	☐	☐	☐	☐
clean your room	☐	☐	☐	☐
make your bed	☐	☐	☐	☐
get up early on weekdays	☐	☐	☐	☐
sleep late on weekends	☐	☐	☐	☐
have a tablet	☐	☐	☐	☐
play video games	☐	☐	☐	☐
listen to rock music	☐	☐	☐	☐
play a musical instrument	☐	☐	☐	☐
play a sport	☐	☐	☐	☐
ride a bicycle	☐	☐	☐	☐
wear braces	☐	☐	☐	☐

argue with your friends

wear braces

make your bed

play a musical instrument

B **PAIR WORK** Join another pair. Tell them what your partner did and didn't do as a child.

"Yu-jin didn't argue with her friends as a child. She cleaned her room."

A What were five important events in your life? Choose four events and add another important event. Then write the years when these events happened in the box.

I was born in . . .

I started elementary school in . . .

I went to my first musical concert in . . .

I opened my first bank account in . . .

I traveled with friends in . . .

I graduated from high school in . . .

I moved to a new place in . . .

I started learning English in . . .

I . . . in . . .

Years
1. _____
2. _____
3. _____
4. _____
5. _____

B **PAIR WORK** Ask your partner about his or her life events.
Your partner will only show you the box with the years.

A: What happened in 2002?
B: I started elementary school.

A: How old were you?
B: I was six.

A You are planning your dream weekend. Write your plans for Saturday and Sunday in the charts. Use these expressions and your own ideas.

go to (the movies/a party)	play (basketball/video games)
go (dancing/shopping)	meet (my friend/teacher)
go (on a trip/picnic)	have dinner with (my brother/parents)
study for (a test/an exam)	visit (my parents/grandparents)
go out with (my girlfriend/boyfriend)	see (the dentist/doctor)

WEEKEND PLANS

Saturday

	Me	My partner
morning		
lunch		
afternoon		
evening		
dinner		
after dinner		

WEEKEND PLANS

Sunday

	Me	My partner
morning		
lunch		
afternoon		
evening		
dinner		
after dinner		

B **PAIR WORK** Compare your plans with your partner. Choose activities to do together.

A: What do you want to do on Saturday morning?
B: Let's go swimming. They opened a new pool at the gym.
A: Oh, I can't swim. Sorry. Maybe we can go bike riding . . .

C **GROUP WORK** Join another pair. Can you decide what to do over the weekend together?

A: So, would you like to go bike riding on Saturday morning?
C: Good idea. And how about a barbecue for lunch?
B: Oh, we don't have time for a barbecue. We want to go to an art festival in the afternoon . . .

Grammar plus

1 My, your, his, her page 3

> ■ Use *his* with males and *her* with females: **His** name is Travis. (NOT: ~~Her name is Travis.~~)
> **Her** name is Nicole. (NOT: ~~His name is Nicole.~~)

Complete the conversations with *my, your, his,* or *her.*

1. **A:** Hello. _____My_____ name is Carlos.
   B: Hi, Carlos. What's _____ last name?
   A: It's Gonzales.
   B: How do you spell _____ last name? Is it G-O-N-Z-A-L-E-Z?
   A: No, it's G-O-N-Z-A-L-E-S. And what's _____ name?
   B: _____ name is Bill Powers. Nice to meet you.

2. **A:** What's Ms. Robinson's first name?
   B: _____ first name is Elizabeth. _____ nickname is Liz.
   A: I'm sorry. What's _____ first name again?
   B: It's Elizabeth. And what's Mr. Weber's first name?
   A: _____ first name is Peter.
   B: That's right. And _____ nickname is Pete.
   A: That's right, too!

2 The verb *be* page 5

> ■ In questions, the verb *be* comes before the noun or pronoun: **Are you** Joshua Brown?
> **Is he** in our English class? **Is she** the teacher?
> ■ Don't use contractions in short answers with *Yes*: Are you in my class?
> Yes, **I am**. (NOT: ~~Yes, I'm.~~)

Complete the conversations with the words in the box.

am	I'm	it's	she's	you're
✓ are	I am	I'm not	you	

1. **A:** Excuse me. _____Are_____ you Layla Moore?
   B: No, _____. _____ over there.
   A: OK. Thanks.

2. **A:** Hi. Are _____ Layla Moore?
   B: Yes, _____.
   A: Nice to meet you. _____ Sergio Oliveira.
   _____ in my English class.
   B: Yes, I _____. _____ nice to meet you too, Sergio.

UNIT 2

1 *This/these; it/they;* plurals page 10

> ■ Don't use a contraction with *What + are*: **What** are these? (NOT: ~~What're these?~~)
> ■ Use *this* with singular nouns: **This** is a laptop. Use *these* with plural nouns: **These** are flash drives.

Choose the correct words.

1. A: **What's** / **What are** these?
   B: **It's** / **They're** my **flash drive** / **flash drives**.
2. A: **What's** / **What are** this?
   B: **It's** / **They're** a / an cell phone.
3. A: **What's** **this** / **these**?
   B: **It's** / **They're** a / an English book.

2 Yes/No and *where* questions with *be* page 11

> ■ In questions with *where*, the verb comes after *Where*: **Where** is my credit card?
> (NOT: ~~Where my credit card is?~~) **Where** are my sunglasses? (NOT: ~~Where my sunglasses are?~~)

A Match the questions with the answers.

1. Is that your wallet? __c__
2. Are these your glasses? _____
3. Where are my keys? _____
4. Is this your bicycle? _____
5. Where's your tablet? _____

a. They're in your backpack.
b. No, it's not.
c. Oh, yes, it is!
d. It's on my desk.
e. No, they're not.

B Complete the conversation. Use the words in the box.

are they	it is	they are	where
it	it's	this	✓ where's

A: ___Where's___ my dictionary?
B: I don't know. Is _____ in your backpack?
A: No, _____ not.
B: Is _____ your dictionary?
A: Yes, _____ Thanks! Now, _____ are my glasses?
B: _____ on your desk?
A: Yes, _____. Thank you!

UNIT 3

1 Negative statements and yes/no questions with be page 17

- Use *be* + *not* to form negative statements: Ana **isn't** a student. (NOT: ~~Ana no is a student.~~)
- *You* is a singular and a plural pronoun: Are **you** from Rio? Yes, **I** am./Yes, **we** are.

A Unscramble the words to write negative statements.

1. is / of Canada / Toronto / the capital / not
   <u>Toronto is not the capital of Canada.</u>

2. Buenos Aires / not / from / we're
   _____

3. not / you and Ashley / in my class / are
   _____

4. is / my first language / Korean / not
   _____

5. from / my mother / not / is / Italy
   _____

6. my parents / not / are / they
   _____

B Complete the conversations.

1. **A:** _____Are_____ you and your friend from Costa Rica?
   B: No, _____ not. _____ from the Dominican Republic.

2. **A:** _____ your first language Spanish?
   B: Yes, it _____. My parents _____ from Ecuador.

3. **A:** _____ Nadia and Rayan Lebanese?
   B: Yes, _____ are. But _____ in France now.

4. **A:** _____ my friends and I late?
   B: No, _____ not. _____ early!

2 Wh-questions with be page 20

- Use *what* to ask about things. Use *where* to ask about places. Use *who* to ask about people. Use *What is/are . . . like?* to ask for a description.
- Use *how* to ask for a description: **How are** you today? Use how old to ask about age: **How old** is he?
- In answers about age, you can use only the number or the number + years old: He's **18**. OR He's **18 years old.** (NOT: ~~He has 18 years.~~)

Complete the questions with *how, what, where,* or *who*. Then match the questions with the answers.

1. <u>Who</u> is that? <u>d</u>
2. _____ is her name? _____
3. _____ is she like? _____
4. _____ old is she? _____
5. _____ your family from? _____
6. _____ is Kyoto like? _____

a. We're from Japan – from Kyoto.
b. She's 18.
c. Her name is Hina.
d. She's my sister.
e. Oh, it's really beautiful.
f. She's very nice and friendly.

1 Possessives `page 24`

- The noun comes after a possessive adjective: This is **my** T-shirt.
- Don't include the noun after a possessive pronoun: This T-shirt is **mine**.
- *Whose* can be used with singular and plural nouns: **Whose** scarf is this? **Whose** sneakers are these?

Complete the conversations. Use the words in the boxes. There are two extra words in each box.

his	mine	my	your	yours	✓ whose

1. **A:** _____Whose_____ jacket is this? Is it _____, Ethan?
   B: No, it's not _____. Ask Matt. I think it's _____.

her	my	mine	your	yours

2. **A:** These aren't _____ gloves. Are they _____?
   B: No, they're not _____. Maybe they are Young-min's.

her	hers	their	theirs	whose

3. **A:** _____ sweaters are these? Are they Rachel's?
   B: No, they're not _____ sweaters. But these shorts are _____.

2 Present continuous statements; conjunctions `page 26`

- The present continuous is the present of *be* + verb + *-ing*: It**'s raining**. She**'s wearing** a raincoat.
- The two negative contractions mean the same: **He's not/He isn't** wearing a coat. **We're not/We aren't** wearing gloves.

Change the affirmative sentences to negative sentences. Change the negative sentences to affirmative sentences.

1. Mr. and Mrs. Liu are wearing green caps. ___Mr. and Mrs. Liu aren't wearing green caps.___
2. It isn't snowing. _____
3. I'm wearing a winter coat. _____
4. You're wearing David's sunglasses. _____
5. Ayumi isn't wearing a scarf. _____

3 Present continuous yes/no questions; adjective + noun `page 27`

- In questions, the present continuous is *be* + subject + verb + *–ing*: I**s** it **raining**? **Are** you **wearing** a raincoat?
- Adjectives can come before nouns or after the verb *be*: He's wearing **a blue hat**. His hat **is blue**.
- Adjectives don't have a plural form: a **green hat**; two **green hats**.

Write questions using the words in parentheses. Then complete the responses.

1. **A.** ___Is Mr. Thomas wearing a dark blue coat?___ (wear, dark blue coat)
   B: No, he _____.
2. **A:** _____ (wear, high heels)
   B: No, we _____.
3. **A:** _____ (wear, a sweater)
   B: Yes, I _____.
4. **A:** _____ (rain)
   B: Yes, it _____.

1 What time is it? / Is it A.M. or P.M.? — page 31

■ Remember: You can say times different ways: 1:15 = *one-fifteen* OR *a quarter after one.*

Write each sentence in a different way.

1. It's a quarter to four. <u>It's three forty-five.</u>
2. It's 7:00 P.M. <u>It's seven in the evening.</u>
3. It's six-fifteen. _____
4. It's 10 o'clock at night. _____
5. It's three-oh-five. _____
6. It's twenty-five to eleven. _____
7. It's one o'clock in the morning. _____
8. It's midnight. _____

2 Present continuous Wh-questions — page 33

■ Use the present continuous to talk about actions that are happening right now:
What **are** you **doing**? **I'm talking** to you!
■ In questions, the *be* verb comes after the question word: What **are you** doing?
■ To form the continuous of verbs ending in *–e*, drop the e and add *–ing*: have → having.
■ For verbs ending in vowel + consonant, double the consonant and add *–ing*: get → getting.

What are the people doing? Write conversations. Use the words in parentheses.

1. A: <u>What's Matt doing?</u> (Matt)
    B: <u>He's swimming.</u> (swim)

2. A: _____ (Jon and Megan)
    B: _____ (shop)

3. A: _____ (you)
    B: _____ (write a message)

4. A: _____ (Chris)
    B: _____ (cook dinner)

5: A: _____ (you and Tyler)
    B: _____ (watch a movie)

6: A: _____ (Sara)
    B: _____ (have pizza)

7. A: _____ (you and Joseph)
    B: _____ (study for the test)

8. A: _____ (Laura and Paulo)
    B: _____ (chat online)

1 Simple present statements `page 37` **and Simple present statements with irregular verbs** `page 38`

> ■ In affirmative statements, verbs with *he/she/it* end in *–s*: He/She **walks** to school. BUT I/You/We/They **walk** to school.
>
> ■ In negative statements, use doesn't with *he/she/it* and don't with all the others: He/She/It **doesn't** live here. I/You/We/They **don't** live here.
>
> ■ Don't add *–s* to the verb: She **doesn't live** here. (NOT: ~~She doesn't lives here.~~)

Elena is talking about her family. Complete the sentences with the correct form of the verbs in parentheses.

My family and I _____live_____ (live) in the city. We _____ (have) an apartment on First Avenue. My sister _____ (go) to school near our apartment, so she _____ (walk) to school. My father _____ (work) in the suburbs, so he _____ (drive) to his job. My mother _____ (use) public transportation – she _____ (take) the bus to her office downtown. She _____ (have) a new job, but she _____ (not like) it very much. And me? Well, I _____ (not work) far from our apartment, so I _____ (not need) a car or public transportation. I _____ (ride) my bike to work!

2 Simple present questions `page 39`

> ■ In questions, use does with *he/she/it* and do with all the others:
> **Does** he/she/it get up early? **Do** I/you/we/they get up early?
>
> ■ Don't add *–s* to the verb: Does she **live** alone? (NOT: ~~Does she lives alone?~~)

A Write questions to complete the conversations.

1. **A:** _Do you use public transportation?_
   B: Yes, I use public transportation.

2. **A:** _____
   B: No, my family doesn't eat dinner at 5:00.

3. **A:** _____
   B: No, my brother doesn't take the bus to work.

4. **A:** _____
   B: No, I don't get up late on weekends.

> ■ Use in with *the morning/the afternoon/the evening*. Use at with *night*:
> I go to school **in** the afternoon and work **at** night.
>
> ■ Use at with clock times: She gets up **at** 8:00.
>
> ■ Use on with days: He sleeps late **on** weekends. She has class **on** Mondays.

B Complete the conversation with *at*, *in*, or *on*.

A: Does your family have breakfast together _____in_____ the morning?

B: Well, we eat together _____ weekends, but _____ weekdays we're all busy. My parents go to work early – _____ 6:30. But we eat dinner together _____ the evening, and we have a big lunch together _____ Sundays. We eat _____ noon. Then _____ the afternoon, we take a walk or go to the movies.

1 Simple present short answers page 45

■ Remember: I/You/We/They **do/don't**. He/She/It **does/doesn't**.

Choose the correct words.

A: **Do /** **Does** your family **live / lives** in an apartment?

B: No, we **don't / doesn't**. We **have / has** a house.

A: That's nice. **Do / Does** your house have two floors?

B: Yes, it **do / does**. It **have / has** four rooms on the first floor. And we **have / has** three bedrooms and a bathroom on the second floor.

A: And **do / does** you and your family **have / has** a yard?

B: Yes, we **do / does**. And how about you, Tim? **Do / Does** you **live / lives** in a house, too?

A: No, I **don't / doesn't**. My wife and I **have / has** a small apartment in the city.

B: Oh. **Do / Does** you **like / likes** the city?

A: Yes, I **do / does**. But my wife **don't / doesn't**.

2 *There is, there are* page 47

■ Use *there is* with singular nouns: **There's** a bed. Use *there are* with plural nouns: **There are** two chairs.

■ Use *some* in affirmative statements: There are **some** chairs in the kitchen. Use *any* in negative statements: There aren't **any** chairs in the bedroom.

Read the information about the Perez family's new house. Write sentences with the phrases in the box.

there's a	there are some
there's no	there are no
there isn't a	there aren't any

1. A living room?	Yes.
2. A dining room?	No.
3. A microwave in the kitchen?	No.
4. A table in the kitchen?	Yes.
5. Curtains on the windows?	Yes.
6. Rugs on the floors?	No.
7. Closets in the bedrooms?	Yes.
8. Bookcases in the bedrooms?	No.

1. *There's a living room.*

2. _____

3. _____

4. _____

5. _____

6. _____

7. _____

8. _____

1 Simple present Wh-questions page 52

> ■ Use *What* to ask about things: **What do** you do? Use *Where* to ask about places: **Where do** you work?
> Use *How do/does . . . like . . . ?* to ask for an opinion: **How does** he **like** his job?

Complete the conversations.

1. A: _What does your husband do_ ?
   B: My husband? Oh, he's a nurse.
   A: Really? Where _____ ?
   B: He works at Mercy Hospital.

2. A: Where _____ ?
   B: I work in a restaurant.
   A: Nice! What _____ ?
   B: I'm a chef.

3. A: How _____ ?
   B: My job? I don't really like it very much.
   A: That's too bad. What _____ ?
   B: I'm a cashier. I work at a clothing store.

4. A: What _____ ?
   B: My brother is a doctor, and my sister is a lawyer.
   A: How _____ ?
   B: They work very hard, but they love their jobs.

2 Placement of adjectives page 54

> ■ Adjectives come after the verb *be*: A doctor's job **is stressful**. Adjectives come before nouns:
> A police officer has a **dangerous job**. (NOT: ~~A police officer has a job dangerous.~~)
> ■ Adjectives have the same form with singular or plural nouns: Firefighters and police officers have stressful
> jobs. (NOT:. . . have ~~stressfuls~~ jobs.)

Use the information to write two sentences.

1. accountant / job / boring
   An accountant's job is boring.
   An accountant has a boring job.

2. salesperson / job / stressful
   _____

   _____

3. security guard / job / dangerous
   _____

   _____

4. actor / job / exciting
   _____

   _____

5. host / job / interesting
   _____

   _____

6. nurse / job / difficult
   _____

   _____

1 Count and noncount nouns; *some* and *any*   page 59

- Count nouns name things you can count: *bananas, crackers, carrots.* Count nouns have a singular and plural form: **1 orange, 2 oranges.** Noncount nouns name things you can't count: *milk, oil, rice.*
- Use *some* in affirmative sentences: We have **some** butter. Use *any* in negative sentences and questions: We don't have **any** lettuce. Do we have **any** tomatoes?

Complete the conversations with *some* or *any*.

1. A: What do you want for lunch?

   B: Let's make _____some_____ sandwiches.

   A: Good idea! We have _____ bread. Do we have _____ cheese?

   B: Yes, I think there's _____ in the refrigerator. Let me see. . . . No, I don't see _____.

   A: Well, let's go to the store. We need _____ milk, too. And do we have _____ cheese?

   B: Yes, we do. There's _____ lettuce here, and there are _____ tomatoes, too.

   A: Do we have _____ mayonnaise? I love _____ mayonnaise on my sandwiches.

   B: Me, too. But there isn't _____ here. Let's buy _____.

2. A: Let's make a big breakfast tomorrow morning.

   B: Good idea! What do we need? Are there _____ eggs?

   A: There are _____ but I think we need to buy _____ more.

   B: OK. And let's get _____ cereal, too. We don't have _____, and I love cereal for breakfast.

   A: Me, too. Do we have _____ blueberry yogurt?

   B: Yes, there's _____ in the refrigerator.

   A: Great! So we don't need to buy _____ at the store.

   B: That's right. Just eggs and cereal!

2 Adverbs of frequency   page 61

- Adverbs of frequency usually go before the main verb: *always, almost always, usually, often, sometimes, hardly ever, almost never, never:* She **never eats** breakfast. I **almost always have** tea in the morning.
  Sometimes can also begin a sentence: **Sometimes** I **eat** broccoli.

Rewrite the conversation. Add the adverbs in the correct places.

A: Where do you have lunch? (usually)   _Where do you usually have lunch?_

B: I go to a restaurant near work. (often)   _____

A: Do you eat at your desk? (ever)   _____

B: No, I stay in for lunch. (hardly ever)   _____

A: And what do you have? (usually)   _____

B: I have soup or a salad. (always)   _____

A: Me, too. I have a big lunch. (never)   _____

1 Simple present Wh-questions page 65

- Remember: *Who* = what person; *where* = what place; *how often* = what frequency; *when* = what days; *what time* = what time of day
- Remember: Use *do* or *does* after the question word.

Complete the questions with the correct question word and *do* or *does*.
Then match the questions with the answers.

1. ___What___ sport ___do___ you like? _c_
2. _____ you go to games with? _____
3. _____ often _____ your team play? _____
4. _____ they play? _____
5. _____ they play? _____
6. _____ time _____ the games start? _____

a. My father and my two brothers.
b. Usually at four o'clock.
c. Soccer. I love to watch my team.
d. Once or twice a month.
e. On Sunday afternoons.
f. At the Olympic Stadium.

2 *Can* for ability page 67

- Use the base form of the verb with *can*. With third-person singular, don't add an –s to *can* or to the base form: She **can play** the piano. (NOT: ~~She can plays the piano.~~)

A Write sentences about the things people can and can't do. Use *can* or *can't* with *and*, *but*, or *or*. (✓ = can, ✗ = can't)

1. Olivia: ride a bike ✓   drive a car ✗
   Olivia can ride a bike, but she can't drive a car.

2. Juan: play the piano ✓   play the violin ✓
   _____

3. Matt and Drew: act ✓   sing ✗
   _____

4. Alicia: snowboard ✓   ice-skate ✗
   _____

5. Ben: take good photos ✓   edit videos ✓
   _____

6. Corinne: write poems ✗   tell good jokes ✓
   _____

B Look at part A. Answer the questions. Write short sentences.

1. Can Matt and Drew sing? _No, they can't._
2. Who can tell good jokes? _____
3. Can Olivia drive a car? _____
4. Can Juan play the piano? _____
5. Who can snowboard? _____
6. What can Matt do? _____

1 The future with *be going to*   page 73

> ■ Use *am/is/are* + *going to* + base form for the future: We**'re going to have** dinner with my parents tonight.
>
> ■ In questions with *be going to*, the *be* verb comes before the subject: **Is he going to buy** me a gift?

A Complete Matthew's story. Use the correct form of *be going to* and the verbs in parentheses.

Tomorrow is _____*going to be*_____ (be) a very exciting day. It's my birthday, and my friends and I _____ (celebrate). In the morning, Stephen and I _____ (drive) to the beach. Our friend Rosa _____ (meet) us there. We _____ (stay) at the beach for a few hours. Then we _____ (have) lunch at my favorite restaurant. After lunch, Stephen _____ (go) to work, and Rosa and I _____ (see) a movie. After the movie, we _____ (go) to our friend Philip's house. He _____ (make) his special homemade pizza for Rosa and me.

B Write questions. Then look at part A and answer the questions.

1. Matthew / celebrate / with his family?
   Q: _Is Matthew going to celebrate with his family?_
   A: _No, he's going to celebrate with his friends._

2. Stephen and Matthew / ride their bikes / to the beach?
   Q: _____
   A: _____

3. the friends / have lunch / at a restaurant?
   Q: _____
   A: _____

4. Rosa and Matthew / go to a museum?
   Q: _____
   A: _____

5. Rosa and Matthew / have pizza / at a restaurant?
   Q: _____
   A: _____

2 Wh-questions with *be going to*   page 75

> ■ Use *is* in questions with *Who* as the subject: **Who's** going to be there? (NOT: ~~Who are going to be there?~~)

Complete the conversation with the correct form of *be going to*.

A: What _____*are*_____ you _____*going to do*_____ (do) this weekend?

B: I _____ (have) a very busy weekend. My friend Amir _____ (visit) me, and we _____ (spend) the weekend in the city.

A: That's nice. _____ you _____ (stay) in a hotel?

B: No, we _____ (stay) with our friend Lara. And Lara _____ (have) a big party on Saturday night.

A: Really? And who _____ (be) at the party? Do you know any of Lara's friends?

B: No, I don't. But Amir and I _____ (meet) everyone on Saturday night.

UNIT 12

1 *Have* + noun; *feel* + adjective page 79

- For most health problems, use *a/an*: I have **a** cold. I have **an** earache. With *flu*, use *the*: I have **the** flu. (NOT: I have a flu.)

Complete the conversation. Use the sentences in the box.

> I think I have a fever.
> Thanks.
> I feel awful, actually.
> Yes. I'm going to call my doctor in a few minutes.
> Yes, I do. And I have a stomachache, too.
> ✓ Hi, Vanessa. How are you?

A: Hi, Vanessa. How are you?

B: I'm terrific, thanks. How about you?

A: _____

B: Oh, no! What's the matter?

A: _____

B: That's too bad. Do you have a headache?

A: _____

B: Are you going to see a doctor?

A: _____

B: Well, feel better soon.

A: _____

2 Imperatives page 82

- Use the base form of the verb in affirmative imperatives: **Go** home and **rest**, Ms. Lake.
- Use *don't* + base form of the verb in negative imperatives. The form doesn't change: **Don't go** to work today, Ms. Lake.

Read the situations. Give the people advice. Use the phrases in the box.

> ✓ drink coffee in the evening
> eat any cold food
> exercise today or tomorrow
> take an antacid
> take two aspirins
> work too hard

1. Dave: "I can't sleep at night." Don't drink coffee in the evening.
2. Corey: "I have a headache." _____
3. Lucia: "I work 12 hours a day." _____
4. William: "My legs hurt." _____
5. Min-ho: "I have a toothache." _____
6. Fatima: "I have an awful stomachache." _____

Unit 12 Grammar plus **143**

1 Prepositions of place page 88

> ■ Use *on* with the names of streets and avenues: The bookstore is **on** Center Street.
> The theater is **on** Park Avenue.
>
> ■ *Across from* is another way of saying *opposite*: The library is **across from** the theater.
> = The library is **opposite** the theater.

Choose the correct words.

A: Excuse me. Is there a post office around here?

B: Yes, there is. It's **in /(on)** Maple Street.

A: Where on Maple?

B: It's **in / on** the corner of Maple Street and Second Avenue.

A: Next **from / to** Charlie's Restaurant?

B: Yes, that's right. It's across the street **from / to** the Windsor Hotel.

A: Thanks. Oh, and where is the bank?

B: It's on Oak Street – **between / next to** the hospital and police station.

A: Great. Thanks very much.

B: You're welcome.

2 Directions page 90

> ■ *Walk up/Go up* mean the same thing. *Walk down/Go down* also mean the same thing.

Jenna doesn't know Manhattan at all. Correct Jenna's directions.
Write the opposite of what she says.

1. Cal How do I get to Washington Square Park?
   Jenna Walk up Fifth Avenue.
   You   _No, don't walk up Fifth Avenue. Walk down Fifth Avenue._

2. Cal How can I get to the Empire State Building?
   Jenna Turn right on 32nd Street.
   You   _____

3. Cal How do I get to Bryant Park from Rockefeller Center?
   Jenna Go down Sixth Avenue.
   You   _____
   Jenna It's on the left.
   You   _____

4. Cal How do I get to Central Park?
   Jenna Walk down Eighth Avenue.
   You   _____

1 **Simple past statements: regular verbs and irregular verbs** _page 93–94_

- Use simple past verbs to talk about the past. Regular verbs end in –ed: I **watched** TV last night. For verbs ending in –e, add –d: _live → lived_. For verbs ending in vowel + consonant, double the consonant and add –ed: _shop → shopped_.

- Use _didn't_ + base form in negative statements. The form doesn't change: He **didn't shop** for groceries yesterday. (NOT: ~~He didn't shopped for groceries yesterday.~~)

Maya wrote an email to a friend. Complete the sentences with the simple past form of the verbs in parentheses.

Hi!

I ___didn't do___ (not do) anything special this weekend, but I _____ (have) a lot of fun. I _____ (not go) out on Friday night. I _____ (stay) home. I _____ (clean) my room and _____ (do) the laundry. I _____ (help) my sister with her homework, and then we _____ (watch) our favorite series. On Saturday, my friend Lori _____ (come) over. She _____ (need) some new shoes, so we _____ (take) the bus downtown to Todd's Shoe Store. We _____ (shop) for a long time, but Lori _____ (not like) any of the shoes at Todd's. She _____ (buy) some purple socks, but she _____ (not buy) any shoes. On our way back to my house, we _____ (stop) at the gym and _____ (exercise). We _____ (not exercise) very hard. I _____ (invite) Lori for dinner, and my dad _____ (cook) hamburgers in the yard. After dinner, Lori and I _____ (talk) and _____ (play) video games. She _____ (not stay) very late – my mother _____ (drive) her home at around ten. On Sunday, my whole family _____ (visit) my mother's best friend and her family. They have a swimming pool, so my sister and I _____ (go) swimming all afternoon.

Tell me about your weekend!

Maya

2 **Simple past yes/no questions** _page 95_

- Use _did_ + base form in questions. The form doesn't change: **Did** you **have** fun yesterday? (NOT: ~~Did you had fun yesterday?~~)

Complete the conversation. Use the simple past form of the verbs in parentheses.

A: ___Did___ you ___enjoy___ (enjoy) your vacation?

B: Yes, I _____. My brother and I _____ (have) a great time.

A: _____ you _____ (make) any videos?

B: No, we _____. But we _____ (take) a lot of pictures.

A: That's good. _____ you _____ (see) a lot of interesting things?

B: Yes, we _____. And we _____ (eat) a lot of new foods. How about you? _____ you (have) a good summer?

A: Well, I _____ (not go) anywhere, but I _____ (read) a lot of good books and _____ (see) some great movies.

1 Past of *be* page 101

■ Present		Past
am/is	→	**was**
are	→	**were**

Complete the conversations with *was*, *wasn't*, *were*, or *weren't*.

1. A: _____Were_____ you here yesterday?

   B: No, I _____. I _____ home in bed.

   A: Oh, _____ you sick?

   B: No. I _____ just really tired.

2. A: Where _____ you born?

   B: I _____ born in Mexico City.

   A: Really? What about your parents? _____ they born here, too?

   B: No, they _____ .They _____ born in Guadalajara.

3. A: Where _____ Jamil last week? _____ he on vacation?

   B: Yes, he _____ . He and his best friend _____ in Portugal.
   They _____ in Oporto.

   A: _____ it a good trip?

   B: Yes, it was. Jamil said it _____ a terrific trip!

2 Wh-questions with *did*, *was*, **and** *were* page 101

   ■ Don't use *did* with the past of *be*: Where **were** you last Tuesday? (NOT: ~~Where did you were last~~ ~~Tuesday?~~) Use *did* in simple past questions with other verbs: Where **did** you **go** last Tuesday?

   ■ *Because* answers the question *Why?*

Complete the questions. Use the words in the box.

✓ how	what	where	why
how old	when	who	

1. A: _____How_____ was your childhood?

   B: I had a fantastic childhood!

2. A: _____ did you grow up?

   B: I grew up in Incheon, a small city in South Korea.

3. A: _____ were you when you started school?

   B: I think I was five or six.

4. A: _____ was your best friend in high school?

   B: My best friend was a boy named Joon-ho.

5. A: _____ did you leave home?

   B: In 2012.

6. A: _____ did you leave Incheon?

   B: Because I wanted to live in a big city.

7: A: _____ was your first job in Seoul?

   B: I worked as a server in a restaurant.

UNIT 16

1 Subject and object pronouns page 107

> ■ Subject pronouns usually come before verbs, and object pronouns go after verbs: **I** saw **him**, but **he** didn't see **me**.

Complete the conversations.

1. **A:** Hello. Is Mr. Chang there?

   B: No, _____he_____ 's not here right now. Can I take a message?

   A: Yes. Please tell _____ to call Todd Harris.

   B: Does _____ have your number?

   A: No, but please give it to _____. It's 555-0987.

2. **A:** Oh, hello, Kimberly!

   A: Hello, Mrs. Sanchez. Is Veronica home?

   B: No, _____ at the mall with her brother. Their dad drove _____ there this morning. Would _____ like to come in?

   A: Thank you, Mrs. Sanchez, but I need to go home. Anyway, my sister and _____ are going to an amusement park tomorrow and maybe Veronica can go with _____. Is that all right?

   B: Sure. I can give _____ your message, or _____ can text her.

   A: Oh, don't worry, Mrs. Sanchez. I'll text _____. Thanks a lot. Bye!

2 Invitations; verb + to page 109

> ■ You can use both *Do you want to . . . ?* and *Would you like to . . . ?* to invite a person to do something.
>
> ■ Don't confuse *would like to* with *like to*. *Would like to* means the same as *want to*.
>
> ■ *I'd (really) like to* and *I'd love to* both mean the same as *I want to*.

Rewrite the conversations. Write the sentences in a different way.

1. **A:** Do you want to see a movie tonight?

   B: Oh, I can't. I need to work.

   A: <u>Would you like to see a movie tonight?</u>

   B: _____

2. **A:** Do you want to play tennis on Saturday?

   B: I'd love to, but I have to help my parents.

   A: _____

   B: _____

3. **A:** I want a job at Carol's café.

   B: You need to speak to her.

   A: _____

   B: _____

4. **A:** Would you like to go to a party with me?

   B: I want to, but I can't. I have to study.

   A: _____

   B: _____

Grammar plus answer key

Unit 1

1 My, your, his, her
1. A: Hello. **My** name is Carlos.
   B: Hi, Carlos. What's **your** last name?
   A: It's Gonzales.
   B: How do you spell **your** last name? Is it G-O-N-Z-A-L-E-Z?
   A: No, it's G-O-N-Z-A-L-E-S. And what's **your** name?
   B: **My** name is Bill Powers. Nice to meet you.
2. A: What's Ms. Robinson's first name?
   B: **Her** first name is Elizabeth. **Her** nickname is Liz.
   A: I'm sorry. What's **her** first name again?
   B: It's Elizabeth. And what's Mr. Weber's first name?
   A: **His** first name is Peter.
   B: That's right. And **his** nickname is Pete.
   A: That's right, too!

2 The verb be
1. A: Excuse me. **Are** you Layla Moore?

   B: No, **I'm not**. **She's** over there.
   A: OK. Thanks.
2. A: Hi. Are **you** Layla Moore?
   B: Yes, **I am**.
   A: Nice to meet you. **I'm** Sergio Oliveira. **You're** in my English class.
   B: Yes, I **am**. **It's** nice to meet you too, Sergio.

Unit 2

1 This/These; it/they; plurals
1. A: **What are** these?
   B: **They're** my flash drives.
2. A: **What's** this?
   B: **It's** a cell phone.
3. A: What's **this**?
   B: **It's an** English book.

2 Yes/No and where questions with be
A
1. c   2. e   3. a   4. b   5. d

B
A: **Where's** my dictionary?
B: I don't know. Is **it** in your backpack?
A: No, **it's** not.
B: Is **this** your dictionary?
A: Yes, **it** is. Thanks! Now, where **are** my glasses?
B: **Are** they on your desk?
A: Yes, **they are**. Thank you!

Unit 3

1 Negative statements and yes/no questions with be
A
2. We're not from Buenos Aires.
3. You and Ashley are not in my class.
4. My first language is not Korean. / Korean is not my first language.
5. My mother is not from Italy.
6. They are not my parents.

B
1. B: No, **are** not. **We're/We are** from the Dominican Republic.
2. A: **Is** your first language Spanish?
   B: Yes, it **is**. My parents **are** from Ecuador.
3. A: **Are** Nadia and Rayan Lebanese?
   B: Yes, **they** are. But **they're/they are** in France now.
4. A: **Are** my friends and I late?
   B: No, **you're/you are** not. **You're/You are** early!

2 Wh-questions with be
2. **What** is her name?   c
3. **What** is she like?   f
4. **How** old is she?   b
5. **Where** is your family from?   a
6. **What** is Kyoto like?   e

Unit 4

1 Possessives
1. A: **Whose** jacket is this? Is it **yours**, Ethan?
   B: No, it's not **mine**. Ask Matt. I think it's **his**.
2. A: These aren't **my** gloves. Are they **yours**?
   B: No, they're not **mine**. Maybe they are Young-min's.
3. A: **Whose** sweaters are these? Are they Rachel's?
   B: No, they're not **her** sweaters. But these shorts are **hers**.

2 Present continuous statements; conjunctions
2. It's snowing.
3. I'm not wearing a winter coat.
4. You're not/You aren't wearing David's sunglasses.
5. Ayumi is wearing a scarf.

3 Present continuous yes/no questions
1. B: No, **he's not/he isn't**.
2. A: **Are you wearing** high heels?
   B: No, **we're not/we aren't**.
3. A: **Are you wearing** a sweater?
   B: Yes, **I am**.
4. A: **Is it** raining?
   B: Yes, **it is**.

Unit 5

1 What time is it? / Is it A.M. or P.M.?
3. It's a quarter after six.
4. It's 10:00 P.M.
5. It's five (minutes) after three.
6. It's ten thirty-five.
7. It's one A.M.
8. It's 12:00 A.M./It's twelve (o'clock) at night.

2 Present continuous Wh-questions
2. A: What are Jon and Megan doing?
   B: They're shopping.
3. A: What are you doing?
   B: I'm writing a message.
4. A: What's Chris doing?
   B: He's cooking dinner.
5. A: What are you and Tyler doing?
   B: We're watching a movie.
6. A: What's Sara doing?
   B: She's having pizza.
7. A: What are you and Joseph doing?
   B: We're studying for a test.
8. A: What are Laura and Paulo doing?
   B: They're chatting online.

Unit 6

1 Simple present statements and Simple present statements with irregular verbs
My family and I **live** in the city. We **have** an apartment on First Avenue. My sister **goes** to school near our apartment, so she **walks** to school. My father **works** in the suburbs, so he **drives** to his job. My mother **uses** public transportation – she **takes** the bus to her office downtown. She **has** a new job, but she **doesn't like** it very much. And me? Well, I **don't work** far from our apartment, so I **don't need** a car or public transportation. I **ride** my bike to work!

2 Simple present questions

A
2. A: Does your family eat dinner at 5:00?
3. A: Does your brother take the bus to work?
4. A: Do you get up late on weekends?

B
B: Well, we eat together **on** weekends, but **on** weekdays we're all busy. My parents go to work early – **at** 6:30. But we eat dinner together **in** the evening, and we have a big lunch together **on** Sundays. We eat **at** noon. Then **in** the afternoon, we take a walk or go to the movies.

Unit 7

1 Simple present short answers
A: **Does** your family **live** in an apartment?
B: No, we **don't**. We **have** a house.
A: That's nice. **Does** your house have two floors?
B: Yes, it **does**. It **has** four rooms on the first floor. And we **have** three bedrooms and a bathroom on the second floor.
A: And **do** you and your family **have** a yard?
B: Yes, we **do**. And how about you, Tim? **Do** you **live** in a house, too?
A: No, I **don't**. My wife and I **have** a small apartment in the city.
B: Oh. **Do** you **like** the city?
A: Yes, I **do**. But my wife **doesn't**.

2 *There is, there are*
2. There's no / There isn't a dining room.
3. There's no / There isn't a microwave in the kitchen.
4. There's a table in the kitchen.
5. There are some curtains on the windows.
6. There are no / There aren't any rugs on the floors.
7. There are closets in the bedrooms.
8. There are no / There aren't any bookcases in the bedroom.

Unit 8

1 Simple present Wh-questions
1. A: Really? Where **does he work**?
2. A: Where **do you work**?
   B: I work in a restaurant.
   A: Nice! What **do you do**?
   B: I'm a chef.
3. A: How **do you like your job**?
   B: My job? I don't really like it very much.
   A: That's too bad. What **do you do**?
   B: I'm a cashier. I work at a clothing store.
4. A: What **do your brother and sister do**?
   B: My brother is a doctor, and my sister is a lawyer.
   A: How **do they like their jobs**?
   B: They work very hard, but they love their jobs.

2 Placement of adjectives
2. A salesperson's job is stressful.
   A salesperson has a stressful job.
3. A security guard's job is dangerous.
   A security guard has a dangerous job.
4. An actor's job is exciting.
   An actor has an exciting job.
5. A host's job is interesting.
   A host has an interesting job.
6. A nurse's job is difficult.
   A nurse has a difficult job.

Unit 9

1 Count and noncount nouns; *some* and *any*
1. A: What do you want for lunch?
   B: Let's make **some** sandwiches.
   A: Good idea! We have **some** bread. Do we have **any** cheese?
   B: Yes, I think there's **some** in the refrigerator. Let me see. . . . No, I don't see **any**.
   A: Well, let's go to the store. We need **some** milk, too. And do we have **any** cheese?
   B: Yes, we do. There's **some** lettuce here, and there are **some** tomatoes, too.
   A: Do we have **any** mayonnaise? I love **some** mayonnaise on my sandwiches.
   B: Me, too. But there isn't **any** here. Let's buy **some**.

2. A: Let's make a big breakfast tomorrow morning.
   B: Good idea! What do we need? Are there **any** eggs?
   A: There are **some** but I think we need to buy **some** more.
   B: OK. And let's get **some** cereal, too. We don't have **any**, and I love cereal for breakfast.
   A: Me, too. Do we have **any** blueberry yogurt?
   B: Yes, there's **some** in the refrigerator.
   A: Great! So we don't need to buy **any** at the store.
   B: That's right. Just eggs and cereal!

2 Adverbs of frequency (page 61)
B: I often go to a restaurant near work.
A: Do you ever eat at your desk?
B: No, I hardly ever stay in for lunch.
A: A: And what do you usually have?
B: I always have soup or a salad.
A: Me, too. I never have a big lunch.

Unit 10

1 Simple present Wh-questions
2. Who do you go to games with? a
3. How often does your team play? d
4. When do they play? e or Where do they play? f
5. Where do they play? f or When do they play? e
6. What time do the games start? b

2 *Can* for ability

A
2. Juan can play the piano, and he can play the violin.
3. Matt and Drew can act, but they can't sing.
4. Alicia can snowboard, but she can't ice-skate.
5. Ben can take good photos, and he can edit videos.
6. Corinne can't write poems but she can tell good jokes.

B
2. Corinne can.
4. Yes, he can.
6. He can act.
3. No, she can't.
5. Alicia can.

Unit 11

1 The future with *be going to*
A Tomorrow **is going to be** a very exciting day. It's my birthday, and my friends and I **are going to celebrate**. In the morning, Stephen and I **are going to drive** to the beach. Our friend Rosa **is going to meet** us there. We**'re going to stay** at the beach for a few hours. Then we**'re going to have** lunch at my favorite restaurant. After lunch, Stephen **is going to go** to work, and Rosa and I **are going to see** a movie. After the movie, we**'re going to go** to our friend Philip's house. He **is going to cook** dinner for Rosa and me.
B Q: Are Stephen and Matthew going to ride their bikes to the beach?
   A: No, they're going to drive to the beach.
4. Q: Are the friends going to have lunch at a restaurant?
   A: Yes, they are.
5. Q: Are Rosa and Matthew going to go to a museum?
   A: No, they're not. (They're going to see a movie.)
6. Q: Are Rosa and Matthew going to have dinner at a restaurant?
   A: No, they're not. (They're going to have dinner at Philip's house.)

2 Wh-questions with *be going to*
A: What **are** you **going to do** this weekend?
B: I**'m going to have** a very busy weekend. My friend Amir **is going to visit** me, and we**'re going to spend** the weekend in the city.
A: That's nice. **Are** you **going to stay** in a hotel?
B: No, we**'re going to stay** with our friend Lara. And Lara **is going to have** a big party on Saturday night.
A: Really? And who**'s going to be** at the party? Do you know any of Lara's friends?
B: No, I don't. But Amir and I **are going to meet** everyone on Saturday night.

Unit 12

1 Have + noun; feel + adjective
A: **Hi, Vanessa. How are you?**
B: I'm terrific, thanks. How about you?
A: **I feel awful, actually.**
B: Oh, no! What's the matter?
A: **I think I have a fever.**
B: That's too bad. Do you have a headache?
A: **Yes, I do. And I have a stomachache, too.**
B: Are you going to see a doctor?
A: **Yes. I'm going to call my doctor in a few minutes.**
B: Well, feel better soon.
A: **Thanks.**

2 Imperatives
2. Take two aspirins.
3. Don't work too hard.
4. Don't exercise today or tomorrow.
5. Don't eat any cold food.
6. Take an antacid.

Unit 13

1 Prepositions of place
A: Excuse me. Is there a post office around here?
B: Yes, there is. It's **on** Maple Street.
A: Where on Maple?
B: It's **on** the corner of Maple Street and Second Avenue.
A: Next **to** Charlie's Restaurant?
B: Yes, that's right. It's across the street **from** the Windsor Hotel.
A: Thanks. Oh, and where is the bank?
B: It's on Oak Street – **between** the hospital and police station.
A: Great. Thanks very much.
B: You're welcome.

2 Directions
2. You: No, don't turn right on 32nd Street. Turn left on 32nd Street.
3. You: No, don't go down Sixth Avenue. Go up First Avenue.
   You: No, it's not on the left. It's on the right.
4. You: No, don't walk down Eight Avenue. Walk up Eighth Avenue.

Unit 14

1 Simple past statements: regular verbs and irregular verbs
Hi!
I **didn't do** anything special this weekend, but I **had** a lot of fun. I **didn't go** out on Friday night. I **stayed** home. I **cleaned** my room and **did** laundry. I **helped** my sister with her homework, and then we **watched** our favorite series. On Saturday, my friend Lori **came** over. She **needed** some new shoes, so we **took** the bus downtown to Todd's Shoe Store. We **shopped** for a long time, but Lori **didn't like** any of the shoes at Todd's. She **bought** some purple socks, but she **didn't buy** any shoes. On our way back to my house, we **stopped** at the gym and **exercised**. We **didn't exercise** very hard. I **invited** Lori for dinner, and my dad **cooked** hamburgers in the yard. After dinner, Lori and I **talked** and **played** video games. She **didn't stay** too late – Mom **drove** her home at around ten. On Sunday, my whole family **visited** my mother's best friend and her family. They have a swimming pool, so my sister and I **went** swimming all afternoon.

2 Simple past yes/no questions
A: **Did** you **enjoy** your vacation?
B: Yes, I **did**. My brother and I **had** a great time.
A: **Did** you **make** a lot any videos?
B: No, we **didn't**. But we **took** a lot of pictures.
A: That's good. **Did** you **see** a lot of interesting things?
B: Yes, we **did**. And we **ate** a lot of new foods. How about you? **Did** you **have** a good summer?
A: Well, I **didn't go** anywhere, but I **read** a lot of good books and **saw** some great movies.

Unit 15

1 Past of be
1. A: **Were** you here yesterday?
   B: No, I **wasn't**. I **was** home in bed.
   A: Oh, **were** you sick?
   B: No. I **was** just really tired.
2. A: Where **were** you born?
   B: I **was** born in Mexico City.
   A: Really? What about your parents? **Were** they born here, too?
   B: No, they **weren't**. They **were** born in Guadalajara.
3. A: Where **was** Jamil last week? **Was** he on vacation?
   B: Yes, he **was**. He and his best friend **were** in Portugal. They **were** in Oporto.
   A: **Was** it a good trip?
   B: Yes, it was. Jamil said it **was** a terrific trip!

2 Wh-questions with did, was, and were
1. A: **How** was your childhood?
   B: I had a fantastic childhood!
2. A: **Where** did you grow up?
   B: I grew up in Incheon, a small city in South Korea.
3. A: **How old** were you when you started school?
   B: I think I was five or six.
4. A: **Who** was your best friend in high school?
   B: My best friend was a boy named Joon-ho.
5. A: **When** did you leave home?
   B: In 2012.
6. A: **Why** did you leave Incheon?
   B: Because I wanted to live in a big city.
7: A: **What** was your first job in Seoul?
   B: I worked as a server in a restaurant.

Unit 16

1 Subject and object pronouns
1. A: Hello. Is Mr. Chang there?
   B: No, **he's** not here right now. Can take a message?
   A: Yes. Please tell **him** to call Todd Harris.
   B: Does **he** have your number?
   A: No, but please give it to **him**. It's 555-0987.
2. A: Oh, hello, Kimberly!
   A: Hello, Mrs. Sanchez. Is Veronica home?
   B: No, **she's** at the mall with her brother. Their dad drove **them** there this morning. Would **you** like to come in?
   A: Thank you, Mrs. Sanchez, but I need to go home. Anyway, my sister and **I** are going to an amusement park tomorrow and maybe Veronica can go with **us**. Is that all right?
   B: Sure. I can give **her** your message, or **you** can text her.
   A: Oh, don't worry, Mrs. Sanchez. I'll text **her**. Thanks a lot. Bye!

2 Invitations; verb + to
1. B: Oh, I can't. I **have** to work.
2. A: **Would you like** to play tennis on Saturday?
   B: **I'd like to,** but I need to help my parents.
3. A: **I'd like** a job at Carol's café.
   B: You **have** to speak to her.
4. A: **Do you want** to go to a party with me?
   B: **I'd like to,** but I can't. I **need** to study.

Credits

The authors and publishers acknowledge the following sources of copyright material and are grateful for the permissions granted. While every effort has been made, it has not always been possible to identify the sources of all the material used, or to trace all copyright holders. If any omissions are brought to our notice, we will be happy to include the appropriate acknowledgements on reprinting and in the next update to the digital edition, as applicable.

Texts

The Roxbury for the adapted text on p. 49. Reproduced with kind permission; Attrap'Rêves for the adapted text on p. 49. Reproduced with kind permission.

Key: B = Below, BL = Below Left, BC = Below Centre, BR = Below Right, B/G = Background, C = Centre, CL = Centre Left, CR = Centre Right, Ex = Exercise, TC = Top Centre, T = Top, TL = Top Left, TR = Top Right.

Illustrations

337 Jon (KJA Artists): 24, 29, 85; **Mark Duffin**: 15, 12(T), 31(T), 44(T), 47, 115, 121; **Thomas Girard** (Good Illustration): 3, 11, 13, 23, 25, 36, 37, 50, 79(T), 89, 100, 102; **Dusan Lakicevic** (Beehive Illustration): 21, 41, 87; **Quino Marin** (The Organisation): 26, 31(B), 79(B); **Gavin Reece** (New Division): 27, 44(B), 45, 101; **Gary Venn** (Lemonade Illustration): 56, 88, 90, 91, 127, 128; **Paul Williams** (Sylvie Poggio Artists): 9, 30, 119.

Photos

Back cover (woman with whiteboard): Jenny Acheson/Stockbyte/GettyImages; Back cover (whiteboard): Nemida/GettyImages; Back cover (man using phone): Betsie Van Der Meer/Taxi/GettyImages; Back cover (woman smiling): PeopleImages.com/DigitalVision/GettyImages; Back cover (name tag): Tetra Images/GettyImages; Back cover (handshake): David Lees/Taxi/GettyImages; p. v: PhotoAlto/Sigrid Olsson/PhotoAlto Agency RF Collections/GettyImages; p. 2 (header), p. vi (unit 1): Paul Bradbury/OJO Images; p. 2 (CR): Paul Bradbury/Caiaimage/GettyImages; p. 2 (BL): Stefania D'Alessandro/WireImage/GettyImages; p. 2 (BR): Steve Granitz/WireImage/GettyImages; p. 4 (Ex 7.1): Maskot/Maskot/GettyImages; p. 4 (Ex 7.2): Design Pics/Ron Nickel/GettyImages; p. 4 (Ex 7.3): Dan Dalton/Caiaimage/GettyImages; p. 4 (Ex 7.4): Squaredpixels/E+/GettyImages; p. 5 (T): Fabrice LEROUGE/ONOKY/GettyImages; p. 5 (C): Erik Dreyer/The Image Bank/GettyImages; p. 5 (B): theboone/E+/GettyImages; p. 6: Maskot/Maskot/GettyImages; p. 7 (T): Peter Dazeley/Photographer's Choice/GettyImages; p. 7 (Ex 14.1): Tim Robberts/The Image Bank/GettyImages; p. 7 (Ex 14.2): Klaus Vedfelt/DigitalVision/GettyImages; p. 7 (Ex 14.3): Nicolas McComber/E+/GettyImages; p. 7 (Ex 14.4): Ariel Skelley/Blend Images/GettyImages; p. 8 (header), p. vi (unit 2): John Slater/Stockbyte/GettyImages; p. 8 (backpack): igor terekhov/iStock/GettyImagesPlus; p. 8 (cellphone): Peter Dazeley/Photographer's Choice/GettyImages; p. 8 (hairbrush): slobo/E+/GettyImages; p. 8 (sunglasses): Fodor90/iStock/GettyImages; p. 8 (wallet): bibikoff/E+/GettyImages; p. 8 (keys): Floortje/E+/GettyImages; p. 8 (umbrella): Picheat Suviyanond/iStock/GettyImages; p. 8 (energy bar): Juanmonino/iStock/Getty Images Plus/GettyImages; p. 8 (book): Image Source/Image Source/GettyImages; p. 8 (notebook): kyoshino/E+/GettyImages; p. 8 (pen): Ann Flanigan/EyeEm/Fuse/GettyImages; p. 8 (eraser): subjug/iStock/GettyImages; p. 8 (clock): GoodGnom/DigitalVision Vectors/GettyImages; p. 9 (tablet): daboost/iStock/Getty Images Plus/GettyImages; p. 9 (box): Guy Crittenden/Photographer's Choice/GettyImages; p. 9 (phone case): Jeffrey Coolidge/DigitalVision/GettyImages; p. 9 (television): Cobalt88/iStock/GettyImages; p. 9 (newspaper): -Oxford-/E+/GettyImages; p. 9 (Id): Daniel Ernst/iStock/Getty Images Plus/GettyImages; p. 9 (clip): Steven von Niederhausern/E+/GettyImages; p. 9 (ticket): Gediminas Zalgevicius/Hemera/GettyImages; p. 9 (purse): Stramyk/iStock/GettyImages; p. 10 (flash drive): zentilia/iStock/Getty Images Plus/GettyImages; p. 10 (laptop): Coprid/iStock/Getty Images Plus/GettyImages; p. 10 (laptops.): karandaev/iStock/GettyImages; p. 10 (keys): krungchingpixs/iStock/GettyImages; p. 10 (backpacks): pavila/iStock/GettyImages; p. 10 (umbrella): Kais Tolmats/E+/GettyImages; p. 10 (sunglasses): Zaharia_Bogdan/iStock/GettyImages; p. 10 (wallet): malerapaso/iStock/GettyImages; p. 10 (window): beright/iStock/GettyImages; p. 10 (credit card): freestylephoto/iStock/GettyImages; p. 10 (headphones): tiler84/iStock/GettyImages; p. 12 (backpack): JulNichols/E+/GettyImages; p. 12 (flash drive): Garsya/iStock/GettyImages; p. 12 (laptop): Creative Crop/Photodisc/GettyImages; p. 12 (newspaper): goir/iStock/GettyImages; p. 12 (computer): AlexLMX/iStock/GettyImages; p. 12 (chair): urfinguss/iStock/GettyImages; p. 12 (wallet): pioneer111/iStock/GettyImages; p. 12 (notebook): drpnncpp/iStock/GettyImages; p. 12 (tv): selensergen/iStock/GettyImages; p. 12 (glasses): bonetta/iStock/GettyImages; p. 15 (cellphone): Manuel Faba Ortega/iStock/GettyImages; p. 15 (cellphones): sunnycircle/iStock/GettyImages; p. 15 (purse): penguenstok/E+/GettyImages; p. 15 (purses): iulianvalentin/iStock/GettyImages; p. 15 (wallet): Nyo09/iStock/GettyImages; p. 15 (wallets): alarich/iStock/GettyImages; p. 16 (header), p. vi (unit 3): stock_colors/iStock/Getty Images Plus/GettyImages; p. 16 (T): Photography by ZhangXun/Moment/GettyImages; p. 16 (BL): Roberto Westbrook/Blend Images/GettyImages; p. 17 (T): Robert Frerck/The Image Bank/GettyImages; p. 17 (B): Jane Sweeney/The Image Bank/GettyImages; p. 18 (Ex 5.1): Dan MacMedan/WireImage/GettyImages; p. 18 (Ex 5.2): Steve Granitz/WireImage/GettyImages; p. 18 (Ex 5.3): Clasos/CON/LatinContent Editorial/GettyImages; p. 18 (Ex 5.4): Koki Nagahama/Getty Images AsiaPac/GettyImages; p. 18 (Ex 5.5): Jeff Spicer/Getty Images Entertainment/GettyImages; p. 19 (TR): SolStock/E+/GettyImages; p. 19 (cellphone): Peter Dazeley/Photographer's Choice/GettyImages; p. 19 (Ben): Hero Images/Hero Images/GettyImage; p. 19 (Nadia): Portra Images/DigitalVision/GettyImages; p. 19 (Ex 7.c.a): Fuse/Corbis/GettyImages; p. 19 (Ex 7.c.b): Purestock/GettyImages; p. 19 (Ex 7.c.c): Lucy Lambriex/Moment/GettyImages; p. 19 (Ex 7.c.d): James Woodson/Photodisc/GettyImages; p. 19 (Ex 7.c.e): Fuse/Corbis/GettyImages; p. 20 (Ex 8.a.1): Alex Barlow/Moment/GettyImages; p. 20 (Ex 8.a.2): Jupiterimages/Stockbyte/GettyImages; p. 20 (Ex 8.a.3): PhotoAlto/Frederic Cirou/PhotoAlto Agency RF Collections/GettyImages; p. 20 (Ex 8.a.4): Hill Street Studios/Blend Images/GettyImages; p. 22 (header), p. vi (unit 4): Sam Edwards/Caiaimage/GettyImages; p. 22 (formal man): Spiderstock/E+/GettyImages; p. 22 (formal woman): Grady Reese/E+/GettyImages; p. 22 (rain coat): EdnaM/iStock/Getty Images Plus/GettyImages; p. 22 (coat): DonNichols/E+/GettyImages; p. 22 (dress): ARSELA/E+/GettyImages; p. 22 (casual woman): BLOOM image/BLOOMimage/GettyImages; p. 22 (pajamas): madtwinsis/E+/GettyImages; p. 22 (swimwear): dendong/iStock/Getty Images Plus/GettyImages; p. 22 (shorts): 487387674/iStock/Getty Images Plus/GettyImages; p. 22 (cap): Steve Zmina/DigitalVision Vectors/GettyImages; p. 25 (brazilian flag): Image Source/Image Source/GettyImages; p. 25 (japanese flag): Jim Ballard/Photographer's Choice/GettyImages; p. 25 (american flag): NirdalArt/iStock/GettyImages; p. 25 (canadian flag): Encyclopaedia Britannica/UIG/Universal Images Group/GettyImages; p. 25 (TL): Andrea Pistolesi/Photolibrary/GettyImages; p. 25 (TR): Photograph by Kangheewan/Moment Open/GettyImages; p. 25 (BL): Bruce Leighty/Photolibrary/GettyImages; p. 25 (BR): EschCollection/Photonica/GettyImages; p. 25 (thermometer): Burke/Triolo Productions/Stockbyte/GettyImages; p. 29: PeopleImages.com/DigitalVision/GettyImages; p. 30 (header), p. vi (unit 5): Driendl Group/Photographer's Choice/GettyImages; p. 30 (Brian): Daniel Grill/GettyImages; p. 30 (Amar): Peter Cade/The Image Bank/GettyImages; p. 31 (Ex 3.a.1): Raimund Koch/The Image Bank/GettyImages; p. 31 (Ex 3.a.2): Science Photo Library/Science Photo Library/GettyImages; p. 31 (Ex 3.a.3): Paul Bricknell/Dorling Kindersley/GettyImages; p. 31 (Ex 3.a.4): SergeiKorolko/iStock/GettyImages; p. 31 (Ex 3.a.5): pagadesign/iStock/GettyImages; p. 31 (Ex 3.a.6): scanrail/iStock/GettyImages; p. 32 (T): Plume Creative/DigitalVision/GettyImages; p. 32 (BR): B. Sporrer/J.Skowronek/StockFood Creative/GettyImages; p. 32 (Jay): B. Sporrer/J.Skowronek/StockFood Creative/GettyImages; p. 32 (Kate): Rafael Elias/Moment Open/GettyImages; p. 33 (TL): Tetra Images/Brand X Pictures/GettyImages; p. 33 (TC): Hola Images/GettyImages; p. 33 (TR): Tim Robberts/The Image Bank; p. 33 (CL): annebaek/iStock/Getty Images Plus/GettyImages; p. 33 (C): Stockbyte/Stockbyte/GettyImages; p. 33 (CR): Caiaimage/Tom Merton/Caiaimage/GettyImages; p. 33 (BL): LWA/Sharie Kennedy/Blend Images/GettyImages; p. 33 (BC): sot/DigitalVision/GettyImages; p. 33 (BR): David Crunelle/EyeEm/EyeEm/GettyImages; p. 34 (dance): Blend Images - Ariel Skelley/GettyImages; p. 34 (drive): Westend61/Westend61/GettyImages; p. 34 (music): Hero Images/Hero Images/GettyImages; p. 34 (basketball): Daniel Grill/Tetra images/GettyImages; p. 34 (read): Peathegee Inc/Blend Images/GettyImages; p. 34 (bycycle): Daniel Milchev/The Image Bank/GettyImages; p. 34 (run): Ty Milford/Aurora Open/GettyImages; p. 34 (shop): BJI/Blue Jean Images/blue jean images/GettyImages; p. 34 (study): JAG IMAGES/DigitalVision/GettyImages; p. 34 (swim): J J D/Cultura/GettyImages; p. 34 (walk): Dougal Waters/Photographer's Choice RF/GettyImages; p. 34 (movie): Blend Images/Andres Rodriguez/Blend Images/GettyImages; p. 35 (Eva35): Sebastian Doerken/fStop/GettyImages; p. 35 (PamL): Denis Schneider/EyeEm/EyeEm/GettyImages; p. 35 (TL): Hero Images/Hero Images/GettyImages; p. 35 (BR): Betsie Van Der Meer/Taxi/GettyImages; p. 36 (header), p. vi (unit 6): Enrique Díaz/7cero/Moment/GettyImages; p. 36 (Ex 1.1): Image Source/DigitalVision/GettyImages; p. 36 (Ex 1.2): Kentaroo Tryman/Maskot/GettyImages; p. 36 (Ex 1.3): Susanne Kronholm/Johner Images Royalty-Free/GettyImages; p. 36 (Ex 1.4): Eternity in an Instant/The Image Bank/GettyImages; p. 36 (Ex 1.5): Marilyn Nieves/iStock/GettyImages; p. 36 (Ex 1.6): Matt Dutile/Image Source/GettyImages; p. 36 (Ex 1.7): Ciaran Griffin/Stockbyte/GettyImages; p. 36 (Ex 1.8): Maria Teijeiro/DigitalVision/GettyImages; p. 38: Robert Daly/Caiaimage/GettyImages; p. 39: Michael Berman/DigitalVision/GettyImages; p. 40: Frank van Delft/Cultura/GettyImages; p. 41: vadimguzhva/iStock/GettyImages; p. 42 (man): James Whitaker/DigitalVision/GettyImages; p. 42 (woman): Tyler Stableford/The Image Bank/GettyImage; p. 43: Pingebat/DigitalVision Vectors; p. 44 (header), p. vi (unit 7): Peter Adams/Photolibrary; p. 45 (lobby): piovesempre/iStock/GettyImages; p. 45 (apartment): Joe_Potato/iStock/GettyImages; p. 45 (house): Ron Evans/Photolibrary/GettyImages; p. 45 (kitchen): ttatty/iStock/GettyImages; p. 46 (armchair): xiaoke ma/E+/GettyImages; p. 46 (stove): taist/iStock/GettyImages; p. 46 (curtains): darksite/iStock/GettyImages; p. 46 (pictures): Glow Decor/Glow/GettyImages; p. 46 (bed): Emevil/iStock/GettyImages; p. 46 (coffee maker): GeorgePeters/E+/GettyImages; p. 46 (table): EdnaM/iStock/GettyImages; p. 46 (coffee table): DonNichols/E+/GettyImages; p. 46 (oven): mbbirdy/E+/GettyImages; p. 46 (refrigerator): JazzIRT/E+/GettyImages; p. 46 (lamps1): Creative Crop/DigitalVision/GettyImages; p. 46 (lamps2): stuartbur/E+/GettyImages; p. 46 (sofa): AnnaDavy/iStock/GettyImages; p. 46 (desk): Hemera Technologies/PhotoObjects.net/GettyImages; p. 46 (bookcase): DonNichols/iStock/GettyImages; p. 46 (dresser): Hemera Technologies/PhotoObjects.net/GettyImages; p. 46 (chairs): Firmafotografen/iStock/Getty Images Plus/GettyImages; p. 46 (mirror): Omer Yurdakul Gundogdu/E+/GettyImages; p. 46 (rug): DEA/G. CIGOLINI/De Agostini Picture Library/GettyImages; p. 46 (cupboards): ChoochartSansong/iStock/GettyImages; p. 47: Marco Baass/GettyImages; p. 48 (loft): Martin Barraud/OJO Images/GettyImages; p. 48 (mountains): Barrett & MacKay/All Canada Photos/GettyImages; p. 48 (villa): Maremagnum/Photolibrary/GettyImages; p. 48 (beach house): catnap72/E+/GettyImages; p. 49 (T): BERTHIER Emmanuel/hemis.fr/hemis.fr/GettyImages; p. 49 (B): Michael Marquand/Lonely Planet Images/GettyImages; p. 50 (header), p. vi (unit 8): iStock/Getty Images Plus/GettyImages; p. 51 (hospital): Vincent Hazat/PhotoAlto Agency RF Collections/GettyImages; p. 51 (office): Peopleimages/E+/GettyImages; p. 51 (store): Maskot/Maskot/GettyImages; p. 51 (hotel): DAJ/amana images/GettyImages; p. 51 (BR): Nevena1987/iStock/GettyImages; p. 51 (Jorden): Sam Edwards/OJO Images/GettyImages; p. 51 (Alicia): Philipp Nemenz/Cultura/GettyImages; p. 52 (BL): Digital Vision./DigitalVision/GettyImages; p. 52 (BC): PeopleImages/DigitalVision/GettyImages; p. 52 (BR): Glow Images, Inc/Glow/GettyImages; p. 53 (lawyer): rubberball/GettyImages; p. 53 (pilot): Katja Kircher/Maskot/GettyImages; p. 53 (photographer): stock_colors/E+/GettyImages; p. 53 (engineer): Thomas Barwick/Iconica/GettyImages; p. 53 (BR): Rubberball/Mike Kemp/Brand X Pictures/GettyImages; p. 53 (Paula): Marc Romanelli/Blend Images/GettyImages; p. 54 (T): Hero Images/Hero Images/GettyImages; p. 54 (B): Jetta Productions/Stone/GettyImages; p. 55 (B): Australian Scenics/Photolibrary/GettyImages; p. 55 (T): Eugenio Marongiu/Cultura/GettyImages; p. 57 (veterinarian): fotoedu/iStock/GettyImages; p. 57 (dentist): XiXinXing/XiXinXing/GettyImages; p. 57 (architect): John Lund/Marc Romanelli/Blend Images/GettyImages; p. 57 (hairstylst): Glow Images, Inc/Glow/GettyImages; p. 58 (header), p. viii (unit 9): Johner Images/GettyImages; p. 58 (apples): Maximilian Stock Ltd/Photolibrary/GettyImages; p. 58 (lemons): osoznaniejizni/iStock/GettyImages; p. 58 (bananas): Burazin/Photographer's Choice/GettyImages; p. 58 (kiwis): serebryakova/iStock/GettyImages; p. 58 (blueberries): Richard Coombs/EyeEm/EyeEm/GettyImages; p. 58 (oranges): David Marsden/Photolibrary/GettyImages; p. 58 (tomatoes): James A. Guilliam/Photolibrary/GettyImages; p. 58 (onions): Joff Lee/StockFood Creative/GettyImages; p. 58 (lettuce): Richard Clark/Photolibrary/GettyImages; p. 58 (carrots): Maximilian Stock Ltd./Photolibrary/GettyImages; p. 58 (potatoes): SvetlanaK/iStock/GettyImages; p. 58 (broccoli): Tsuji/E+/GettyImages; p. 58 (pasta): Dave King Dorling Kindersley/Dorling Kindersley/GettyImages; p. 58 (noodles): Yoyochow23/iStock/GettyImages; p. 58 (rice): Maximilian Stock Ltd/Photolibrary/GettyImages; p. 58 (crackers): Richard Griffin/iStock/GettyImages; p. 58 (bread): Pavlo_K/iStock/GettyImages; p. 58 (cereal): Graham Day/Photolibrary/GettyImages; p. 58 (butter): DustyPixel/E+/GettyImages; p. 58 (mayonnaise): Suzifoo/E+/GettyImages; p. 58 (oil): John E. Kelly/Photolibrary/GettyImages; p. 58 (cheese): jjwithers/E+/GettyImages; p. 58 (milk): PhotoObjects.net/PhotoObjects.net/GettyImages; p. 58 (cream): malerapaso/E+/GettyImages; p. 58 (yogurt): Science Photo Library/Science Photo Library/GettyImages; p. 58 (beans): malerapaso/iStock/GettyImages; p. 58 (nuts): Maximilian Stock Ltd./Photographer's Choice/GettyImages; p. 58 (eggs): ermingut/E+/GettyImages; p. 58 (beef): Lew Robertson/StockFood Creative/GettyImages; p. 58 (chicken): Andrea Bricco/StockFood Creative/GettyImages; p. 58 (fish): angorius/iStock/GettyImages; p. 59 (TR):

RyanJLane/E+/GettyImages; p. 59 (potato salad): JFsPic/iStock/GettyImages; p. 59 (potato): -massmedia-/iStock/Getty Images Plus/GettyImages; p. 59 (celery): anna1311/iStock/GettyImages; p. 59 (onions): prwstd/iStock/GettyImages; p. 59 (mayonnaise): BWFolsom/iStock/GettyImages; p. 59 (apple): Raimondas/iStock/GettyImages; p. 60 (oranges): JannHuizenga/iStock/Getty Images Plus/GettyImages; p. 60 (apples): joanek/iStock/GettyImages; p. 60 (lettuce): Foodcollection RF/GettyImages; p. 60 (potatoes): RBOZUK/iStock/GettyImages; p. 60 (tomatoes): S847/iStock/Getty Images Plus/GettyImages; p. 60 (celery): Stefano Oppo/Stockbyte/GettyImages; p. 60 (bananas): PavlinaGab/iStock/GettyImages; p. 60 (kiwis): nullplus/iStock/Getty Images Plus/GettyImages; p. 60 (lemons): Michael Paul/StockFood Creative/GettyImages; p. 60 (carrots): RBOZUK/iStock/GettyImages; p. 60 (onions): IJdema/iStock/GettyImages; p. 60 (broccoli): Marco Vacca/Photographer's Choice RF/GettyImages; p. 60 (blueberries): billnoll/iStock/Getty Images Plus/GettyImages; p. 60 (BL): Rohit Seth/iStock/GettyImages; p. 60 (BC): MIXA/GettyImages; p. 60 (BR): Alberto Coto/Photodisc/GettyImages; p. 61 (TR): artparadigm/Taxi Japan/GettyImages; p. 61 (BR): Luis Alvarez/Taxi/GettyImages; p. 62: LiudmylaSupynska/iStock/Getty Images Plus/GettyImages; p. 63 (CR): Mardis Coers/Moment/GettyImages; p. 63 (TL): BIEL ALINO/AFP/GettyImages; p. 63 (CL): gnomeandi/iStock/GettyImages; p. 63 (BR): Danita Delimont/Gallo Images/GettyImages; p. 64 (header), p. viii (unit 10): Mike Powell/Allsport Concepts/GettyImages; p. 64 (racket): Arijuhani/iStock/Getty Images Plus/GettyImages; p. 64 (volleyball): Burazin/Photographer's Choice/GettyImages; p. 64 (goggles): Image Source/Image Source/GettyImages; p. 64 (football): Image Source/Image Source/GettyImages; p. 64 (hockey): C Squared Studios/Photodisc/GettyImages; p. 64 (baseball): PhotoObjects.net/PhotoObjects.net/GettyImages; p. 64 (basketball): Andrew Dernie/Stockbyte/GettyImages; p. 64 (skates): RedKoalaDesign/iStock/GettyImages; p. 64 (snowboard): Stockbyte/Stockbyte/GettyImages; p. 64 (bike): hamurishi/iStock/GettyImages; p. 64 (hiking boots): Don Bayley/E+/GettyImages; p. 64 (soccer): Lazi & Mellenthin/Westend61/GettyImages; p. 64 (BR): Blend Images - Jose Luis Pelaez Inc/Brand X Pictures/GettyImages; p. 64 (Victor): Blend Images - Jose Luis Pelaez Inc/Brand X Pictures/GettyImages; p. 64 (Tara): Tom Merton/Caiaimage/GettyImages; p. 65 (T): Michael DeYoung/Design Pics/First Light/GettyImages; p. 65 (B): Lewis Mulatero/Taxi/GettyImages; p. 66 (T): Jupiterimages/Stone/GettyImages; p. 66 (B): shaunl/iStock/Getty Images Plus/GettyImages; p. 67 (Ex 7.a.1): Alexander Rhind/Stone/GettyImages; p. 67 (Ex 7.a.2): leaf/iStock/Getty Images Plus/GettyImages; p. 67 (Ex 7.a.3): innovatedcaptures/iStock/Getty Images Plus/GettyImages; p. 67 (Ex 7.a.4): Spaces Images/Blend Images/GettyImages; p. 67 (Ex 7.a.5): alfalfa126/Moment/GettyImages; p. 67 (Ex 7.a.6): Gazimal/The Image Bank/GettyImages; p. 68 (Ex 9.1): Nicola Tree/Taxi/GettyImages; p. 68 (Ex 9.2): Westend61/Westend61/GettyImages; p. 68 (Ex 9.3): MarioGuti/iStock/GettyImages; p. 68 (Ex 9.4): Kyle Monk/Blend Images/GettyImages; p. 68 (Ex 9.5): Chad Springer/Image Source/GettyImages; p. 68 (Ex 9.6): olegkalina/iStock/GettyImages; p. 68 (Ex 9.7): Roberto Cerruti/Hemera/GettyImages; p. 68 (Ex 9.8): Tatomm/iStock/GettyImages; p. 69 (TL): Carlos Osorio/Toronto Star/GettyImages; p. 69 (Centre): SAM PANTHAKY/AFP/GettyImages; p. 69 (TR): Raul Sifuentes/Guiness World Records/Newscom; p. 71 (chef): Jetta Productions/Iconica/GettyImages; p. 71 (mechanic): Tanya Constantine/Blend Images/GettyImages; p. 71 (artist): Lisa Stirling/The Image Bank/GettyImages; p. 71 (musician): Hill Street Studios/Blend Images/GettyImages; p. 72 (header), p. viii (unit 11): Caiaimage/Tom Merton/Caiaimage/GettyImages; p. 72 (BR): Dorling Kindersley/Dorling Kindersley/GettyImages; p. 72 (Ava): LWA/Larry Williams/Blend Images/GettyImages; p. 72 (Martin): Marcos Ferro/GettyImages; p. 73 (Ex 3.a.1): Dave and Les Jacobs/Lloyd Dobbie/Blend Images/GettyImages; p. 73 (Ex 3.a.2): Mike Svoboda/DigitalVision/GettyImages; p. 73 (Ex 3.a.3): Kathrin Ziegler/Taxi/GettyImages; p. 73 (Ex 3.a.4): UpperCut Images/UpperCut Images/GettyImages; p. 73 (Ex 3.a.5): Jetta Productions/Iconica/GettyImages; p. 73 (Ex 3.a.6): Caiaimage/Paul Bradbury/OJO+/GettyImages; p. 73 (Ex 3.a.7): Nicolas McComber/E+/GettyImages; p. 73 (Ex 3.a.8): John Eder/The Image Bank/GettyImages; p. 74 (Morgan): Image Source/Image Source/GettyImage; p. 74 (Issac): T.T./Iconica/GettyImages; p. 74 (Lauren): PeopleImages/DigitalVision/GettyImages; p. 74 (Brian): Eugenio Marongiu/Cultura/GettyImages; p. 74 (Ex 7: photo1): tiridifilm/E+/GettyImages; p. 74 (Ex 7: photo2): Gail Shumway/Photographer's Choice/GettyImages; p. 74 (Ex 7: photo3): Zeb Andrews/Moment/GettyImages; p. 74 (Ex 7: photo4): PeopleImages.com/DigitalVision/GettyImages; p. 74 (Ex 7: photo5): Tetra Images/Tetra images/GettyImages; p. 74 (Ex 7: photo6): Rudi Von Briel/Photolibrary/GettyImages; p. 75 (Allie): Louise Morgan/Moment/Getty Images; p. 75 (Jim): Louise Morgan/Moment/Getty Images; p. 75 (TR): Vegar Abelsnes Photography/Photodisc/GettyImages; p. 76 (special cloth): William Tang/Design Pics/Perspectives/GettyImages; p. 76 (food): Ronnie Kaufman/Larry Hirshowitz/Blend Images/GettyImages; p. 76 (decorate): Photo by Glenn Waters in Japan/Moment/GettyImages; p. 76 (give gifts): Fastrum/iStock/GettyImages; p. 76 (play music): Derek E. Rothchild/Photolibrary/GettyImages; p. 76 (parade): Oliver Strewe/Lonely Planet Images/GettyImages; p. 76 (picnic): uniquely india/photosindia/GettyImages; p. 76 (fireworks): Ichiro Murakami/EyeEm/EyeEm/GettyImages; p. 76 (blossom festival): Bohistock/Moment/GettyImages; p. 76 (carnival): Yadid Levy/robertharding/robertharding/GettyImages; p. 77 (TL): Foodcollection RF/Foodcollection/GettyImages; p. 77 (CR): Emilia Krysztofiak Rua Photography/Moment/GettyImages; p. 77 (BL): Thomas Fricke/First Light/GettyImages; p. 77 (BR): Kelly Cheng Travel Photography/Moment Open/GettyImages; p. 78 (header), p. viii (unit 12): Mark Alcarez/Photolibrary/GettyImages; p. 78 (man): Eric Audras/ONOKY/GettyImages; p. 78 (holding volleyball): Stockbyte/GettyImages; p. 80 (Ex 4.a.1): Predrag Vuckovic/iStock/GettyImages; p. 80 (Ex 4.a.2): Ghislain & Marie David de Lossy/Cultura/GettyImages; p. 80 (Ex 4.a.3): Lawren/Moment/GettyImages; p. 80 (Ex 4.a.4): g-stockstudio/iStock/GettyImages; p. 80 (chamomile tea): Maximilian Stock Ltd./Photographer's Choice/GettyImages; p. 80 (cough syrup): Comstock/Stockbyte/GettyImages; p. 80 (chicken soup): Shawn Gearhart/E+/GettyImages; p. 80 (cold medicine): MakiEni's photo/Moment Open/GettyImages; p. 80 (eye drops): BananaStock/BananaStock/GettyImages; p. 80 (aspirin): Diane Macdonald/Photographer's Choice RF/GettyImages; p. 80 (antacid): STEVE HORRELL/SPL/Science Photo Library/GettyImages; p. 80 (nasal spray): hamikus/iStock/GettyImages; p. 80 (ice pack): Hero Images/Hero Images/GettyImages; p. 81: Chad Baker/Jason Reed/Ryan McVay/Photodisc/GettyImages; p. 82 (Ex 10.a.1): diego_cervo/iStock/GettyImages; p. 82 (Ex 10.a.2): BSIP/UIG/Universal Images Group/GettyImages; p. 82 (Ex 10.a.3): Garry Wade/The Image Bank/GettyImages; p. 82 (Ex 10.a.4): ViewStock/View Stock/GettyImages; p. 83: pixologicstudio/iStock/Getty Images Plus/GettyImages; p. 85 (TL): Paul Bradbury/OJO Images/GettyImages; p. 85 (TC): BartekSzewczyk/iStock/GettyImages; p. 85 (TR): Image Source/Photodisc/GettyImages; p. 85 (BL): baona/iStock/GettyImages; p. 85 (BC): Manuel Faba Ortega/iStock/GettyImages; p. 85 (BR): Jamie Grill/The Image Bank/GettyImages; p. 86 (header), p. viii (unit 13): Andy Ryan/Stone/GettyImages; p. 86 (Ex 1.a.a): Tetra Images/Tetra images/GettyImages; p. 86 (Ex 1.a.b): Musketeer/DigitalVision/GettyImages; p. 86 (Ex 1.a.c): PhotoAlto/James Hardy/Brand X Pictures/GettyImages; p. 86 (Ex 1.a.d): Bloomberg/Bloomberg/GettyImages; p. 86 (Ex 1.a.e): Deborah Cheramie/iStock/GettyImages; p. 86 (Ex 1.a.f): Jetta Productions/The Image Bank/GettyImages; p. 86 (Ex 1.a.g): Inti St Clair/Blend Images/GettyImages; p. 86 (Ex 1.a.h): David Nevala/Aurora/GettyImages; p. 89 (TL): David Henderson/Caiaimage/GettyImages; p. 89 (TC): Chris Mellor/Lonely Planet Images/GettyImages; p. 89 (TR): Medioimages/Photodisc/Photodisc/GettyImages; p. 89 (BL): Cultura RM Exclusive/Christoffer Askman/Cultura Exclusive/GettyImages; p. 89 (BC): STAN HONDA/AFP Creative/GettyImages; p. 89 (BR): Chris Mellor/Lonely Planet Images/GettyImages; p. 91 (TL): Fandrade/Moment/GettyImages; p. 91 (TC): Anton Petrus/Moment/GettyImages; p. 91 (TR): Karina Vera/Moment/GettyImages; p. 91 (CL): Rebeca Mello/Moment Open/GettyImages; p. 91 (BL): Bettmann/Bettmann/GettyImages; p. 91 (BR): Alfredo Herms/STR/LatinContent WO/GettyImages; p. 92 (header), p. viii (unit 14): Adam Burton/robertharding/GettyImages; p. 92 (Ex 1: photo 1): Caiaimage/Paul Bradbury/Riser/GettyImages; p. 92 (Ex 1: photo 2): Maskot/GettyImages; p. 92 (Ex 1: photo 3): Fabrice LEROUGE/ONOKY/GettyImages; p. 92 (Ex 1: photo 4): Holger Mette/iStock/Getty Images Plus/GettyImages; p. 92 (Ex 1: photo 5): Ariel Skelley/Blend Images/GettyImages; p. 92 (Ex 1: photo 6): David Jakle/Image Source/GettyImages; p. 92 (Ex 1: photo 7): Andersen Ross/Blend Images/GettyImages; p. 92 (Ex 1: photo 8): Hero Images/GettyImages; p. 92 (BR): Absodels/ABSODELS/GettyImages; p. 93: A. Chederros/ONOKY/GettyImages; p. 94 (TL): Djura Topalov/iStock/Getty Images Plus/GettyImages; p. 94 (TC): JGI/Jamie Grill/Blend Images/GettyImages; p. 94 (TR): KNSY/Picture Press/GettyImages; p. 94 (CL): svetikd/E+/GettyImages; p. 94 (C): Ghislain & Marie David de Lossy/Cultura/GettyImages; p. 94 (CR): Kevin Kozicki/Image Source/GettyImages; p. 95 (TR): Greg Elms/Lonely Planet Images/GettyImages; p. 95 (Kim): Sam Edwards/Caiaimage/GettyImages; p. 95 (Martin): Jetta Productions/Blend Images/GettyImages; p. 95 (BR): Thomas Barwick/Taxi/GettyImages; p. 96: Matthew Micah Wright/Lonely Planet Images/GettyImages; p. 97 (Nick): William King/The Image Bank/GettyImages; p. 97 (Jessie): Caiaimage/Sam Edwards/OJO+/GettyImages; p. 97 (Armando): Daniel Ernst/iStock/Getty Images Plus/GettyImages; p. 97 (Juliette): Robert Daly/Caiaimage; p. 99 (T): David Wall Photo/Lonely Planet Images/GettyImages; p. 99 (C): Emma Innocenti/Taxi/GettyImages; p. 99 (B): Robert Deutschman/DigitalVision/GettyImages; p. 100 (header), p. viii (unit 15): David Oliver/The Image Bank/GettyImages; p. 100 (Ex 1.1): Jeff Kravitz/FilmMagic, Inc/GettyImages; p. 100 (Ex 1.2): Gary Gershoff/WireImage/GettyImages; p. 100 (Ex 1.3): Bruce Glikas/FilmMagic/GettyImages; p. 100 (Ex 1.4): G Fiume/Getty Images Sport/GettyImages; p. 100 (Ex 1.5): Kevork Djansezian/Getty Images News/GettyImages; p. 102 (TR): John Eder/The Image Bank/GettyImages; p. 104: Ridofranz/iStock/GettyImages; p. 105 (map): Richard Sharrocks/iStock/Getty Images Plus/GettyImages; p. 105 (boy): Tim Kitchen/DigitalVision/GettyImages; p. 105 (B/G): Mark Miller Photos/Photolibrary/GettyImages; p. 106 (header), p. viii (unit 16): Lumina Images/Blend Images; p. 106 (CL): PhotoAlto/Frederic Cirou/PhotoAlto Agency RF Collections/GettyImages; p. 106 (CR): Caiaimage/Sam Edwards/Caiaimage/GettyImages; p. 106 (BL): REB Images/Blend Images/GettyImages; p. 106 (BR): Gary Burchell/Taxi/GettyImages; p. 106 (BR): Cultura RM Exclusive/Gary John Norman/Cultura Exclusive/GettyImages; p. 107: Marc Romanelli/Blend Images/GettyImages; p. 108 (camping): Hero Images/Hero Images/GettyImages; p. 108 (amusement park): Joe McBride/Iconica/GettyImages; p. 108 (street fair): Patti McConville/Photographer's Choice/GettyImages; p. 108 (concert): PeopleImages.com/DigitalVision/GettyImages; p. 108 (barbecue): Hero Images/Hero Images/GettyImages; p. 108 (play): Caiaimage/Robert Daly/OJO+/GettyImages; p. 108 (Nathan): Ezra Bailey/Taxi/GettyImages; p. 108 (Julie): Mike Chick/Stone/GettyImages; p. 108 (BR): Image Source/Image Source/GettyImages; p. 109: NT Photography/Image Source/GettyImages; p. 110 (TR): B Busco/Photographer's Choice/GettyImages; p. 110 (BR): monkeybusinessimages/iStock/GettyImages; p. 111 (T): Cooper Neill/Getty Images Entertainment/GettyImages; p. 112 (Audrey Hepburn): Michael Ochs Archives/Moviepix/GettyImages; p. 112 (Nelson Mandela): Per-Anders Pettersson/Hulton Archive/GettyImages; p. 112 (Paul Walker): Jason Merritt/FilmMagic/GettyImages; p. 113: PeopleImages/DigitalVision/GettyImages; p. 114 (CR): Pascal Le Segretain/Getty Images Entertainment/GettyImages; p. 114 (BR): Amanda Edwards/WireImage/GettyImages; p. 116 (Bradley Cooper): Steve Granitz/WireImage/GettyImages; p. 116 (Rashida Jones): Stefanie Keenan/WireImage/GettyImages; p. 116 (Neymar): David Ramos/Getty Images; p. 116 (Ronaldo): Anthony Harvey/Getty Images Entertainment/GettyImages; p. 116 (Idris Elba): Dave J Hogan/Getty Images Entertainment/GettyImages; p. 116 (Scarlett Johansson): Ray Tamarra/WireImage/GettyImages; p. 117 (Ariana Grande): Christopher Polk/Getty Images Entertainment/GettyImages; p. 117 (John Cho): John M. Heller/Getty Images Entertainment/GettyImages; p. 117 (Ang Lee): Pascal Le Segretain/Getty Images Entertainment/GettyImages; p. 117 (Kate Middleton): Anwar Hussein/WireImage/GettyImages; p. 117 (Zoe Saldana): Jon Kopaloff/FilmMagic/GettyImages; p. 117 (Liam Hemsworth): Joe Scarnici/Getty Images Entertainment/GettyImages; p. 118: PeopleImages.com/DigitalVision/GettyImages; p. 120 (TR): Garry Wade/The Image Bank/GettyImages; p. 120 (CR): Indeed/ABSODELS/GettyImages; p. 120 (BR): Joos Mind/Photographer's Choice/GettyImages; p. 122 (CR): urbancow/iStock/GettyImages; p. 122 (TR): George Doyle/Stockbyte/GettyImages; p. 122 (BL): Dennis K. Johnson/Lonely Planet Images/GettyImages; p. 122 (BR): baona/E+/GettyImages; p. 123 (almonds): Ljupco/iStock/GettyImages; p. 123 (vegetables): Bill Arce/StockFood Creative/GettyImages; p. 123 (cake): bluestocking/E+/GettyImages; p. 123 (candy): Diana Taliun/iStock/GettyImages; p. 123 (chocolates): pilcas/iStock/GettyImages; p. 123 (cookies): bluestocking/E+/GettyImages; p. 123 (chips): sunstock/iStock/GettyImages; p. 123 (grapes): Donald Erickson/E+/GettyImages; p. 123 (hot dogs): IngaNielsen/iStock/GettyImages; p. 123 (Icecream): Donald Erickson/E+/GettyImages; p. 123 (peanuts): Suwanmanee99/iStock/GettyImages; p. 123 (pineapple): Marek Mnich/E+/GettyImages; p. 123 (pizza): david franklin/E+/GettyImages; p. 123 (popcorn): Korovin/iStock/GettyImages; p. 123 (potato chips): rimglow/iStock/GettyImages; p. 123 (watermelon): mkos83/iStock/GettyImages; p. 124 (CL): Brand New Images/Stone/GettyImages; p. 124 (C): Hero Images/Hero Images/GettyImages; p. 124 (CR): Westend61/Westend61/GettyImages; p. 124 (BL): Tara Moore/The Image Bank/GettyImages; p. 124 (BC): Ron Krisel/Stone/GettyImages; p. 124 (BR): Art Vandalay/Photodisc/GettyImages; p. 125 (remote): Gary Ombler/Dorling Kindersley/GettyImages; p. 125 (cheese): Thomas Firak Photography/Photolibrary/GettyImages; p. 125 (BR): Ian Logan/The Image Bank/GettyImages; p. 125 (clock): Korvit78/iStock/GettyImages; p. 125 (BC): arkady2013/iStock/Getty Images Plus/GettyImages; p. 125 (BL): Sally Anscombe/Moment/GettyImages; p. 126 (car): Pgiam/E+/GettyImages; p. 126 (woman sleeping): Tanya Constantine/Blend Images/GettyImages; p. 126 (man): PeopleImages/E+/GettyImages; p. 126 (girl clicking): Plume Creative/DigitalVision/GettyImages; p. 129 (BR): Inti St Clair/Blend Images/GettyImages; p. 129 (BL): David Young-Wolff/The Image Bank/GettyImages; p. 129 (TL): Wavebreakmedia/iStock/GettyImages; p. 129 (CL): Jonathan Kirn/The Image Bank/GettyImages; p. 130 (TL): JGI/Tom Grill/Blend Images/GettyImages; p. 130 (TC): Tetra Images - Erik Isakson/Brand X Pictures/GettyImages; p. 130 (TR): AlenPopov/iStock/GettyImages; p. 130 (CL): Thinkstock/Stockbyte/GettyImages; p. 130 (C): Debbie Fortes/EyeEm/EyeEm/GettyImages; p. 130 (CR): Monashee Frantz/OJO Images/GettyImages; p. 130 (BL): George Doyle/Stockbyte/GettyImages; p. 130 (BC): Erik Isakson/Tetra images/GettyImages; p. 130 (BR): DamianPalus/iStock/GettyImages.

interchange

FIFTH EDITION

intro

Video Activity
Worksheets

Jack C. Richards
Revised by Karen Davy

CAMBRIDGE
UNIVERSITY PRESS

Credits

Illustration credits

Ralph Butler: 20, 29, 41, 54, 61; Mark Collins: 17, 30, 46, 56; Paul Daviz: 34, 58; Chuck Gonzales: 4, 13, 18, 62; Dan Hubig: 8 (*bottom*), 14, 16, 37, 57, 65; Kja-Artists.com: 5 (*top*), 25, 33, 45, 49; Trevor Keen: 38; Joanna Kerr: 8 (*top*), 26; Monika Melnychuk/i2iart.com: 6, 9, 28; Karen Minot: 50; Ortelius Design: 10, 12; Robert Schuster: 5 (*bottom*), 36, 47; Russ Willms: 48, 63; James Yamasaki: 2, 22, 53

Photo Acknowledgements

The authors and publishers acknowledge the following sources of copyright material and are grateful for the permissions granted. While every effort has been made, it has not always been possible to identify the sources of all the material used, or to trace all copyright holders. If any omissions are brought to our notice, we will be happy to include the appropriate acknowledgements on reprinting and in the next update to the digital edition, as applicable.

Key: L = Left, R = Right, B = Below,
TL = Top Left, TCL = Top Centre Left,
TCR = Top Centre Right, TR = Top Right,
CL = Centre Left, C = Centre, CR = Centre Right,
BL = Below Left, BCL = Below Centre Left,
BC = Below Centre, BCR = Below Centre Right,
BR = Below Right, BG = Background.

p. 10 (C): GUY NEEDHAM/National Geographic My Shot/National Geographic Stock; p. 10 (L): age fotostock/SuperStock; p. 10 (R): Best View Stock/age fotostock; p. 12: © Leonid Plotkin/Alamy; p. 24 (B): Simon Willms/Lifesize/Getty Images; p. 24 (C): DAJ/Getty Images; p. 24 (CR): Jodi & Jake/age fotostock; p. 24 (CR): Jose Luis Pelaez Inc/age fotostock; p. 36 (TL): Bonchan/Shutterstock; p. 36 (TCL), p. 36 (TR): iStockphoto/Thinkstock; p. 36 (TCR): laylandmasuda/istock/Getty Images; p. 40 (BL): © Jim Cummins/The Image Bank/Getty Images; p. 40 (TL): Flirt/SuperStock; p. 40 (CL): IMAGEMORE Co.,Ltd./Getty Images; p. 40 (CR): Image Source/Photodisc/Getty Images; p. 40 (TR): Bruce Obee/All Canada Photos/Getty Images; p. 40 (BC): Comstock/Getty Images; p. 40 (BG): Ryan McVay/Stockbyte/Getty Images; p. 40 (BR): SerKucher/iStock/Getty Images; p. 42 (TL): Corbis/Superstock; p. 42 (TCL): age fotostock/SuperStock; p. 42 (BCR): Gregory Dale/National Geographic Stock; p. 42 (TR): fstockfoto/Shutterstock; p. 42 (BL): © James Quine/Alamy; p. 42 (TCR): Glowimages/Getty Images; p. 42 (BR): russellkord.com/age fotostock; p. 42 (BCL): Glowimages/Getty Images; p. 44 (CR): Evy Mages/The Washington Post/Getty Images; p. 44 (C): Alex Wong/Getty Images; p. 44 (BR): GlowImages/age fotostock; p. 44 (CL): © JIM LO SCALZO/epa/Corbis; p. 44 (BC): © JIM YOUNG/Reuters/Corbis; p. 44 (BL): Stock Connection/SuperStock; p. 44 (BG): LightScribe/iStock/Getty Images; p. 58 (photo 2A.1): Andrew H. Walker/Getty Images; p. 58 (photo 2A.2): © Walter McBride/Retna Ltd/Corbis; p. 58 (photo 2A.3): Julie Jacobson/AP Images; p. 58 (photo 2A.4): Stuart Ramson/AP Images; p. 58 (photo 2A.5): Eduardo Parra/FilmMagic/Getty Images; p. 58 (photo 2A.6): Bruce Glikas/FilmMagic/Getty Images; p. 59 (C): Zoonar/Paul Hakimata/age footstock.

Plan of Intro Video

1 Welcome! Two students have trouble finding their class on the first day of school.
Functional Focus Introducing oneself; asking for and giving information
Grammar The verb *be*; personal pronouns
Vocabulary Letters, numbers, greetings

2 My passport! Sofia and Jessica search their apartment for Sofia's passport so she can make her flight to Brazil.
Functional Focus Asking for and giving locations
Grammar Questions with *be*; prepositions of place
Vocabulary Location words; furniture items

3 Newcomers High School At a very interesting high school in New York, students from around the world talk about their countries of origin.
Functional Focus Asking for and giving information about countries, languages, and cultures
Grammar Questions and short answers with *be*
Vocabulary Countries, languages; describing places and people

4 What are you wearing? People talk about the clothes they have on.
Functional Focus Asking about and describing clothing
Grammar Present continuous with the verb *wear*
Vocabulary Clothing

5 Everybody's having fun. To avoid studying, Peter talks to several friends to find out what they are doing.
Functional Focus Telling time; asking about and describing current activities
Grammar Present continuous statements and questions
Vocabulary Common activities

6 My life Vanessa introduces her family, describes her daily routine, and shares her dream – stand-up comedy!
Functional Focus Talking about routines
Grammar Simple present statements and questions
Vocabulary Daily routines

7 Richdale Street In their new apartment, Sofia and Jessica get a surprise visit from Jessica's mother.
Functional Focus Asking about and describing homes
Grammar There is/There are
Vocabulary Rooms and objects in a home

8 The night shift People who work at night talk about their jobs and their unusual routines.
Functional Focus Talking about work; describing jobs
Grammar Simple present tense: summary; adjectives
Vocabulary Jobs

9 At the diner People in a popular diner talk about what they're having for brunch.
Functional Focus Talking about eating habits
Grammar Adverbs of frequency
Vocabulary Breakfast foods

10 What's your sport? People at Flushing Meadows Park in New York talk about their favorite sports to play and to watch.
Functional Focus Talking about abilities and interests
Grammar *Can* for ability
Vocabulary Sports

11 A trip to Washington, D.C. People talk about what they plan to do during their visit to the United States capital.
Functional Focus Talking about plans
Grammar Future with *be going to*
Vocabulary Sightseeing activities

12 Where does it hurt? Peter, who doesn't feel well, goes to see Dr. Smith and ends up solving the doctor's health problem.
Functional Focus Talking about health problems; giving advice
Grammar Imperatives
Vocabulary Action verbs; health problems

13 Across the bridge A young couple visits the Capilano Suspension Bridge in Vancouver, British Columbia, Canada.
Functional Focus Describing physical locations
Grammar Prepositions of place
Vocabulary Direction words

14 How was your vacation? Back at work, Hugo tells his coworker about his disastrous vacation.
Functional Focus Talking about activities in the recent past
Grammar Past tense of regular and irregular verbs
Vocabulary Vacation activities

15 On Broadway People who work in the Broadway theater world talk about their jobs and their dreams.
Functional Focus Giving personal information
Grammar Past tense of *be*; Wh-questions with *did*, *was*, and *were*
Vocabulary Words related to theater and musicals

16 Then he said … At school, Abby describes to her friend her strange but eventful date with Greg.
Functional Focus Accepting and refusing invitations; making excuses
Grammar Verb + *to* + verb; subject and object pronouns
Vocabulary Social activities

Welcome!

1 VOCABULARY *People and names*

PAIR WORK Fill in the blanks. Use the words in the box. Then compare with a partner.

> ✓ first   friends   last   student   teacher

1. Hi. My ....first.... name is Caroline. My .... call me Carol.

2. Ms. Lee is my .... I'm her .... My name's Alex Sims.

3. Hello. I'm Eduardo. My .... name is Robles.

2 INTRODUCTIONS

A Check (✓) the correct responses. Then compare with a partner.

1. Hello.
   - ☐ Excuse me.
   - ☑ Hi.

2. My name is Molly. What's your name?
   - ☐ I'm Peter.
   - ☐ My friends call me Molly.

3. Hi, Pete. It's nice to meet you.
   - ☐ Nice to meet you, too.
   - ☐ Yes, I am.

4. Hello. I'm Peter Krum.
   - ☐ Hello. What's your name?
   - ☐ Hi, Peter. Nice to meet you.

B **PAIR WORK** Practice the conversations in part A. Use your own names.

3 WHAT DO YOU SEE?

Watch the first 30 seconds of the video with the sound off. Check (✓) the correct answers.

1. Peter is
   - ☐ a student.
   - ☐ a teacher.

2. Molly is
   - ☐ a student.
   - ☐ a teacher.

4 GET THE PICTURE

A Check your answers to Exercise 3.
Are they correct?

B Match. Then compare with a partner.

1. ....c.... Molly

2. .... Peter

3. .... Mrs. Smith

4. .... Miss Taylor

C Match the first names or titles with the
last names. Then compare with a partner.

A	B
1. Miss	a. Krum
2. Mrs.	b. Lin
3. Peter	c. Smith
4. Molly	d. Taylor

5 WATCH FOR DETAILS

Check (✓) the correct answers. Then compare with a partner.

1. Peter's nickname is
   ☐ Krum.
   ✓ Pete.

2. Molly's friends call her
   ☐ Molly.
   ☐ Holly.

3. Peter is Molly's
   ☐ friend.
   ☐ classmate.

4. Molly and Peter's class is at
   ☐ 8:00.
   ☐ 9:00.

5. Mrs. Smith
   ☐ is Molly and Peter's teacher.
   ☐ is not Molly and Peter's teacher.

6. Miss Taylor's class is in Room
   ☐ 201.
   ☐ 203.

Write the sentences under the correct picture. Then compare with a partner.

He's Molly's classmate.	She's Peter's teacher.	His class is not in Room 201.
Her last name is Taylor.	She's the teacher in Room 203.	Her last name is Smith.
Her room is 201.	His teacher is Miss Taylor.	She's Peter's classmate.
✓ She's not a teacher.	She's not Molly's teacher.	Her teacher is Miss Taylor.

She's not a teacher.

Follow-up

7 NICE TO MEET YOU

A Match.

A
1. It's nice to meet you, Sarah.
2. Hello. I'm Paul Thompson.
3. Are you a student here?

B
a. Yes, I am.
b. Nice to meet you, too.
c. Hi. My name is Sarah Long.

B **PAIR WORK** Put the sentences in order. Then practice the conversation.

A: Hello. I'm Paul Thompson.

B: Hi. My name is Sarah Long.

A: ....

B: ....

A: ....

B: ....

C **CLASS ACTIVITY** Now introduce yourself around the class. Use your own information.

☰ Language close-up

8 WHAT DID THEY SAY?

Watch the video and complete the conversation. Then practice it.

Molly and Peter are at school.

Molly: Excuse me. Um, ...hello............ .

Peter: .... !

Molly: .... name is Molly.
What's .... name?

Peter: .... Peter. My .... call me Pete.

Molly: My friends .... me . . . Molly.
Hi, Pete. It's nice to .... you.

Peter: It's nice to meet you, ...

Molly: Are you a .... here?

Peter: ...., I am. My .... is at
nine o'clock with .... Taylor.

Molly: Miss Taylor? .... my teacher. You're in
.... class.

Peter: .... !

9 THE VERB BE *Asking for and giving information*

 A Complete the conversations with the correct forms of *be*.
Then practice with a partner.

1. A: Excuse me. ......Are...... you Sam?
   B: No, I .... Luis. Sam .... over there.

2. A: I .... Celia. What .... your name?
   B: My name .... Dan.

3. A: .... this Mrs. Costa's classroom?
   B: No. Her class .... in Room 105.

4. A: What .... your email address?
   B: It .... marymary@email.com.

5. A: What .... your phone number?
   B: It .... (646) 555-7841.

B **PAIR WORK** Practice the conversations again.
Use your own information.

C **GROUP WORK** Now ask five students from
your class for their contact information.

A: What's your phone number, David?
B: It's (201) 555-3192.
A: 555-3182?
B: No, 3192.
A: OK, thanks.

2 My passport!

1 VOCABULARY Prepositions

A Look at the pictures. Where are these things? Circle the correct locations.

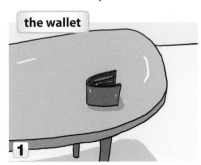

the wallet

1

in / (on)
the table

the keys

2

under / behind
the sofa

the umbrella

3

next to / under
the door

the cell phone

4

in / on
the TV

the passport

5

in front of / behind
the bag

the camera

6

in front of / behind
the books

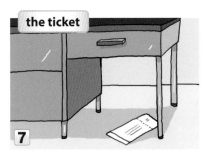

the ticket

7

on / under
the desk

the notebooks

8

in front of / in
the drawer

the books

9

next to / on
the table

B **PAIR WORK** Ask and answer questions about the things in part A.

A: Where is the wallet?
B: It's on the table.

A: Where are the keys?
B: They're . . .

Interchange Intro VRB © Cambridge University Press 2012   Photocopiable

2 *WHAT DO YOU SEE?*

Watch the video with the sound off. Check (✓) **True** or **False**.
Correct the false sentences. Then compare with a partner.

	True	False
1. The ticket is ~~under~~ *on* the TV.	☐	✓
2. The camera is in a box next to the sofa.	☐	☐
3. The keys are on the TV.	☐	☐
4. The passport is behind the desk.	☐	☐

☰ Watch the video

3 *GET THE PICTURE*

What things do Sofia and Jessica find? Number the things from
1 to 7 in the order they are found. Then compare with a partner.

.... her bag   .... her ticket

.... her camera   .... her umbrella

.... her keys   ....1..... her wallet

.... her passport

4 *WATCH FOR DETAILS*

Check (✓) the correct answers. Then compare with a partner.

1. At the beginning of the story, it's
   ☐ nine o'clock.
   ✓ ten o'clock.

2. Sofia's flight is at
   ☐ twelve-thirty.
   ☐ two-thirty.

3. Sofia's trip is to
   ☐ Peru.
   ☐ Brazil.

4. Sofia's desk is in the
   ☐ bedroom.
   ☐ living room.

5. Sofia is on a plane to
   ☐ Brazil.
   ☐ Budapest.

5 WHERE IS IT?

A Where are these things in the video? Fill in the blanks. Then compare with a partner.

1. The pen is ......*on*...... the TV.

2. The magazines are .... the coffee table.

3. The lamp is .... the TV.

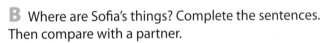

4. The coffee table is .... the sofa.

B Where are Sofia's things? Complete the sentences. Then compare with a partner.

1. Sofia's wallet is _in her bag_..................... .
2. Her ticket is on the TV, ...
3. Her camera is ....
4. Her keys are ....
5. Her passport is ....
6. Her bag is ....
7. Her umbrella is ....

☰ Follow-up

6 TRUE OR FALSE?

PAIR WORK Your partner puts some of your things in different places. Can you guess where?

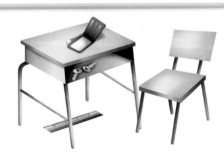

A: My keys are in the desk.
B: True.

A: My ruler is on the desk.
B: False. It's under the desk.

Interchange Intro VRB © Cambridge University Press 2012   Photocopiable

7 WHAT DID THEY SAY?

Watch the video and complete the conversation. Then practice it.

Sofia is looking for her things.

Jessica: Sofia! Where's your ......*passport*...... ?

Sofia: .... it's . . . maybe it's .... a box!

Jessica: Oh!

Sofia: Maybe it's. . . . It's probably .... the chair.

Jessica: No, ... not here.

Sofia: OK. Maybe it's .... to the ....

Jessica: Sofia! .... this?

Sofia: My .... I'm going to need that. . . .

My .... !

Jessica: Is it .... the books? No.

Sofia: Oh, no!

Jessica: Sofia, are those .... keys, in .... of the TV?

Sofia: Yes, those are .... keys. . . . My passport, Jessica!

Wait a minute. Wait a minute. It's on the .... in the bedroom!

8 PREPOSITIONS OF PLACE *Describing location*

A Complete the sentences about the things in the picture.
Use each preposition only once. Then compare with a partner.

behind	in	in front of	✓next to	on	under

1. The purse *is next to the sofa* ....
2. The notebooks ....
3. The wallet ....
4. The lamp ....
5. The sunglasses ....
6. The clock ....

B Write similar sentences about things in your classroom.
Then read your sentences to your partner.

1. ....
2. ....
3. ....
4. ....
5. ....
6. ....

3 Newcomers High School

1 VOCABULARY Countries and regions

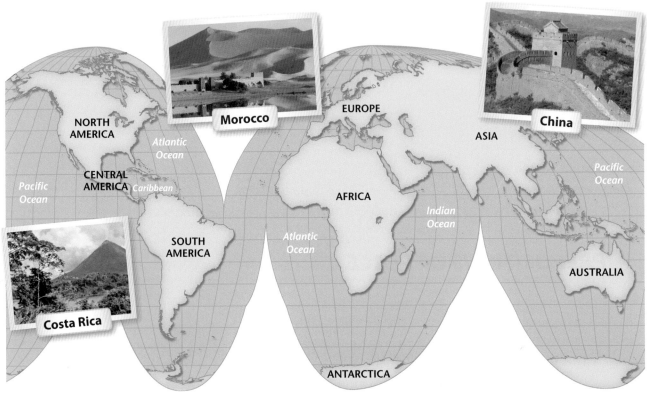

Countries	Regions
..b.. 1. China	a. Africa
.... 2. Costa Rica	b. Asia
.... 3. the Dominican Republic	c. Europe
.... 4. Italy	d. Central America
.... 5. Mexico	e. North America
.... 6. Morocco	f. South America
.... 7. Uruguay	g. the Caribbean
.... 8.	
.... 9.	

A Match. Then add two more countries to the list.

B PAIR WORK Ask and answer questions about the places in part A.

A: Where's China?
B: It's in Asia. **or**
   I think it's in . . . **or**
   I'm not sure. Is it in . . . ?

2 GUESS THE FACTS

Complete the chart. Use the words in the box.
Then compare with a partner.

Arabic	✓ Casablanca	San José
Cantonese	Hong Kong	Spanish

A: Casablanca is in Morocco.
B: Yes, that's right. **or**
　　No, it's not. It's in . . .

B: They speak Spanish in Morocco.
A: No, they speak . . .

Country	City	Language
1. Morocco	*Casablanca*	....
2. Costa Rica	....	....
3. China	....	....

☰ Watch the video

3 GET THE PICTURE

A Check your answers to Exercise 2.

B Where are they from?
Check (✓) the correct answers.

	Fatima	**Camilia**	**Cai**
China	☐	☐	☐
Costa Rica	☐	☐	☐
Morocco	✓	☐	☐

4 WATCH FOR DETAILS

Check (✓) the correct answers. Then compare with a partner.

1. Newcomers High School is in
   ☐ Washington, D.C.
   ✓ New York City.

2. The students at Newcomers High School
   ☐ are from the U.S.
   ☐ aren't from the U.S.

3. Morocco is on the
   ☐ ocean.
   ☐ river.

4. Camilia says the rain forest is
   ☐ fun.
   ☐ large.

5. Cai's brother is
   ☐ 20.
   ☐ 22.

6. Cai's brother is
   ☐ talkative.
   ☐ serious.

7. Fatima speaks
   ☐ two languages.
   ☐ three languages.

8. *Ma'a salama* means
   ☐ "Thank you."
   ☐ "Good-bye."

5 WHERE IS IT?

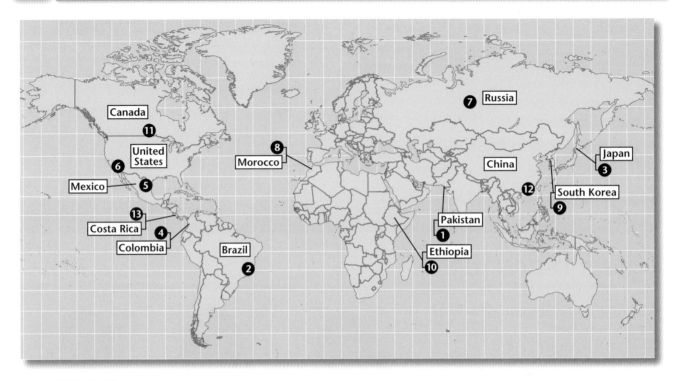

A **PAIR WORK** Students from Newcomers High School come from these cities.
Find the cities on the map.

Casablanca	Hong Kong	San José

A: Where's Casablanca?
B: I think it's here, in . . . It's number . . .
A: You're right. **or** No. It's number . . . It's here, in . . .

B **PAIR WORK** Now take turns finding these cities.

Addis Ababa	Inchon	Monterrey	Sapporo	Winnipeg
Cali	Karachi	San Diego	St. Petersburg	Vitória

A: Where's Cali?
B: I think it's in Colombia. It's number 4.
A: Yes, that's right. **or** No, it's not. It's here, number . . .

C **GROUP WORK** Write five cities on five pieces of paper.
Mix them up. Pick a city. Where is it?

A: Where's . . . ?
B: I think it's in . . .
A: That's right. **or** No, it's in . . .

Cali, Colombia

Interchange Intro VRB © Cambridge University Press 2012   Photocopiable

6 WHAT DID THEY SAY?

Watch the video and complete the conversation. Then practice it.

Rachel Park is talking to Camilia, a student at Newcomers High School.

Rachel: ....Hello........ . Where .... you from, Camilia?
Are .... from Morocco, too?

Camilia: No, I'm .... from Costa Rica.

Rachel: .... is Costa Rica, Camilia?

Camilia: .... in Central America.
I'm .... San José, the ....

Rachel: What's San José .... ?

Camilia: It's very .... I like it a lot.

Rachel: What are .... ?

Camilia: These .... photos of the rain forest in my ....
The rain forest is .... and interesting. It's fun, ...

Rachel: It looks fun! .... you, Camilia.

7 PRESENT TENSE OF BE *Countries and regions*

A Complete the conversations. Then practice them.

1. A: How ....are........ you today?
   B: I .... fine, thank you.
   A: Where .... you from, Carlos?
   B: I .... from Mexico. How about you?
   A: I .... from Canada.
   B: Oh, ... you from Montreal?
   A: Yes, I ....

2. A: Where .... Rachel from?
   B: She .... from the U.S.
   A: .... she from New York?
   B: No, she .... not from New York.
   She .... from Chicago originally.

3. A: Where .... Ji-son and Hyo from?
   B: Ji-son .... from Pusan, and
   Hyo .... from Seoul.
   A: Oh, so they .... both from South Korea.
   B: Yes, they ....

Where are you from, Ji-son?

I'm from Pusan. How about you?

I'm from Seoul.

B CLASS ACTIVITY Now find out what cities (or countries) your classmates are from.

What are you wearing?

1 VOCABULARY *Clothing*

A Find these things in the picture. Match.

1. ___d___ a dark blue suit	5. .... white socks	9. .... a backpack	13. .... a scarf
2. .... a brown tie	6. .... a gray skirt	10. .... boots	14. .... a yellow dress
3. .... black shoes	7. .... a white blouse	11. .... jeans	15. .... a pink hat
4. .... a briefcase	8. .... a blue jacket	12. .... a sweater	16. .... a red shirt

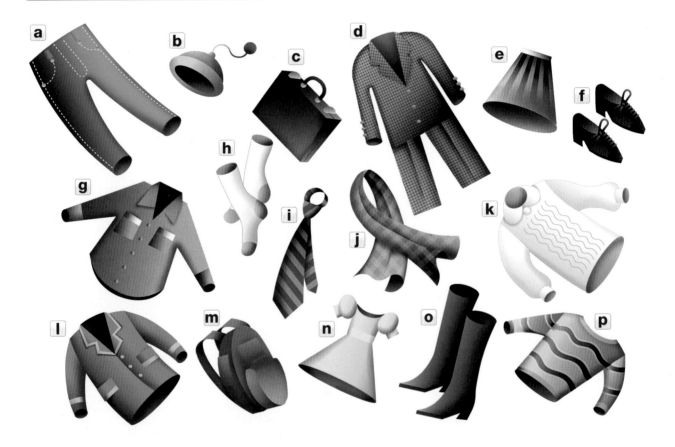

B PAIR WORK Cover the words in part A. Then ask about things in the picture.

A: What's this?
B: It's a dark blue suit.
A: What are these?
B: They're black shoes.

Interchange Intro VRB © Cambridge University Press 2012   Photocopiable

2 WHAT DO YOU SEE?

Watch the video with the sound off. Answer the questions.
Check (✓) all correct answers.

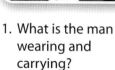

1. What is the man wearing and carrying?

- ☐ a blue suit
- ✓ a brown tie
- ☐ brown shoes
- ✓ a black briefcase

2. What is the uniform for the girl's school?

- ☐ white socks
- ☐ a red skirt
- ☐ a white blouse
- ☐ a green sweater

3. What are the mother and baby wearing?

- ☐ sneakers
- ☐ jeans
- ☐ a T-shirt
- ☐ a scarf
- ☐ yellow pants
- ☐ a pink hat

4. What is Jamal wearing today?

- ☐ black pants
- ☐ a green shirt
- ☐ a coat

☰ Watch the video

3 GET THE PICTURE

Check your answers to Exercise 2. Then compare with a partner.

4 WATCH FOR DETAILS

Watch the video again. This time, cross out the wrong items in Exercise 2. Write the correct ones. Then compare with a partner.

- ☐ ~~a blue suit~~ *a gray striped suit*
- ✓ a brown tie
- ☐ ~~brown shoes~~ *black shoes*
- ✓ a black briefcase

5 DO YOU REMEMBER?

Check (✓) the correct answers. Then compare with a partner.

1. The season is
   - ☐ spring.
   - ☐ fall.

2. The weather is cool and
   - ☐ cloudy.
   - ☐ sunny.

3. Megan's backpack is yellow, and Jasmin's backpack is
   - ☐ blue.
   - ☐ black.

4. Sheila and Julie are wearing
   - ☐ casual clothes.
   - ☐ formal clothes.

☰ Follow-up

6 WHAT'S YOUR OPINION?

A Do you like these people's clothes? Check (✓) your answers.

1. ☐ yes ☐ no

2. ☐ yes ☐ no

3. ☐ yes ☐ no

4. ☐ yes ☐ no

5. ☐ yes ☐ no

6. ☐ yes ☐ no

B **PAIR WORK** Compare your answers to part A.

A: I like his clothes. I like his gray suit.
B: I like his gray suit, and I like his brown tie.

> The negative of *like* is *don't like*.

"I like his gray suit, but I don't like his red tie."

Interchange Intro VRB © Cambridge University Press 2012   Photocopiable

7 WHAT DID THEY SAY?

Watch the video and complete the conversations.

Jamal Greene is asking people about their clothes.

1. Jamal: Excuse me. Hello!
   Man: ....Hello........ there.
   Jamal: .... talking to people about ....
   What are you .... today?
   Man: I'm wearing a .... striped suit,
   brown .... , and black ....
   Jamal: Is it a .... suit?
   Man: .... , it's for cool ....
   It's good for the fall and ....
   Jamal: Very .... , very formal.
   Man: Yes, I'm .... today, so I'm wearing
   formal ....
   Jamal: I ....

2. Jamal: So .... are you wearing .... ?
   Sheila: We're just wearing .... clothes.
   I have on boots and jeans, a .... ,
   a light jacket, and .... sunglasses.
   Jamal: And a very pretty .... scarf.
   Sheila: Thank you.
   Jamal: And what is Julie .... ?
   Sheila: She's wearing blue .... , a white .... ,
   a pink hat. It's her .... hat.

8 PRESENT CONTINUOUS *Asking about and describing clothing*

A Complete these conversations with the present continuous of *wear*.

1. A: ....Are........ you ....wearing.... pants today?
   B: No, I .... a skirt.

2. A: What .... our teacher .... today?
   B: She .... a black sweater, a blue blouse, and a gray skirt.

3. A: What color shoes .... you .... ?
   B: I .... white shoes today.

4. A: .... your classmates .... coats today?
   B: No, they .... coats, but they .... sweaters.

5. A: What colors .... you .... today?
   B: I .... yellow, blue, brown, and green.

B **PAIR WORK** Practice the conversations again.
Use your own information.

Everybody's having fun.

1 VOCABULARY Actions

A Write the actions under the pictures. Then compare with a partner.

answering the phone	looking up a phone number	sleeping
babysitting	making popcorn	✓ studying
having dinner together	ordering a pizza	watching movies

1. studying

2. _____

3. _____

4. _____

5. _____

6. _____

7. _____

8. _____

9. _____

B **PAIR WORK** Ask and answer questions about the people in part A.

A: What's Mimi doing?
B: She's studying.
A: What are Blake and Sam doing?
B: They're . . .

Interchange Intro VRB © Cambridge University Press 2012   Photocopiable

2 WHAT DO YOU SEE?

Watch the video with the sound off. Put the pictures in order from 1 to 7.

.... Peter is studying. ....

....

....

....

Watch the video

3 GET THE PICTURE

A Check your answers to Exercise 2.

B Now write the correct description under each picture in Exercise 2. Use the ideas in the box. Then compare with a partner.

Peter / Kate / Doug / Emi is . . .
answering the phone.   sleeping.
babysitting.   ✓ studying.
calling a friend.   watching movies.
going out.

Peter

Kate

Doug

Emi

4 WATCH FOR DETAILS

Check (✓) the correct answers. Then compare with a partner.

1. At the beginning of the video, it's
   - ☐ 6:00.
   - ✓ 7:00.

2. Peter is studying
   - ☐ at home.
   - ☐ in school.

3. Kate thinks babysitting
   - ☐ is fun.
   - ☐ isn't fun.

4. Peter calls Doug at
   - ☐ 8:25.
   - ☐ 7:25.

5. Doug is having dinner
   - ☐ with his grandparents.
   - ☐ at his girlfriend's house.

6. Emi calls Peter at
   - ☐ 9:20.
   - ☐ 8:20.

7. Emi, Ivan, and Carla are at
   - ☐ Carla's place.
   - ☐ Emi's place.

8. Emi, Ivan, and Carla are making
   - ☐ a pizza.
   - ☐ popcorn.

Follow-up

5 WHAT AM I DOING?

PAIR WORK Take turns acting out an action and guessing the action.
Use the verbs in the box or your own ideas.

cook	drive	get up	read	shop	study
dance	eat	play	run	sleep	(swim)

A: What am I doing?
B: Are you dancing?
A: No, I'm not.
B: Are you swimming?
A: Yes, I am.

Interchange Intro VRB © Cambridge University Press 2012   Photocopiable

WHAT DID THEY SAY?

Watch the video and complete the conversation. Then practice it.

Emi is calling Peter.

Peter: Uh, ... *hello* .... ?
Emi: Hi, Peter. .... Emi.
Um, ... you OK?
Peter: I'm ....
Emi: .... not studying. You're .... !
Peter: OK, OK. I'm .... But I'm .... ,
too! .... are you doing, Emi?
Emi: I'm hanging out .... Ivan
and Carla.
Peter: .... ? Sounds like fun.
Emi: Yeah. We're .... movies at my place.
.... you busy?
Peter: Well, I'm studying for a test that I have
on ....
Emi: We're .... popcorn.
Peter: What .... is it?
Emi: It's .... after nine. Ivan is .... a pizza.
Peter: OK! I'm ....

 PRESENT CONTINUOUS *Describing current activities*

A Complete these conversations. Use the correct present continuous
forms of the verbs in parentheses. Then practice with a partner.

1. A: What *'s* .... Pablo .... *doing* .... (do)?
   B: He .... (study).

2. A: What .... Mariko .... (read)?
   B: She .... (read) a really good book.

3. A: What .... your family .... (do) right now?
   B: My parents .... (work), and my brother and sister
   .... (talk) on the phone.

4. A: What .... our teacher .... (do)?
   B: He .... (have) lunch.
   A: Really? I .... (get) hungry, too.

5. A: .... you .... (speak) Spanish right now?
   B: No, I .... (speak) English!

B **PAIR WORK** Now ask and answer similar questions about your classmates,
friends, and family. Use your own information.

My life

Preview

1 VOCABULARY Daily routines

Look at Vanessa's daily routine. Write the sentences under the pictures.
Then compare with a partner.

I walk to work.	Every night, I write jokes.
✓ Weekdays, I get up at 7:30.	I have breakfast with my parents.
At 5:00, I finish work.	I start work at 9:00.
At 1:30, I take a lunch break.	On Saturdays, I tell my jokes at a comedy club.

1. Weekdays, I get up at 7:30.

2. ....

3. ....

4. ....

5. ....

6. ....

7. ....

8. ....

GUESS THE FACTS

Look again at the sentences in Exercise 1. Where do you think Vanessa works? Check (✓) your answer.

☐ She works at a school.

☐ She works in an office.

☐ She works at home.

    Interchange Intro VRB © Cambridge University Press 2012   Photocopiable

3 WHAT DO YOU SEE?

Watch the first minute of the video with the sound off. Check your answer to Exercise 2.

≡ Watch the video

4 GET THE PICTURE

A Complete the description.

On weekdays, Vanessa ...*designs web pages*... all day,
and she .... at night.

B Check (✓) **True** or **False**. Then compare with a partner.

	True	False
1. Vanessa lives with her brother.	☐	✓
2. Vanessa's mother is a teacher.	☐	☐
3. Vanessa's father walks to work.	☐	☐
4. In the evening, Vanessa writes stories.	☐	☐
5. On Saturdays, Vanessa goes to a comedy club.	☐	☐
6. Vanessa gets home early from the club.	☐	☐
7. On Sundays, Vanessa works all day.	☐	☐

5 WATCH FOR DETAILS

Check (✓) the correct answers. Then compare with a partner.

1. How old is Vanessa?
   ☐ 25
   ✓ 22

2. What is Vanessa's brother's name?
   ☐ Wynton
   ☐ William

3. What time does Vanessa's mother take the bus?
   ☐ 8:30 A.M.
   ☐ 9:00 A.M.

4. What time does Vanessa's father start work?
   ☐ 9:00 A.M.
   ☐ 9:30 P.M.

5. What time does the show at the club start?
   ☐ 8:00 P.M.
   ☐ 9:00 P.M.

6. When does Vanessa usually go home from the club?
   ☐ Around 11:00 P.M.
   ☐ Around 12:00 A.M.

DO YOU REMEMBER?

PAIR WORK Complete the chart. Check (✓) the words that describe Vanessa's routine.

	On weekdays	At night	On weekends
Designs web pages	☐	☐	☐
Writes jokes	☐	☐	☐
Tells jokes	☐	☐	☐
Goes downtown	☐	☐	☐

☰ Follow-up

7 A DAY IN THE LIFE

A **PAIR WORK** Choose one of these people. Describe a day in the person's life.
Use the ideas in the box below or your own ideas. Your partner guesses the person.

A: He gets up at 1:00 in the afternoon. He starts work at 10:00 at night.
B: I think he's a musician.

a musician

a reporter

a teacher

a waiter

He/She . . .
gets up at 5:00 in the morning.
gets up at 1:00 in the afternoon.
finishes work at 3:00 in the morning.
has breakfast at work.
starts work at 10:00 at night.
wears a white shirt and black pants at work.
finishes work at 3:00 in the afternoon.
works for a television station.
doesn't work on weekends.
sometimes has lunch with students.
writes on the board.

B **GROUP WORK** Now share your descriptions with another pair. Your partners
guess who you're describing.

     Interchange Intro VRB © Cambridge University Press 2012   Photocopiable

8 WHAT DID SHE SAY?

Watch the video and complete the descriptions. Then practice it.

Vanessa is talking about her life.

Hi, I'm Vanessa. Welcome to my .... home .... I live ....
Come on in! This is my .... , and this is my ....
This is my .... , Wynton. He doesn't ....
with us. He has his own .... He's ....
I'm 22, so that makes him .... big brother.

.... , I get up around 7:30. We ....
breakfast at about eight .... , right here. My mom is
a teacher. She .... in the school. She takes the
.... to work. The bus comes at .... , and she gets
home about .... My dad .... to work. He works
.... the clinic. .... a doctor. He starts work at
.... o'clock and gets home at ....

9 SIMPLE PRESENT TENSE *Talking about routines*

A Complete these conversations with the correct verb forms.
Then practice the conversations.

1. A: .... Do .... (Do/Does) you live in the city?
   B: No, I .... (don't/doesn't). I .... (live/lives)
      in the suburbs. My sister .... (live/lives) in the city.
      She .... (have/has) a good job there.

2. A: How .... (do/does) you go to school?
   B: I .... (take/takes) the bus because
      I .... (don't/doesn't) have a car.

3. A: What time .... (do/does) you go to school?
   B: Well, the bus .... (come/comes) at 7:00.

4. A: .... (Do/Does) you have breakfast every day?
   B: Yes, I .... (do/does). My parents ....
      (don't/doesn't) work in the morning, but they ....
      (get up/gets up) early and .... (have/has) breakfast with
      me. Then my father .... (drive/drives) me to the bus.

5. A: Where .... (do/does) you have dinner?
   B: My friends and I .... (go/goes) to a restaurant after class,
      so I .... (don't/doesn't) have dinner with my family.

B **PAIR WORK** Ask and answer the questions again. Use your
own information.

Richdale Street

1 VOCABULARY A new apartment

A Find these places in the picture.
Match. Then compare with a partner.

1. ...f... bathroom
2. .... bedroom
3. .... closet
4. .... kitchen
5. .... living room
6. .... yard

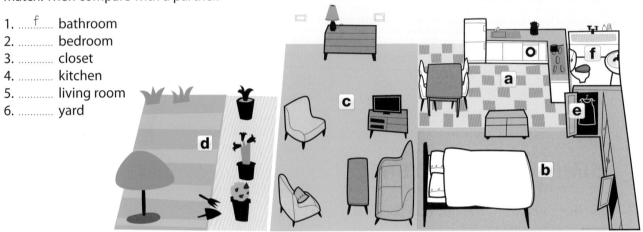

B **PAIR WORK** What do you need in a new apartment? Number
the things from 1 (most important) to 10 (least important).

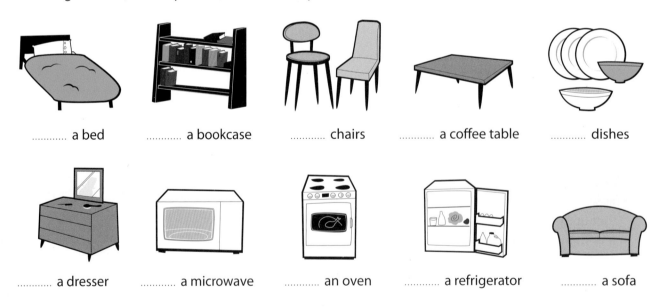

.... a bed   .... a bookcase   .... chairs   .... a coffee table   .... dishes

.... a dresser   .... a microwave   .... an oven   .... a refrigerator   .... a sofa

C **GROUP WORK** Now compare your answers. Use your own ideas, too.

A: I think you need a refrigerator for the kitchen.
B: And you also need a sofa for the living room.
C: Well, I think you need . . .

Interchange Intro VRB © Cambridge University Press 2012   Photocopiable

2 WHAT DO YOU SEE?

Watch the video with the sound off. What things do the two roommates have? Check (✓) them. Then compare with a partner.

- ✓ a sofa
- ☐ shelves
- ☐ a refrigerator
- ☐ a dresser
- ☐ a coffee table
- ☐ a microwave
- ☐ dishes
- ☐ a bed
- ☐ chairs
- ☐ a stove
- ☐ a coffeemaker
- ☐ a television

Watch the video

3 GET THE PICTURE

Jessica tells her mother about her apartment. What information is true, and what information is false? Check (✓) the correct answers. Then compare with a partner.

	True	False
1. Sofia waves hello to Jessica's mom.	✓	☐
2. There's no microwave.	☐	☐
3. The kitchen is very sunny.	☐	☐
4. There's a modern refrigerator.	☐	☐
5. The kitchen is clean.	☐	☐
6. The bedroom has a lot of windows.	☐	☐
7. The bedroom has a great view.	☐	☐
8. There's a closet in the bedroom.	☐	☐
9. They don't have a yard.	☐	☐
10. The vase is in the living room.	☐	☐

4 WATCH FOR DETAILS

Check (✓) the correct answers. Then compare with a partner.

1. Who is on the phone?
   - ✓ Jessica's mother.
   - ☐ Sofia's mother.

2. What's the view from Jessica's bedroom?
   - ☐ A park.
   - ☐ A wall.

3. What's the present from Jessica's mother?
   - ☐ A lamp.
   - ☐ A vase.

4. What's Jessica and Sofia's address?
   - ☐ 238 Richdale Street.
   - ☐ 283 Richdale Street.

5. Where is Jessica's mother calling from?
   - ☐ The suburbs.
   - ☐ The city.

6. What does Jessica's mother say about the apartment?
   - ☐ She says it's nice.
   - ☐ She says it's perfect.

5 WHAT'S YOUR OPINION?

What important things do you think Jessica and Sofia still need? Check (✓) them.
Then compare with a partner.

☐ an armchair

☐ a rug

☐ curtains

☐ a microwave

☐ a dining table

☐ pictures

A: I think they need . . .
B: But they don't really need . . .

☰ Follow-up

6 ROLE PLAY

A What questions do you think Jessica's mother asks about the new apartment?
Write six more questions.

1. *Do you like your new apartment?*
2. *How many rooms are there?*
3. ....
4. ....
5. ....
6. ....
7. ....
8. ....

B **GROUP WORK** Now ask and answer questions.
Two people play the roles of Jessica and Sofia.

A: Do you like your new apartment?
B: Yes, we do.
A: How many rooms are there?
C: There are four rooms.

We have an oven, but we don't have a microwave.

Interchange Intro VRB © Cambridge University Press 2012   Photocopiable

7 WHAT DID SHE SAY?

Watch the video and complete the conversation. Then practice it.

Jessica is talking to her mother on the phone and answering her questions.

Jessica: She's asking about our apartment. . . . Yeah, I .... *like* .... it.

Well, let me see. There are .... rooms: the living
room, the .... , and two bedrooms. Oh, and of
course, a ....

The .... room? Well, it's really big. The kitchen
is .... , too.

No, we don't have a .... We just ....
a regular oven.

Yes, the kitchen is very .... There is a
modern ....

Clean? Yeah, of course, ... clean.

The bedroom? Actually, there are a .... of big
windows. And the .... is really ....

8 THERE IS/THERE ARE *Describing a home*

A Complete these sentences with **there's**, **there are**, and **there aren't**.

1. .... *There are* .... eight rooms in our house,
   and .... a garage, too.
2. .... some trees in the yard,
   but .... any flowers.
3. .... some armchairs in the living room,
   and .... a large table in the dining room.
4. .... any pictures in the dining room,
   but .... some in the living room.
5. .... a stove and a refrigerator in the kitchen,
   but .... no microwave oven.
6. .... three bedrooms in the house,
   and .... one bathroom.

B Rewrite the sentences in part A so that they are true for
your house or apartment. Then compare with a partner.

8 The night shift

1 VOCABULARY *Jobs*

A Write the jobs under the pictures. Then compare with a partner.

> ambulance driver   ✓ doctor   taxi driver   waiter

1. _doctor_

2. ....

3. ....

4. ....

B **PAIR WORK** Choose a job from part A. Say what you do. Use the sentences in the box or your own ideas. Your partner guesses the job.

I take people to the emergency room.	I wear a uniform.
I work at night.	I help sick people.
I sit all day / all night.	I stand all day / all night.
I work in a hospital.	I work in a restaurant.

A: I stand all day.
B: Are you a doctor?
A: No, I'm a waiter.

  Interchange Intro VRB © Cambridge University Press 2012   Photocopiable

2 WHAT DO YOU SEE?

Watch the video with the sound off. Write each person's job. Then compare with a partner.

1. ....

2. ....

3. ....

4. ....

☰ Watch the video

3 GET THE PICTURE

A Check your answers to Exercise 2. Were they correct?

B These people work at night. What time do they start? What time do they finish?
Write the times. Then compare with a partner.

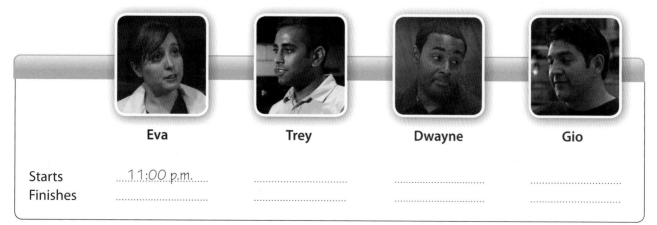

	Eva	Trey	Dwayne	Gio
Starts	11:00 p.m.	....	....	....
Finishes	....	....	....	....

Check (✓) the correct answers. Then compare with a partner.

Eva

1. Eva North thinks her job is ....
   - ☐ dangerous
   - ✓ stressful

2. Eva .... her job.
   - ☐ likes
   - ☐ doesn't like

Trey

3. Trey thinks his job is ....
   - ☐ busy, but interesting
   - ☐ difficult, but exciting

4. Trey works for .... hours, and then he has a breakfast break.
   - ☐ five
   - ☐ seven

Dwayne

5. Dwayne goes to school in the ....
   - ☐ morning
   - ☐ afternoon

6. Dwayne wakes up about ....
   - ☐ 10:00 P.M.
   - ☐ 12:00 P.M.

7. .... is a hard day for Dwayne.
   - ☐ Tuesday
   - ☐ Thursday

Gio

8. Taxi drivers on the night shift often work .... hours.
   - ☐ 10 to 15
   - ☐ 12 to 14

9. It's .... when Rachel speaks to Gio.
   - ☐ 6:00 A.M.
   - ☐ 7:00 A.M.

10. Gio thinks he .... hard.
    - ☐ works
    - ☐ doesn't work

Follow-up

5 ROLE PLAY

PAIR WORK Play the roles of the people in the video. Give your real opinion of the jobs. Use the words in the box.

dangerous	easy	interesting	relaxing	stressful
difficult	exciting	pleasant	safe	unpleasant

A: What do you do, Eva?
B: I'm a doctor.
A: Oh, that's an exciting job!
B: Yes, but it's very stressful.

Interchange Intro VRB © Cambridge University Press 2012   Photocopiable

6 WHAT DID THEY SAY?

Watch the video and complete the conversation. Then practice it.

A reporter is talking to people who work at night.

Rachel: I'm Rachel Park, and I'm ......standing...... in front of
Memorial Hospital with Eva North. She works
.... in the hospital. Eva, ...
do you do?

Eva: I'm a ....

Rachel: .... do you work, exactly?

Eva: Right here in the emergency ....

Rachel: Is it .... at night?

Eva: Yes, yes, it ....

Rachel: Really?

Eva: All .... and all night.

Rachel: .... do you like your job?

Eva: It's .... I work .... hours – from
11:00 to 7:00. But .... day
in the hospital is different. I .... it. . . . Oh,
actually, I'm .... I have to go.

7 SIMPLE PRESENT TENSE *Talking about work and school*

A Complete these conversations. Use the correct forms of the verb. Then practice the conversations.

1. A: ......Does...... Dwayne ......work...... (work) at night?

   B: Yes, he .... (do). He .... (go) to school in the morning
   and .... (do) his homework in the afternoon.

   A: When .... he .... (sleep)?

   B: That's a good question!

2. A: Where .... Eva and Trey .... (work)?

   B: They .... (work) at a hospital.

   A: What .... they .... (do), exactly?

   B: Eva .... (take) care of sick people, and Trey
   .... (drive) an ambulance.

B **PAIR WORK** Now ask your partner these questions.

1. Do you have classes during the day? What time do you go to school?
2. How do you go to school? How do you go home?
3. When do you do your homework? Where do you do it?
4. Do you have a job? Do you work at night?

9 At the diner

1 VOCABULARY Brunch

A Find these things in the picture. Match. Then compare with a partner.

1. ...g.. broccoli
2. .... coffee
3. .... corn
4. .... eggs
5. .... a fruit salad
6. .... granola
7. .... a green salad
8. .... jam
9. .... orange juice
10. .... pancakes with syrup
11. .... steak and eggs
12. .... tea
13. .... toast with butter
14. .... yogurt

a

b

c

d

e

f

g

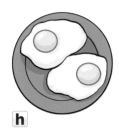
h

i

j

k

l

m

n

B GROUP WORK What do your classmates have for breakfast? Ask them.

A: What do you usually have for breakfast?
B: I usually have eggs and toast.
C: I always have coffee and fruit.
D: I never eat breakfast.

Interchange Intro VRB © Cambridge University Press 2012   Photocopiable

2 WHAT DO YOU SEE?

Watch the video with the sound off. Which of these foods do you see? Check (✓) your answers.

- ☐ broccoli and corn
- ✓ coffee
- ☐ eggs

- ☐ fruit salad
- ☐ muffins
- ☐ orange juice

- ☐ pancakes
- ☐ rice
- ☐ steak and eggs

- ☐ tea
- ☐ toast
- ☐ yogurt and granola

Watch the video

3 GET THE PICTURE

Match the people with their brunches.
Check (✓) all correct answers.

	1	2	3	4
coffee	☐	☐	☐	☐
eggs	☐	☐	☐	☐
a fruit salad	☐	☐	☐	☐
granola	☐	☐	☐	☐
a green salad	☐	☐	☐	☐
orange juice	☐	☐	☐	☐
pancakes	☐	☐	☐	☐
tea	☐	☐	☐	☐
toast	☐	☐	☐	☐
water	☐	☐	☐	☐
yogurt	☐	☐	☐	☐

4 WATCH FOR DETAILS

Check (✓) the correct answers. Then compare with a partner.

1. The young man .... jam for his toast.
   - ☐ wants
   - ✓ doesn't want

3. The woman .... sugar in her tea.
   - ☐ likes
   - ☐ doesn't like

5. The brunch special today at Sunny's is ....
   - ☐ steak and eggs
   - ☐ bacon and eggs

7. The boy's name is ....
   - ☐ Richie
   - ☐ Ricky

2. The man .... has coffee in the morning.
   - ☐ always
   - ☐ usually

4. She is visiting from ....
   - ☐ California
   - ☐ Canada

6. The man .... the special.
   - ☐ wants
   - ☐ doesn't want

8. The boy likes ....
   - ☐ broccoli
   - ☐ corn

5 WHAT'S YOUR OPINION?

PAIR WORK Which of these meals do you like? Tell your partner why.

A: I like this meal. I love yogurt.
B: Really? I hate yogurt!

6 PLAN A MENU

PAIR WORK You work at the Happy Day Restaurant. Plan eight brunch dishes for the menu. List drinks, too. Then compare menus around the class.

A: Let's serve two eggs with toast.
B: That sounds good. Let's also serve . . .

7 WHAT DID THEY SAY?

Watch the video and complete the conversation. Then practice it.

Jamal Greene is talking to people about brunch.

Student: And I'll have ......two...... ......eggs...... , some toast with
.... , and some orange juice, ...

Server: Do you want any .... with your toast?

Student: No, ...

Jamal: Hi. I see you're having some .... , too.

Student: Yes, I am.

Jamal: Do you .... have coffee with your meal?

Student: Yes, I do. I .... late at night, and I'm sleepy
in the ....

Jamal: Now, today is .... , and there's a special brunch
menu. Do you ever have .... here on weekdays?

Student: No. On weekdays, I .... breakfast at home.

Jamal: What .... lunch?

Student: I .... have lunch at school with my ....

Jamal: OK. Well, enjoy your ....

Student: Thanks.

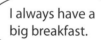

8 ADVERBS OF FREQUENCY *Talking about eating habits*

A Complete the sentences. Choose adverbs that are true for you. Then compare
with a partner.

always	never	seldom	sometimes	usually

1. I .... have a big breakfast.
2. People in my country .... eat steak and eggs for breakfast.
3. I .... drink orange juice with my breakfast.
4. I .... drink coffee in the morning.
5. I .... have time for breakfast.
6. On weekends, I .... have a big breakfast.

B CLASS ACTIVITY Do you and your partner have the same
or different breakfast habits? Tell the class.

"I seldom have a big breakfast, but Laura always has a big breakfast."

I always have a
big breakfast.

10 What's your sport?

Preview

1 VOCABULARY Sports

A Match. Then compare with a partner.

| baseball | cricket | handball | tennis |
| basketball | ✓ golf | soccer | |

1. _golf_

2. ....

3. ....

4. ....

5. ....

6. ....

7. ....

B **PAIR WORK** What sports can your partner play? Ask him or her.
Use the words in part A or your own ideas.

A: Can you play baseball?
B: Yes, I can, but not very well. Can you play golf?
A: No, I can't.

2 WHAT DO YOU SEE?

Watch the first minute of the video with the sound off. Which of these
sports do you see? Check (✓) your answers.

☑ baseball ☐ bike riding ☐ golf ☐ soccer
☐ basketball ☐ cricket ☐ hockey ☐ tennis

Interchange Intro VRB © Cambridge University Press 2012   Photocopiable

3 GET THE PICTURE

A What sports do these people enjoy? Check (✓) all correct answers.

	1	2	3	4
cricket	☐	☐	☐	☐
golf	☐	☐	☐	☐
soccer	✓	☐	☐	☐
tennis	☐	☐	☐	☐

B One of the people in part A doesn't play a sport. What does that person say? Complete the sentence.
I don't *play* .... I .... it.

4 WATCH FOR DETAILS

Check (✓) the correct answers. Then compare with a partner.

Omar

1. The players on Omar's team are from the same ....
   ☐ city
   ✓ country

2. They practice every ....
   ☐ day
   ☐ weekend

Ian

3. Ian's sport .... very popular in the U.S.
   ☐ is
   ☐ isn't

4. There are .... people on a cricket team.
   ☐ 7
   ☐ 11

Diane

5. Diane says she .... tennis.
   ☐ likes
   ☐ loves

6. Diane .... tennis.
   ☐ plays
   ☐ doesn't play

Susan

7. Susan's .... takes the kids to the playground.
   ☐ husband
   ☐ sister

8. Susan thinks her favorite sport is ....
   ☐ relaxing
   ☐ exciting

5 ROLE PLAY A day at the park

PAIR WORK Choose a partner. Your partner is a reporter. Answer his or her questions.
Use the questions in the box and your own ideas.

> Can you play . . . ?   What sports do you like?
>
> Who do you play with?   How often do you practice?

Start like this:
A: Hi. Can I ask you some questions about sports?
B: Sure! What do you want to know?

6 FIND SOMEONE WHO . . .

CLASS ACTIVITY Go around the class. Ask questions and complete the chart with classmates' names.

	Name		Name
Find someone who . . .			
1. plays a sport every week.	....	5. can play tennis.	....
2. doesn't like sports.	....	6. can't swim.	....
3. can play volleyball.	....	7. loves to watch baseball.	....
4. likes to play handball.	....	8. can play soccer well.	....

7 WHAT DID SHE SAY?

Watch the video and complete the information. Then practice it.

Lisa Kim is talking about a popular park in Queens, New York.

Lisa: Flushing Meadows ....has........... something for everyone.

And you don't need to .... sports to enjoy the

.... You .... also just take it

.... There are many .... places to

.... in the park. Like this.

Best of all, you can .... to Flushing Meadows easily on

the .... from Manhattan. The Number 7 ....

takes you right to the park.

.... where do you get .... the train? Just

.... for the Unisphere. This giant globe ....

you that you're in Flushing Meadows. .... great,

huh? Flushing Meadows welcomes .... from all

around the world to play sports, ... sports, or just

.... a day in this beautiful park.

8 TALKING ABOUT ABILITIES AND INTERESTS

A Answer these questions with your own information.
Choose from the sentences in the box.

Yes, I do.	Yes, I can.
No, I don't.	No, I can't.

1. A: Can you ski?
   B: ....

2. A: Do you like basketball?
   B: ....

3. A: Can you do gymnastics?
   B: ....

4. A: Do you play soccer?
   B: ....

5. A: Do you like golf?
   B: ....

6. A: Can you play tennis?
   B: ....

B Write five more questions about sports.
Then ask and answer the questions with a partner.

11 A trip to Washington, D.C.

1 VOCABULARY *Sightseeing activities*

A Here are some things you can do in Washington, D.C. Match. Then compare with a partner.

1. __c__ walk around the National Mall
2. .... visit museums
3. .... take a tour of the Capitol
4. .... watch the fireworks on the National Mall

5. .... see the Lincoln Memorial
6. .... go to the top of the Washington Monument
7. .... take a tour of the White House
8. .... get on a sightseeing bus

B **GROUP WORK** What is the most interesting activity? Compare ideas.

A: What are you going to do in Washington, D.C.?
B: I'm going to take a tour of the Capitol.
C: I'm going to . . .

2 WHAT DO YOU SEE?

Watch the video with the sound off. Which activities can you see?
Check (✓) your answers.

✓ take a walk in the park
☐ visit museums
☐ go shopping

☐ see a movie
☐ take a tour of the Capitol
☐ watch the fireworks on the National Mall

☐ see some monuments
☐ ride the subway
☐ get on a sightseeing bus

Interchange Intro VRB © Cambridge University Press 2012   Photocopiable

3 GET THE PICTURE

What are these people going to do in Washington, D.C.? Check (✓) all correct answers.

1. ☐ go shopping at the mall
   ☑ visit some museums
   ☐ see some monuments
   ☑ have lunch at a museum café

2. ☐ take a tour of the Capitol
   ☐ see the Lincoln Memorial
   ☐ watch the fireworks on the National Mall
   ☐ visit some museums

3. ☐ walk around the National Mall
   ☐ ride the subway
   ☐ go to the top of the Washington Monument
   ☐ take a tour of the White House

4 WATCH FOR DETAILS

Check (✓) the correct answers. Then compare with a friend.

1. The girl is with her ....
   ☐ aunt
   ☑ mother

2. It's the girl's .... birthday.
   ☐ 16th
   ☐ 17th

3. She wants to be a .... someday.
   ☐ pilot
   ☐ flight attendant

4. The kids think Washington is really ....
   ☐ interesting
   ☐ fun

5. The kids are with their ....
   ☐ family
   ☐ class

6. The fireworks are going to start at ....
   ☐ 9:00
   ☐ 10:00

7. The woman is going to visit some ....
   ☐ monuments
   ☐ museums

8. The man is going to .... to the White House.
   ☐ drive
   ☐ walk

9. Marc is going to ....
   ☐ walk around the National Mall
   ☐ get on a sightseeing bus

5 WHAT THE PEOPLE SAY

What do these people say? Complete the sentences. Then compare with a partner.

1. There are .... ,
.... ,
famous buildings, and lots of
monuments.

2. ....
the National Air and Space
Museum.

3. I'm an artist, so I want to
see the art museum. So,
....
the whole day there.

Follow-up

6 A DAY IN WASHINGTON, D.C.

A **GROUP WORK** Plan a day in Washington, D.C. Decide on two things to do in the morning, two things to do in the afternoon, and something to do in the evening.

Washington, D.C.

Take a ride on the Metro.

Eat in a restaurant in Chinatown.

Attend a concert at the Kennedy Center.

Watch the boats at Washington Harbor.

Visit the National Zoo.

Go shopping in Georgetown.

B **CLASS ACTIVITY** Share your plans with the class.

"In the morning, we're going to . . ."
"Then we're going to . . ."

Interchange Intro VRB © Cambridge University Press 2012   Photocopiable

VIDEO ACTIVITIES

7 WHAT DID THEY SAY?

Watch the video and complete the conversation. Then practice it.

Marc Jones is interviewing people on the National Mall in Washington, D.C.

Marc: And who are you ....with.......... ?

Woman: This is my .... Today's her 16th
.... We're ....
Washington, D.C., for her birthday.

Marc: Well, ... birthday!

Girl: Thanks!

Marc: So, ... are you going to .... ?

Girl: Well, we're going to visit some ....
And then, we're going to .... lunch at
a café in the museum.

Marc: Nice! .... museum are you going to
.... ?

Girl: I want to .... the National Air and Space
Museum. I .... to be a pilot someday.

Marc: Great! .... , have a good day.

8 FUTURE WITH BE GOING TO *Talking about plans*

A Complete these conversations. Use the correct future with
be going to forms of the verbs in parentheses.

1. A: ......Are...... you ....going to do.... (do)
   anything on Friday night?
   B: Yes, I .... (see) a movie.

2. A: What time .... you .... (leave)
   school today?
   B: I .... (go) home at 7:00 P.M.

3. A: What .... you .... (have)
   for dinner tonight?
   B: We .... (have) fish.

4. A: .... you .... (study) English tonight?
   B: No. I .... (watch) TV.

B **PAIR WORK** Practice the conversations in part A. Use your own information.

Where does it hurt?

☰ Preview

1 VOCABULARY *Health problems*

A Write the health problems under the pictures. Then compare with a partner.

I feel dizzy.	I have a backache.	✓ I have an earache.
I feel tired.	I have a cough.	I have a fever.

1. I have an earache.

2. ....

3. ....

4. ....

5. ....

6. ....

B **PAIR WORK** Ask and answer questions about the people in part A.

A: What's the matter with the woman?
B: She has an earache.

2 WHAT DO YOU SEE?

Watch the video with the sound off. Check (✓) all correct answers.

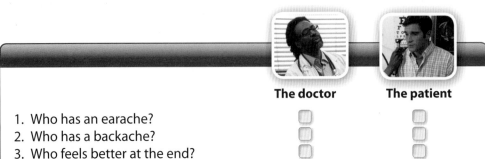

	The doctor	The patient
1. Who has an earache?	☐	☐
2. Who has a backache?	☐	☐
3. Who feels better at the end?	☐	☐

Interchange Intro VRB © Cambridge University Press 2012   Photocopiable

3 GET THE PICTURE

A Check your answers to Exercise 2. Were they correct?

B Complete the doctor's notes about the patient. Then compare with a partner.

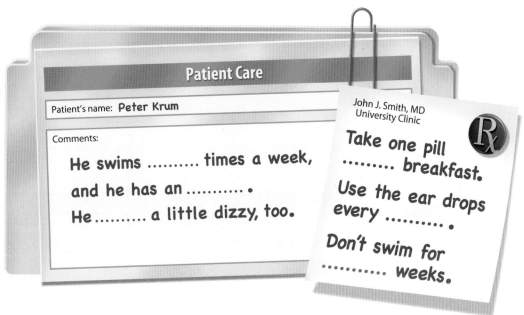

Patient Care

Patient's name: **Peter Krum**

Comments:

He swims .... times a week, and he has an ....
He .... a little dizzy, too.

John J. Smith, MD
University Clinic

℞

Take one pill .... breakfast.
Use the ear drops every ....
Don't swim for .... weeks.

4 WATCH FOR DETAILS

Check (✓) the correct answers. Then compare with a partner.

1. When does Peter feel the pain?
   ☐ Constantly.
   ✓ From time to time.

2. What is wrong with Peter?
   ☐ He has extra wax in his ear.
   ☐ He has a serious fever.

3. When does the doctor's back hurt?
   ☐ When he stands a lot.
   ☐ All the time.

4. Why does Peter know how to fix backaches?
   ☐ His father is a doctor.
   ☐ His father has the same problem.

5. What does Peter tell the doctor to do first?
   ☐ Pull his left knee up.
   ☐ Turn his body to the side.

6. Which way does Peter tell the doctor to turn?
   ☐ To the right.
   ☐ To the left.

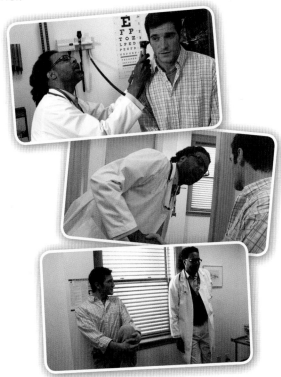

5 DO YOU REMEMBER?

What does the doctor ask the patient? Check (✓) the correct questions.
Then compare with a partner.

- ☐ Why are you here today?
- ☑ How are you feeling today?
- ☐ Do you have a cold?
- ☐ Do you have a headache?
- ☐ Do you have a cough?
- ☐ Do you have a fever?
- ☐ Do you have a sore throat?
- ☐ Do you feel terrible?
- ☐ Do you feel tired?
- ☐ Do you exercise often?
- ☐ Do you go swimming every day?
- ☐ Do you need some medicine?

Follow-up

6 ROLE PLAY At the doctor's office

A PAIR WORK Take turns playing the roles of the patient and the doctor.
Act out the first part of their conversation. Use the checked questions in Exercise 5.

A: How are you feeling today?
B: Not so good, Doc.

B PAIR WORK Talk about your health. Use the problems below or your own ideas.

| the flu | a headache | a stomachache | sore eyes | a toothache |

A: Do you ever get the flu?
B: I seldom get the flu. What about you? Do you get the flu?
A: Yes, I do, sometimes.

Interchange Intro VRB © Cambridge University Press 2012   Photocopiable

Language close-up

7 WHAT DID THEY SAY?

Watch the video and complete the conversation. Then practice it.

Dr. Smith is examining Peter to find out why Peter doesn't feel well.

Dr. Smith: So, do you go swimming ...*every*... ...*day*... ?

Peter: No, not every day. .... three times a ....

Dr. Smith: I think I .... the problem.

Peter: Is it .... ?

Dr. Smith: Oh, ... You have some ....
wax in your ear, probably .... you swim so much.
I'm going to .... you some .... ,
and you should feel .... in a week.

Peter: OK. .... good.

Dr. Smith: I'm going to give you some .... and
some pills. .... one pill .... breakfast.
Use the ear drops before ....

Peter: One pill .... the morning, ear drops .... night.

Dr. Smith: That's .... !

8 IMPERATIVES *Giving advice*

A Complete the conversations. Choose from the advice in the box. Then compare with a partner.

Don't lift heavy things.	Drink a lot of orange juice.	Stay in bed for two days.
Don't try new foods.	✓ Drink hot tea with lemon.	Take two aspirin and close your eyes.

1. A: I have a sore throat.
   B: Drink hot tea with lemon.

2. A: I have a headache.
   B: ....

3. A: I have a backache.
   B: ....

4. A: I have the flu.
   B: ....

5. A: I have a stomachache.
   B: ....

6. A: I have a cold.
   B: ....

I have a sore throat.

Drink hot tea with lemon.

B Now complete the conversations in part A with your own ideas. Then compare your advice in groups.

Across the bridge

1 VOCABULARY Directions

Look at the map of the Capilano Suspension Bridge area. Complete the sentences with the words in the box. Then compare with a partner.

across	behind	left	✓ right
around	in front of	past	up

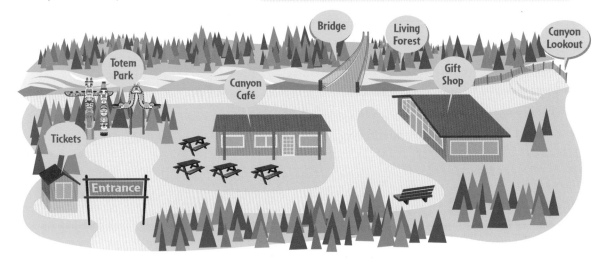

1. After you enter the park, turn ....right.......... . Walk .... the
   path, ... the Canyon Café. The bridge is on the ....

2. At the bridge, turn to your right and the gift shop is directly .... you.
   To get to the Canyon Lookout, walk .... the gift shop to the left.
   The Lookout is .... the gift shop.

3. To visit the Living Forest exhibition, go .... the bridge.

2 GUESS THE FACTS

The Capilano Suspension Bridge is a famous tourist attraction in Canada. What other things do you think visitors can find at the park? Check (✓) your guesses. Then compare with a partner.

⬜ a gift shop
⬜ a nature center
⬜ a rain forest
⬜ a restaurant

⬜ a zoo
⬜ an amusement park
⬜ an art museum
⬜ totem poles

totem poles

Interchange Intro VRB © Cambridge University Press 2012   Photocopiable

3 WHAT DO YOU SEE?

Watch the video with the sound off. Number the pictures in order from 1 to 6.

Ben and Sara arrived at the park.

Watch the video

4 GET THE PICTURE

A Check your answers to Exercise 3. Were they correct?

B Write the correct description under each picture in Exercise 3. Use the ideas in the box. Then compare with a partner.

Ben and Sara looked at the bridge.	✓ Ben and Sara arrived at the park.
Ben helped Sara cross the bridge.	Ben took pictures of Sara.
Sara got scared on the bridge and froze.	Sara took pictures of Ben.

Interchange Intro VRB © Cambridge University Press 2012   Photocopiable

5 WATCH FOR DETAILS

Check (✓) the correct answers. Then compare with a partner.

1. Sara says the bridge is one of .... most popular tourist attractions.
   - ☑ Vancouver's
   - ☐ Seattle's

2. Ben wants to go to the .... first.
   - ☐ totem poles
   - ☐ restaurant

3. The totem poles are .... the gift shop.
   - ☐ next to
   - ☐ across from

4. Sara tells Ben to stand .... two totem poles.
   - ☐ behind
   - ☐ between

5. Ben wants to buy a .... at the gift shop.
   - ☐ present for his mother
   - ☐ picture of the bridge

6. Ben admits that he .... high places.
   - ☐ likes
   - ☐ doesn't like

7. Sara .... angry with Ben.
   - ☐ gets
   - ☐ doesn't get

8. Sara freezes when she looks ....
   - ☐ down from the bridge
   - ☐ across the bridge

Follow-up

6 DIRECTIONS

GROUP WORK Write directions to two places in or near your school. Use the expressions in the box. Then share the directions with another group.

Go right / left . . .	It's on the corner of . . . and . . .	It's next to . . .
Walk one block . . .	It's between . . . and . . .	It's behind . . .
Turn right / left . . .	It's across from . . .	It's in front of . . .

Place 1: ....   Place 2: ....

....

....

Start like this:

A: How do I get to . . . ?
B: Walk out the door and . . .
C: Then . . .

7 **WHAT DID THEY SAY?**

Watch the video and complete the conversation. Then practice it.

Ben and Sara are visiting the Capilano Suspension Bridge.

Sara: We got some great ....*photos*.......... . Now .... go cross that bridge.

Ben: Oh! I just .... !

Sara: .... ?

Ben: We have to get a .... for my mom. We ....

Sara: Yeah?

Ben: The gift shop's just .... there. We can get her something .... nice . . .

Sara: Ben . . .

Ben: . . . and then we can .... to the restaurant, and we can .... something to eat.

Sara: Ben?

Ben: What?

Sara: What's .... on?

Ben: What do you mean?

Sara: Well, ... you wanted to go to Totem Park. .... you want to go to the gift shop. What .... the bridge?

Ben: Well, ... , I don't like .... places. I get scared, and I freeze up.

Sara: So you .... want to go .... the bridge?

 8 **OPPOSITES** *Giving directions*

These people need to go the other way. Complete the answers. Then practice the conversations with a partner.

1. A: Do I walk up this path?
   B: No, not up. Walk ......*down*...... the path.

2. A: Is the restaurant around the corner on the left?
   B: It's around the corner, but it's on the ....

3. A: Is the restroom in front of the ticket booth?
   B: No, it's .... the ticket booth.

4. A: Are the totem poles far from here?
   B: No, they're really ....

5. A: Do I turn right at the sign?
   B: No, you turn ....

6. A: Is the café two blocks west of the school?
   B: No, it's two blocks .... of the school.

How was your vacation?

1 VOCABULARY Vacation problems

Look at the problems that people had on vacation. Write the sentences under the pictures. Then compare with a partner.

> **Was** is the past tense of **is**.

I got sunburned.	There was no air-conditioning.	The hotel was too noisy.
✓ I lost my passport.	They canceled my flight.	I didn't like the food.
I was in an accident.	I forgot my camera.	

1. I lost my passport.

2. ....

3. ....

4. ....

5. ....

6. ....

7. ....

8. ....

2 WHAT DO YOU SEE?

Watch the first 40 seconds of the video with the sound off.
Why do you think Hugo's arms and back hurt?

- ☐ He was in an accident.
- ☐ He exercised a lot.
- ☐ He got sunburned.

 Interchange Intro VRB © Cambridge University Press 2012   Photocopiable

3 GET THE PICTURE

A Check your answer to Exercise 2. Was it correct?

B These statements are false. Change one word to correct them.
Then compare with a partner.

Evan

Hugo

Hugo
1. ~~Evan~~ was on vacation last week.

2. Evan slaps Hugo's face.

3. The first day, Hugo ran on the beach.

4. Evan and Hugo's co-worker, Harry, is working.

5. The elevator at Hugo's hotel didn't work.

6. Hugo bought a new suitcase for his trip.

7. Hugo remembered to pack his camera.

8. Hugo came back from his vacation on Saturday.

4 WATCH FOR DETAILS

Check (✓) the correct answers. Then compare with a partner.

1. Evan wants to hear about Hugo's ....
   ☐ business trip   ✓ vacation

2. Hugo tells Evan that his vacation was ....
   ☐ great   ☐ OK

3. Hugo went to the beach ....
   ☐ one time   ☐ two times

4. Hugo says that his hotel was really ....
   ☐ hot   ☐ cold

5. Hugo didn't .... well on his vacation.
   ☐ eat   ☐ sleep

6. Hugo didn't take any pictures because he left his camera at ....
   ☐ home   ☐ work

7. Hugo spent Saturday night at the ....
   ☐ hotel   ☐ airport

8. Evan is going to .... tomorrow.
   ☐ Chicago   ☐ Morocco

5 VACATION ACTIVITIES

A Match. Then compare with a partner.

1.	...c...	stay home	Yes	No
2.	....	visit family	Yes	No
3.	....	go swimming	Yes	No
4.	....	take pictures	Yes	No
5.	....	play sports	Yes	No
6.	....	eat new foods	Yes	No
7.	....	meet interesting people	Yes	No
8.	....	go dancing	Yes	No

B Did you do any of the things in part A on your last vacation? Circle **Yes** or **No**.

C **PAIR WORK** Now ask and answer questions about your last vacation.

A: Did you stay home on your last vacation?
B: Yes, I did. **or** No, I didn't.

6 WHAT DID THEY SAY?

Watch the video and complete the conversation. Then practice it.

Hugo just got back from his vacation.

Hugo: I was really happy when I ....got......... there.
It was .... The water was so .... , and
the sand was .... There were palm ....
and cool breezes. I couldn't wait to hit the ....

Evan: Lucky .... So what did you .... first?

Hugo: Well, the first day I .... relaxed on the beach.
I even fell asleep ....

Evan: Kind of like Harry there?

Hugo: Yeah. Like ....

Evan: So you fell asleep .... the beach. That
sounds ....

Hugo: Yeah, it was, except I didn't use .... sunscreen.

Evan: Uh-oh.

Hugo: And I got sunburned .... over.

Evan: Ouch! So that explains the . . .

Hugo: ....

7 PAST TENSE Talking about vacations

A Complete these conversations with the past tense of the verbs
in parentheses. Then practice the conversations.

1. A: ......Did...... you ......visit...... (visit) your family on your vacation?
   B: Yes, I did. I .... (go) home because my sister ....
      (get) married last Saturday. She .... (wear) a beautiful
      white dress.

2. A: .... you .... (go) anywhere interesting on
      your last vacation?
   B: Yes. I .... (go) to Mexico and .... (take) a
      Spanish class.

3. A: .... you .... (have) fun on your vacation?
   B: Yes, we did. We .... (have) a great time. We .... (eat)
      a lot of new foods and .... (meet) some interesting people.

4. A: .... you .... (do) anything interesting on
      your vacation?
   B: No, not really. I .... (stay) home and .... (work)
      around the house. I .... (paint) the front porch and
      .... (clean) the basement. Oh, I .... (see) a few good movies, too.

B **PAIR WORK** Practice the conversations again. Use your own information.

15 On Broadway

Preview

1 VOCABULARY *The theater*

Do you know these theater words? Match them to the pictures. Then compare with a partner.

> actor   dancers   musical   musician   ✓play   usher

1. play ....
2. ....
3. ....

4. ....
5. ....
6. ....

2 THEATER QUIZ

A **PAIR WORK** Here are some popular musicals. They began on Broadway and then became popular around the world. How many do you know? Match.

1. The Lion King
2. Beauty and the Beast
3. Mary Poppins
4. Billy Elliot
5. West Side Story
6. Hairspray

B **PAIR WORK** Talk about these questions.

1. Did you ever go to the theater to see a play or a musical? If so, what did you see?
2. The musicals in part A are also movies. Which of the movies did you see? Did you like each movie? Why or why not?
3. Look again at the musicals in part A. Which one(s) do you think you'd like to see – either at the theater or at the movies? Why?

    Interchange Intro VRB © Cambridge University Press 2012   Photocopiable

3 WHAT DO YOU SEE?

A *Watch the video with the sound off.* Does each person have a job in the theater?
Circle **Yes** or **No**.

1. Yes   No

2. Yes   No

3. Yes   No

B Where is Broadway?
Check (✓) the correct answer.
Then compare with a partner.

- ☐ Chicago
- ☐ Denver
- ☐ Los Angeles
- ☐ Miami
- ☐ New York
- ☐ San Francisco
- ☐ Seattle

☰ Watch the video

4 GET THE PICTURE

A Check your answers to Exercise 3. Were they correct?

B Where are these people from? Match.

Sylvia

Frank

Andrea

1. .... Sylvia   a. New York

2. .... Frank   b. Mexico

3. .... Andrea   c. Colorado

5 WATCH FOR DETAILS

A Check (✓) all correct answers.

☐ Sylvia came to New York four years ago.

✓ Sylvia came to New York to be an actress.

☐ Before she came to New York, she studied acting.

☐ Her parents were happy when she came to New York.

☐ Her parents thought New York was a big, interesting city.

☐ Her parents love New York now.

☐ Andrea is a musician.

☐ She works five days a week.

☐ There are two shows on Tuesdays.

☐ The theater is closed on Mondays.

☐ Andrea was born and raised in Brazil.

☐ Andrea studied dance in college.

☐ Frank is an actor.

☐ He took this job because he needed the money.

☐ He doesn't like his job.

☐ He meets a lot of nice people.

☐ He came to New York to study acting.

☐ He wants to write movies.

B Look again at the sentences in part A. Correct the false statements. Then compare with a partner.

Sylvia came to New York ~~four~~ five years ago.

C **PAIR WORK** Now ask and answer questions about the people in part A.

A: Did Sylvia come to New York to be an actress?
B: Yes, she did. Is she working as a Spanish teacher?
A: No, she isn't. She's working as a yoga teacher.

Follow-up

6 INTERVIEW

A You're interviewing a young actor. First, match the questions with the answers. Then, practice the interview with a partner.

1. ..._b_... When did you come to New York?

2. .... Where did you grow up?

3. .... Did you study acting in school?

4. .... What did you do before you came here?

5. .... What was the name of your first show?

a. *Broadway Dreams.*

b. I came here three years ago.

c. In a small town in Arizona.

d. No, but I'm studying it now.

e. I worked in a restaurant.

B **PAIR WORK** Now interview each other. Use the questions in part A. Answer with your own ideas.

Interchange Intro VRB © Cambridge University Press 2012   Photocopiable

☰ Language close-up

7 WHAT DID THEY SAY?

Watch the video and complete the conversation. Then practice it.

Rachel Park is interviewing people on Broadway.

Rachel: Times Square. Midtown Manhattan. And the heart and the ....home........ of the theater
district: Broadway! .... is New York City! And no .... to New York is
complete until you go to a Broadway .... or musical. Broadway
is a .... and exciting place to be. It's .... the dream
of thousands of actors, ... , musicians, and other artists. Let's
.... with some of the people who actually work here on Broadway.

Rachel: Hi, Sylvia.
Sylvia: Hi.
Rachel: .... is Sylvia Santiago. Sylvia, were you ....
in New York?
Sylvia: No. I .... born in Mexico.
Rachel: And when did you .... to New York?
Sylvia: I .... here five years ago. I .... to be an actress.
Rachel: Wow. Do you want to be in a Broadway .... ?
Sylvia: Yes! That's .... dream.
Rachel: Did you study .... before you came to New York?
Sylvia: No, I .... I studied ....

8 PAST TENSE *Giving personal information*

A Complete this interview with a Broadway actor. Use **was, were,
did**, or **didn't**. Then practice the interview with a partner.

A: Where .....did..... you grow up?
B: In Australia.
A: .... you study music when you .... a child?
B: Yes, I .... I studied the violin. Later, I studied acting.
A: .... your parents actors, too?
B: Yes and no. My father .... a professional actor, but my mother
.... a musician. Now they're both teachers.
A: When .... you come to the U.S.?
B: In 2003.
A: .... you get an acting job right away?
B: Yes, I .... I .... lucky. I got a job with the touring company
of a musical. So I .... have to get a day job to support myself, like most actors.

B CLASS ACTIVITY Find out about your classmates. Write five more questions.
Then go around the class and ask them.

1. *Where were you born?* ....
2. ....
3. ....
4. ....
5. ....
6. ....

16 Then he said . . .

1 VOCABULARY *Dating activities*

A **PAIR WORK** What's the perfect date? Add two more activities to the list below.
Then rate each activity from 1 (you like it a lot) to 5 (you don't like it very much).

I like to . . .

a. eat in nice restaurants.

b. go to art fairs.

c. go to sporting events.

d. go to the movies.

e. go to amusement parks.

f. go to dance clubs.

g. go to parties.

h. go to concerts.

Your suggestions: i. .... ☐   j. .... ☐

B **GROUP WORK** Talk about your dating suggestions in part A.

A: I like to . . . on dates.
B: I like to . . .
C: I don't like to . . . on dates. I like to . . .

2 GOOD EXCUSES

A Sometimes people invite us to do something, but we can't accept, or don't want to accept.
Look at these excuses. Number them from 1 (the best excuse) to 8 (the worst excuse).

.... I have to babysit.	.... I need to clean my room.	.... I'm reading a new book.
.... My family and I have plans.	.... I have dance class.	.... My grandparents are
.... I have an appointment.	.... I'm going to study.	coming over.

B **PAIR WORK** Take turns choosing an activity from
Exercise 1 and an excuse from part A of Exercise 2.

A: Do you want to go to the movies tonight?
B: I'm really sorry, but I can't. I have to babysit.

Interchange Intro VRB © Cambridge University Press 2012   Photocopiable

3 GUESS THE FACTS

Watch the first 45 seconds of the video with the sound on.
Guess where Abby went on her date. Check (✓) your answer.

She went to . . .

- ☐ a basketball game.
- ☐ an amusement park.
- ☐ an art fair.
- ☐ the movies.

☰ Watch the video

4 GET THE PICTURE

A Check your answer to Exercise 3. Was it correct?

B Put the pictures in order from 1 to 7. Then write the correct sentence under each picture. Compare with a partner.

Abby refused Greg's invitations.

Abby got sick and had to sit down.
✓ Abby refused Greg's invitations.
Abby's family and Greg had lunch.
Abby's sister gave Greg his wallet.

Greg accepted Abby's invitation.
Greg and Abby went on a roller coaster.
Greg bought Abby's sister ice cream.

Check (✓) the correct answers. Then compare with a partner.

Abby

Peter

1. At the beginning of the video, why does Peter want to go outside?
   - [ ] He wants to have lunch with Abby.
   - [ ] He wants to hear Abby's story.
   - [ ] He wants to find Greg.

2. What does Peter mean when he says, "I'm all ears"?
   - [ ] I can't hear you.
   - [ ] I have an earache.
   - [ ] I'm listening.

3. Why did Abby refuse Greg's invitation to the game?
   - [ ] She likes some sports, but she hates basketball.
   - [ ] She likes Greg, but she doesn't want to see him.
   - [ ] She likes Greg, but she doesn't like sports.

4. What day did Abby see Greg?
   - [ ] Friday.
   - [ ] Saturday.
   - [ ] Sunday.

5. When did Greg lose his wallet?
   - [ ] On the roller coaster.
   - [ ] During lunch.
   - [ ] At the ice-cream stand.

6. At the end of the video, why does Abby refuse Greg's invitations?
   - [ ] She's really embarrassed.
   - [ ] She doesn't like him.
   - [ ] She's very busy.

☰ Follow-up

6 **MAKE WEEKEND PLANS**

A Complete the chart with your own ideas. Then compare with a partner.

Weekend activities	Excuses for not accepting an invitation
go to the movies see a ball game go to a dance club	I have to work late. I have a date with a friend. I have to stay in and study.
....	....
....	....
....	....

B **CLASS ACTIVITY** Go around the class and invite people to do something with you this weekend. They should say they can't and give you an excuse.

A: Hi, Sammi. Would you like to go to a dance club with me this weekend?
B: Oh, sorry. I can't. I have a date with a friend.
A: OK. Maybe some other time, then.
B: Sure.

Language close-up

WHAT DID THEY SAY?

Watch the video and complete the conversation. Then practice it.

Abby starts to tell Peter about her plans with Greg.

Peter: Great! So you ......went...... to the movies together.

Abby: No, I .... because of my little sister. I had to babysit. So then he .... if I wanted to go to the basketball game the .... night.

Peter: Oh, so you .... to the game Saturday night.

Abby: No. I turned him ....

Peter: What? Are you crazy? .... ? What was your excuse?

Abby: No .... I told him that I like him, but I .... do not like sports. But, um, he was really .... about it, and he even asked me to go to the art fair with him on ....

Peter: So you went to the art fair. I was .... , but I didn't .... you.

Abby: No, we didn't go. I couldn't. On Sunday, I had .... with my family to go to the amusement park.

Peter: So you .... see him.

Abby: Yes, I ....

Peter: OK, wait a minute. I'm confused. .... did you see him?

WANT TO, NEED TO, HAVE TO *Making excuses*

Reply to these invitations, giving your own excuses. Then practice the conversations with a partner.

1. A: Let's see a movie tonight.
   B: I can't. I have to ....

2. A: Do you want to go downtown after class?
   B: Sorry, I can't. I need to ....

3. A: Do you want to go to a party on Friday night?
   B: Friday night? Oh, I'm not free. I have to ....

4. A: Let's go dancing on Saturday night.
   B: Gee, I can't. I have to .... Sorry. ....

5. A: Do you want to go to a concert on Sunday afternoon?
   B: Sorry, I can't. I need to ....

I can't go. I have to write a paper for school.

VIDEO ACTIVITIES

This page is intentionally left blank

interchange

FIFTH EDITION

intro

Workbook

Jack C. Richards

CAMBRIDGE
UNIVERSITY PRESS

This page is intentionally left blank

Contents

Credits

The authors and publishers acknowledge the following sources of copyright material and are grateful for the permissions granted. While every effort has been made, it has not always been possible to identify the sources of all the material used, or to trace all copyright holders. If any omissions are brought to our notice, we will be happy to include the appropriate acknowledgements on reprinting and in the next update to the digital edition, as applicable.

Key: B = Below, BC = Below Centre, BL = Below Left, BR = Below Right, C = Centre, CL = Centre Left, CR = Centre Right, Ex = Exercise, L = Left, R = Right, T = Top, TC = Top Centre, TL = Top Left, TR = Top Right.

Illustrations

337 Jon (KJA Artists): 11, 21, 81; **417 Neal** (KJA Artists): 1, 58; **Mark Duffin**: 7, 12, 26, 37, 41, 52, 70; **Thomas Girard** (Good Illustration): 10, 63, 68, 84; **John Goodwin** (Eye Candy Illustration): 23, 71; **Dusan Lakicevic** (Beehive Illustration): 57; **Quino Marin** (The Organisation): 19, 69, 92, 94; **Gavin Reece** (New Division): 5, 39; **Gary Venn** (Lemonade Illustration): 25, 74, 77; **Paul Williams** (Sylvie Poggio Artists): 6, 29, 67.

Photos

Back cover (woman with whiteboard): Jenny Acheson/Stockbyte/GettyImages; Back cover (whiteboard): Nemida/GettyImages; Back cover (man using phone): Betsie Van Der Meer/Taxi/GettyImages; Back cover (woman smiling): PeopleImages.com/DigitalVision/GettyImages; Back cover (name tag): Tetra Images/GettyImages; Back cover (handshake): David Lees/Taxi/GettyImages; p. 2 (TL): Yellow Dog Productions/Iconica/GettyImages; p. 2 (CR): Morsa Images/DigitalVision/GettyImages; p. 2 (BL): Johnny Greig/iStock/Getty Images Plus/GettyImages; p. 3: Nicolas McComber/E+/GettyImages; p. 4: MichaelDeLeon/iStock/Getty Images Plus/GettyImages; p. 5: Steve Debenport/E+/GettyImages; p. 8 (TL): hudiemm/E+/GettyImages; p. 8 (TC): Marek Mnich/E+/GettyImages; p. 8 (TR): Dorling Kindersley/Dorling Kindersley/GettyImages; p. 8 (CL): Tpopova/iStock/Getty Images Plus/GettyImages; p. 8 (C): Tpopova/iStock/Getty Images Plus/GettyImages; p. 8 (CR): Creative Crop/DigitalVision/GettyImages; p. 8 (BR): Betsie Van Der Meer/Taxi/GettyImages; p. 9 (TR): michaeljung/iStock/Getty Images Plus/GettyImages; p. 9 (B): Milk & Honey Creative/Stockbyte/GettyImages; p. 13: Martin Barraud/OJO Images/GettyImages; p. 14 (TL): Lumina Images/Blend Images/GettyImages; p. 14 (TR): Elyse Lewin/Photographer's Choice/GettyImages; p. 14 (BL): Fabrice LEROUGE/ONOKY/GettyImages; p. 14 (BR): Susan Chiang/iStock/Getty Images Plus/GettyImages; p. 15 (TL): franckreporter/E+/GettyImages; p. 15 (TR): AWL Images/AWL Images/GettyImages; p. 15 (CL): Image Source/Image Source/GettyImages; p. 15 (CR): Matthias Tunger/Photolibrary/GettyImages; p. 15 (BL): MATTES RenÃ©/hemis.fr/hemis.fr/GettyImages; p. 15 (BR): Luis Davilla/Photolibrary/GettyImages; p. 16: Bruce Glikas/FilmMagic/GettyImages; p. 17 (TL): Digital Vision/Digital Vision/GettyImages; p. 17 (CL): Thomas Barwick/Iconica/GettyImages; p. 17 (C): skynesher/E+/GettyImages; p. 17 (BC): Hans Neleman/The Image Bank/GettyImages; p. 17 (BL): RunPhoto/Photodisc/GettyImages; p. 17 (CR): Portra Images/Taxi/GettyImages; p. 17 (BR): Terry Vine/Blend Images/GettyImages; p. 18: Jupiterimages/Stockbyte/GettyImages; p. 20: Hero Images/Hero Images/GettyImages; p. 22 (TL): Gabriela Tulian/Moment/GettyImages; p. 22 (TR): James A. Guilliam/Photolibrary/GettyImages; p. 22 (CL): Stuart Stevenson photography/Moment/GettyImages; p. 22 (CR): Cultura RM Exclusive/Stephen Lux/Cultura Exclusive/GettyImages; p. 22 (BL): Robert Daly/Caiaimage/GettyImages; p. 22 (BR): noelbesuzzi/RooM/GettyImages; p. 24 (TL): Tim Robberts/Taxi/GettyImages; p. 24 (TR): Jan Scherders/Blend Images/GettyImages; p. 24 (BL): Chris Whitehead/Cultura/GettyImages; p. 24 (BR): A J James/Photodisc/GettyImages; p. 26: Paul Bradbury/Caiaimage/GettyImages; p. 27 (TL): Caiaimage/Trevor Adeline/Caiaimage/GettyImages; p. 27 (TC): Hero Images/Hero Images/GettyImages; p. 27 (TR): Westend61//GettyImages; p. 27 (CL): Susan Chiang/E+/GettyImages; p. 27 (C): shapecharge/E+/GettyImages; p. 27 (CR): Image Source/Image Source/GettyImages; p. 27 (BL): Henrik Sorensen/Iconica/GettyImages; p. 27 (BC): Hero Images/Hero Images/GettyImages; p. 27 (BR): Dougal Waters/DigitalVision/GettyImages; p. 28 (Ex 6.1): Hoxton/Tom Merton/Hoxton/GettyImages; p. 28 (Ex 6.2): Mike Harrington/The Image Bank/GettyImages; p. 28 (Ex 6.3): Alexander Rhind/Stone/GettyImages; p. 28 (Ex 6.4): Vico Collective/Alin Dragulin/Blend Images/GettyImages; p. 28 (Ex 6.5): Leonardo Patrizi/E+/GettyImages; p. 28 (Ex 6.6): JGI/Tom Grill/Blend Images/GettyImages; p. 28 (Ex 6.7): elenaleonova/iStock/Getty Images Plus/GettyImages; p. 28 (Ex 6.8): Thomas Barwick/Iconica/GettyImages; p. 30: Tetra Images/Tetra Images/GettyImages; p. 31 (TL): Caiaimage/Sam Edwards/Caiaimage/GettyImages; p. 31 (TR): Shestock/Blend Images/GettyImages; p. 31 (C): Marc Romanelli/Blend Images/GettyImages; p. 32: Dave & Les Jacobs/Blend Images/Getty Images Plus/GettyImages; p. 33: Dan Porges/Photolibrary/GettyImages; p. 33: Sam Edwards/Caiaimage/GettyImages; p. 34: Hero Images/Hero Images/GettyImages; p. 35: Hero Images/Hero Images/GettyImages; p. 36: XiXinXing/XiXinXing/GettyImages; p. 38: Mint Images - Tim Robbins/Mint Images RF/GettyImages; p. 40 (T): Klaus Tiedge/Blend Images/GettyImages; p. 40 (B): nwinter/iStock/Getty Images Plus/GettyImages; p. 43 (Ex 1a): Daniel Allan/Photographer's Choice/GettyImages; p. 43 (Ex 1b): Gary John Norman/Iconica/GettyImages; p. 43 (Ex 1c): Paul Bradbury/Caiaimage/GettyImages; p. 43 (Ex 1d): Dave and Les Jacobs/Lloyd Dobbie/Blend Images/GettyImages; p. 43 (Ex 1e): Hero Images/Hero Images/GettyImages; p. 43 (Ex 1f): BJI/Blue Jean Images/GettyImages; p. 43 (Ex 1g): XiXinXing/GettyImages; p. 43 (Ex 1h): Phil Boorman/Cultura/GettyImages; p. 43 (Ex 1i): Gary John Norman/The Image Bank/GettyImages; p. 43 (Ex 1j): Cultura RM Exclusive/yellowdog/Cultura Exclusive/GettyImages; p. 44 (Ex 2.1): Portra Images/Taxi/GettyImages; p. 44 (Ex 2.2): Paper Boat Creative/DigitalVision/GettyImages; p. 44 (Ex 2.3): Monty Rakusen/Cultura/GettyImages; p. 44 (Ex 2.4): Hero Images/Stone/GettyImages; p. 44 (Ex 2.5): diego_cervo/iStock/Getty Images Plus/GettyImages; p. 44 (Ex 2.6): Caiaimage/Robert Daly/OJO+/GettyImages; p. 45 (TL): Jetta Productions/Iconica/GettyImages; p. 45 (TR): Dana Neely/Stone/GettyImages; p. 45 (BL): Rob Daly/OJO Images/GettyImages; p. 45 (BR): vgajic/E+/GettyImages; p. 46 (T): Hero Images/Hero Images/GettyImages; p. 46 (B): zoranm/E+/GettyImages; p. 47 (T): HAYKIRDI/iStock/Getty Images Plus/GettyImages; p. 47 (B): onepony/iStock/Getty Images Plus/GettyImages; p. 48 (Ex 6.1): Klaus Vedfelt/Taxi/GettyImages; p. 48 (Ex 6.2): Caiaimage/Sam Edwards/Caiaimage/GettyImages; p. 48 (Ex 6.3): Inti St Clair/Blend Images/GettyImages; p. 48 (Ex 6.4): Monty Rakusen/Cultura/GettyImages; p. 48 (Ex 6.5): JGI/Tom Grill/Blend Images/GettyImages; p. 48 (Ex 6.6): Caiaimage/Tom Merton/Caiaimage/GettyImages; p. 49 (Ex 1.1): Rosemary Calvert/Photographer's Choice/GettyImages; p. 49 (Ex 1.2): Bruno Crescia Photography Inc/First Light/GettyImages; p. 49 (Ex 1.3): Roger Dixon/Dorling Kindersley/GettyImages; p. 49 (Ex 1.4): Alexander Bedrin/iStock/Getty Images Plus/GettyImages; p. 49 (Ex 1.5): Kaan Ates/iStock/Getty Images Plus/GettyImages; p. 49 (Ex 1.6): David Marsden/Photolibrary/GettyImages; p. 49 (Ex 1.7): RedHelga/E+/GettyImages; p. 49 (Ex 1.8): rimglow/iStock/Getty Images Plus/GettyImages; p. 49 (Ex 1.9): Suwanmanee99/iStock/Getty Images Plus/GettyImages; p. 49 (Ex 1.10): Creative Crop/DigitalVision/GettyImages; p. 49 (Ex 1.11): Dorling Kindersley/Dorling Kindersley/GettyImages; p. 49 (Ex 1.12): mm88/iStock/Getty Images Plus/GettyImages; p. 49 (Ex 1.13): kbwills/iStock/Getty Images Plus/GettyImages; p. 49 (Ex 1.14): Steve Wisbauer/Photolibrary/GettyImages; p. 49 (Ex 1.15): Tomas_Mina/iStock/Getty Images Plus/GettyImages; p. 49 (Ex 1.16): Freila/iStock/Getty Images Plus/GettyImages; p. 49 (Ex 1.17): Paul Poplis/Photolibrary/GettyImages; p. 49 (Ex 1.18): Dorling Kindersley/Dorling Kindersley/GettyImages; p. 49 (Ex 1.19): Science Photo Library/Science Photo Library/GettyImages; p. 49 (Ex 1.20): Gary Sergraves/Dorling Kindersley/GettyImages; p. 50 (Ex 2.1): Dave King Dorling Kindersley/Dorling Kindersley/GettyImages; p. 50 (Ex 2.2): fcafotodigital/E+/GettyImages; p. 50 (Ex 2.3): Susan Trigg/E+/GettyImages; p. 50 (Ex 2.4): Davies and Starr/The Image Bank/GettyImages; p. 50 (Ex 2.5): Kai Schwabe/StockFood Creative/GettyImages; p. 50 (Ex 2.6): Kevin Summers/Photographer's Choice/GettyImages; p. 50 (Ex 3.1): 109508Liane Riss/GettyImages; p. 51 (T): Digital Vision/Photodisc/GettyImages; p. 51 (B): Lisa Hubbard/Photolibrary/GettyImages; p. 53 (T): MIXA/GettyImages; p. 53 (B): Tom Grill/The Image Bank/GettyImages; p. 54: Jake Curtis/Iconica/GettyImages; p. 55 (Ex 1a): Shell_114/iStock/Getty Images Plus/GettyImages; p. 55 (Ex 1b): C Squared Studios/Photodisc/GettyImages; p. 55 (Ex 1c): Image Source/ Image Source/GettyImages; p. 55 (Ex 1d): inxti/iStock/Getty Images Plus/GettyImages; p. 55 (Ex 1e): skodonnell/E+/GettyImages; p. 55 (Ex 1f): by_nicholas/E+/GettyImages; p. 55 (Ex 1g): koosen/iStock/Getty Images Plus/GettyImages; p. 55 (Ex 1h): Creativ Studio Heinemann/GettyImages; p. 55 (Ex 1i): Lazi & Mellenthin/GettyImages; p. 55 (Ex 1j): stockbymh/iStock/Getty Images Plus/GettyImages; p. 56 (T): John P Kelly/The Image Bank/GettyImages; p. 56 (B): Nicola Tree/The Image Bank/GettyImages; p. 59 (T): Zave Smith/Photolibrary/GettyImages; p. 59 (C): XiXinXing/GettyImages; p. 59 (B): Steve Mcsweeny/Moment/GettyImages; p. 60: Dougal Waters/Taxi/GettyImages; p. 61 (spring): Maria Viola/EyeEm/EyeEm/GettyImages; p. 61 (summer): Dothan Nareswari/EyeEm/EyeEm/GettyImages; p. 61 (fall): Plattform/GettyImages; p. 61 (winter): juliannafunk/iStock/Getty Images Plus/GettyImages; p. 64 (T): VisitBritain/Britain On View/GettyImages; p. 64 (B): GM Visuals/Blend Images/GettyImages; p. 65 (Ex 6.1): T.T./Taxi/GettyImages; p. 65 (Ex 6.2): Jade/Blend Images/GettyImages; p. 65 (Ex 6.3): Hero Images/Hero Images/GettyImages; p. 65 (Ex 6.4): Todor Tsvetkov/E+/GettyImages; p. 65 (Ex 6.5): Hero Images/Hero Images/GettyImages; p. 65 (Ex 6.6): Lucia Lambriex/Taxi/GettyImages; p. 65 (Ex 6.7): Er Creatives Services Ltd/Iconica/GettyImages; p. 65 (Ex 6.8): Susan Chiang/E+/GettyImages; p. 65 (Ex 6.9): PhotoAlto/Teo Lannie/PhotoAlto Agency RF Collections/GettyImages; p. 66 (TL): Maximilian Stock Ltd/Photolibrary/GettyImages; p. 66 (TR): Grafner/iStock/Getty Images Plus/GettyImages; p. 66 (CL): Freek Gout/EyeEm/EyeEm/GettyImages; p. 66 (CR): Vstock LLC/GettyImages; p. 66 (BL): mashabuba/E+/GettyImages; p. 66 (BR): Tom Merton/Caiaimage/GettyImages; p. 70: Nicolas McComber/iStock/Getty Images Plus/GettyImages; p. 73 (bank): Keith Brofsky/Photodisc/GettyImages; p. 73 (coffee shop): Jake Curtis/Iconica/GettyImages; p. 73 (petrol pump): David Lees/Taxi/GettyImages; p. 73 (book store): Jetta Productions/The Image Bank/GettyImages; p. 73 (clothing store): Blend Images - Erik Isakson/Brand X Pictures/GettyImages; p. 73 (post office): Matt Cardy/Stringer/Getty Images Europe/GettyImages; p. 73 (supermarket): Johner Images/GettyImages; p. 73 (pharmacy): Caiaimage/Rafal Rodzoch/Caiaimage/GettyImages; p. 76: Leonardo Patrizi/E+/GettyImages; p. 79 (Ex 1.1): Y.Nakajima/un/ANYONE/amana images/GettyImages; p. 79 (Ex 1.2): John Lund/Marc Romanelli/Blend Images/GettyImages; p. 79 (Ex 1.3): Maskot/Maskot/GettyImages; p. 79 (Ex 1.4): UniversalImagesGroup/Universal Images Group/GettyImages; p. 79 (Ex 1.5): ullstein bild/ullstein bild/GettyImages; p. 79 (Ex 1.6): Geography Photos/Universal Images Group/GettyImages; p. 79 (Ex 1.7): CommerceandCultureAgency/The Image Bank/GettyImages; p. 79 (Ex 1.8): Jose Luis Pelaez Inc/Blend Images/GettyImages; p. 80 (Alisha): Dougal Waters/DigitalVision/GettyImages; p. 80 (Kim): Hero Images/Hero Images/GettyImages; p. 82: ullstein bild/ullstein bild/GettyImages; p. 83: Tetra Images - Chris Hackett/Brand X Pictures/GettyImages; p. 85: Westend61/GettyImages; p. 86 (T): Walter Bibikow/AWL Images/GettyImages; p. 86 (C): Michele Falzone/Photolibrary/GettyImages; p. 86 (B): Takashi Yagihashi/amana images/GettyImages; p. 87 (Ex 3.1): Photos.com/PHOTOS.com>>/Getty Images Plus/GettyImages; p. 87 (Ex 3.2): Piero Pomponi/Hulton Archive/GettyImages; p. 87 (Ex 3.3): KMazur/WireImage/GettyImages; p. 87 (Ex 3.4): Nancy R. Schiff/Hulton Archive/GettyImages; p. 87 (Ex 3.5): API/Gamma-Rapho/GettyImages; p. 87 (Ex 3.6): Jack Mitchell/Archive Photos/GettyImages; p. 88: Christopher Futcher/E+/GettyImages; p. 89: Mel Melcon/Los Angeles Times/GettyImages; p. 90 (T): Kevin Dodge/Blend Images/GettyImages; p. 90 (B): Thomas Barwick/Taxi/GettyImages; p. 91 (L): Stockbyte/Stockbyte/GettyImages; p. 91 (R): nyul/iStock/Getty Images Plus/GettyImages; p. 93: freemixer/iStock/Getty Images Plus/GettyImages; p. 94: Echo/Cultura/GettyImages; p. 95: Stockbyte/Stockbyte/GettyImages; p. 96 (T): Thanks for viewing! www.johnsteelephoto.com/Moment/GettyImages; p. 96 (B): Giordano Cipriani/The Image Bank/GettyImages.

1 What's your name?

1 Complete the conversations. Use the names in the box.

☐ John   ☐ Mr. Garcia   ☐ Ms. Baker   ☑ Nancy

Hi, ____Nancy____.

Hello, _____.

It's nice to meet you, _____.

Nice to meet you, too, _____.

2 Complete the conversations. Use *my*, *your*, *his*, or *her*.

1. A: Hi. What's _____your_____ name?

   B: _____ name is Lisa. And what's _____ name?

   A: _____ name is James.

2. A: What's _____ name?

   B: _____ name is Michael.

   A: And what's _____ name?

   B: _____ name is Susan.

3 Complete the conversations.

1. **A:** Hello, _____Mr._____ Wilson.
   B: _____ morning, David.
      _____ are you?
   A: _____ OK, thank you.

2. **A:** Hi. How are _____ , Mrs. Turner?
   B: I'm just _____ , thank you. How about _____ , _____ Smith?
   A: Pretty _____ , thanks.

3. **A:** How's it _____ , Ken?
   B: Great. _____ are you doing?
   A: Pretty good.

4 Choose the correct responses.

1. A: Hi, Tony.

   B: _____ Hello. _____
- Hello.
- It's nice to meet you.

2. A: My name is Ellen Miller.

   B: _____
- It's Williams.
- I'm Rob Williams.

3. A: Hello, Carol. How's it going?

   B: _____
- Fine, thanks.
- Nice to meet you, too.

4. A: How do you spell your last name?

   B: _____
- R-O-G-E-R-S.
- It's Rogers.

5. A: I'm Rich Martinez.

   B: _____
- Nice to meet you, too.
- It's nice to meet you.

5 Spell the numbers.

1. 2 _____ two _____

2. 3 _____

3. 8 _____

4. 1 _____

5. 7 _____

6. 10 _____

7. 5 _____

8. 6 _____

9. 0 _____

10. 9 _____

11. 4 _____

6 Write the telephone numbers and email addresses.

1. two-one-two, five-five-five, six-one-one-five   <u>212-555-6115</u>

2. A-M-Y dash L-O-P-E-Z eight-two at C-U-P dot O-R-G   <u>amy-lopez82@cup.org</u>

3. six-oh-four, five-five-five, four-seven-three-one   _____

4. nine-four-nine, five-five-five, three-eight-oh-two   _____

5. B-R-I-A-N dot J-O-H-N-S-O-N zero-three-nine at C-U-P dot O-R-G   _____

6. seven-seven-three, five-five-five, one-seven-seven-nine   _____

7. M-A-R-I-A-B-R-A-D-Y underscore seven at C-U-P dot O-R-G   _____

8. T-I-N-A dash F-O-X underscore nine-five-two at C-U-P dot O-R-G   _____

7 Complete the conversations. Write 'm, 're, or 's.

1. **A:** What <u>'s</u> your name?

   B: I _____ Momoko Sato.

   A: It _____ nice to meet you, Momoko.

2. **A:** Hello. I _____ Josh Brown. I _____ in your English class.

   B: Yes, and you _____ in my math class, too.

3. **A:** What _____ his name?

   B: It _____ Chris Allen.

   A: He _____ in our English class.

   B: You _____ right!

8 Complete the conversations. Use the words in the box.

☐ am ☐ he's ☐ I'm not ☐ it's ☐ you
☐ are ☐ I'm ☐ is ☑ me ☐ you're

1. **Amy:** Excuse _____me_____ . Are
   _____ Alex Walker?

   Carlos: No, _____ .
   _____ over there.

   Amy: Oh, _____ sorry.

2. **Amy:** Excuse me. _____ you
   Alex Walker?

   Alex: Yes, I _____ .

   Amy: Hi, Alex. My name _____
   Amy Clark.

   Alex: Oh, _____ in my English class.

   Amy: That's right. _____ nice to meet you.

   Alex: Nice to meet you, too.

9 Complete the conversation. Use the questions in the box.

☐ What's your name? ☐ And what's your email address?
☐ And how do you spell your last name? ☐ What's your phone number?
☑ Are you Andrea Nelson? ☐ How do you spell your first name?

A: Hi. <u>Are you Andrea Nelson?</u> _____

B: No, I'm not.

A: Oh, I'm sorry. _____

B: Kerry Moore.

A: _____

B: K-E-R-R-Y.

A: _____

B: M-O-O-R-E.

A: _____

B: It's 618-555-7120.

A: _____

B: It's kmoore19@cup.org.

10 Hello and good-bye!

A Complete the conversations. Use the words in parentheses.

1. A: _Hi._

(Hi. / Excuse me.) How are you?

B: I'm fine, thanks.

2. A: _____

(Hello. / Good-bye.)

B: See you tomorrow.

3. A: _____

(Excuse me. / Thank you.) Are you
Min-ji Park?

B: Yes, I am. It's nice to meet you.

4. A: _____

(Good evening. / Good night.)

B: Hello.

B Match the pictures with the conversations in part A.

a. _1_

b. _____

c. _____

d. _____

2 Where are my keys?

1 What are these things?

A What's in the picture? Write the things.

1. <u>a backpack</u>
2. _____
3. _____
4. _____
5. _____
6. _____
7. _____
8. _____

B What's in the picture? Write sentences.

1. <u>This is a backpack.</u>
2. _____
3. _____
4. _____
5. _____
6. _____
7. _____
8. _____

2 Complete the chart with the words in the box.

✓ doors	☐ purses	☐ desks	☐ energy bars
✓ books	☐ umbrellas	☐ hairbrushes	☐ tablets
✓ quizzes	☐ laptops	☐ keys	☐ boxes

/z/		/s/		/ɪz/	
doors	_____	books	_____	quizzes	_____
_____	_____	_____	_____	_____	_____

3 Complete the questions with *this* or *these*. Then answer the questions.

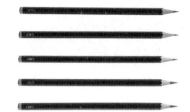

1. **A:** What's _____this_____ ?
   B: _It's a cell phone._____

2. **A:** What's _____ ?
   B: _____

3. **A:** What are _____ ?
   B: _____

4. **A:** What are _____ ?
   B: _____

5. **A:** What are _____ ?
   B: _____

6. **A:** What's _____ ?
   B: _____

4 Complete the conversation. Use the words in the box.

| ☐ a | ☐ 's | ☐ this | ☐ they | ☐ you |
| ☐ an | ☑ it's | ☐ these | ☐ they're | ☐ you're |

Clara: Wow! What's this?

Kevin: _____It's_____ a purse.

Clara: Oh, cool. Thank _____ , Kevin.

Kevin: _____ welcome.

Eva: Now open _____ box.

Clara: OK. What _____ this?

Eva: It's _____ tablet case.

Clara: Oh, thank you, Eva. And what are _____ ?

Eva: _____ 're sunglasses.

Clara: Thanks! _____ great!

Laura: Open this, too!

Clara: Oh, it's _____ umbrella. Thanks, Laura!

5 Complete the conversations. Use the answers in the box.

| ☐ Yes, I am. | ☐ Yes, it is. | ☐ Yes, they are. | ☐ It's |
| ☐ No, I'm not. | ☐ No, it's not. | ☑ No, they're not. | ☐ They're |

1. **A:** Are these your books?

   B: _No, they're not._ My books are in my bag.

2. **A:** Excuse me. Is this the math class?

   B: _____ And I'm your teacher.

3. **A:** Is my purse on the chair?

   B: _____ It's under the table.

4. **A:** Where's my laptop?

   B: _____ in your backpack.

5. **A:** Where are your glasses?

   B: _____ in my purse.

6. **A:** Hi. Are you in my math class?

   B: _____ And I'm in your English class, too!

7. **A:** Are these your keys?

   B: _____ Thank you.

8. **A:** Excuse me. Are you Min-soo Cho?

   B: _____ My name is Jin-ho Han. Min-soo isn't in this class.

6 Complete the conversations.

1. A: Oh no! Where ____is____ my tablet?

  B: Is _____ in your backpack?

  A: No, it's _____ .

  B: Hmm. _____ it under your math book?

  A: Yes, it is! Thank you!

2. A: _____ this my cell phone?

  B: No, _____ not. It's my cell phone.

  A: Sorry. _____ is my cell phone?

  B: Is _____ in your purse?

  A: Oh, yes, it _____ . Thanks.

3. A: Where _____ my keys?

  B: Are _____ in your pocket?

  A: No, they're _____ .

  B: _____ they on the table?

  A: Hmm. Yes, _____ are. Thanks.

4. A: _____ my notebook in your backpack?

  B: No, _____ not. Sorry.

  A: Hmm. _____ is my notebook?

  B: _____ it behind your laptop?

  A: Let me see. Yes, it _____ . Thank you!

7 Answer the questions. Use your own information.

1. Are you a teacher?

No, I'm not. I'm a student.

2. Is your name Akiko Nakayama?

_____

3. Is your workbook on your desk?

_____

4. Is your phone number 806-555-0219?

_____

5. Are you in a math class?

_____

8 Complete the sentences. Use the prepositions in the box.

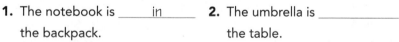

☐ behind   ☑ in   ☐ in front of   ☐ next to   ☐ on   ☐ under

1. The notebook is ____in____ the backpack.

2. The umbrella is _____ the table.

3. The keys are _____ the wallet.

4. The pen is _____ the purse.

5. The laptop is _____ the desk.

6. The wastebasket is _____ the chair.

9 Where are these things?

A Look at the picture. Write questions and answers about the things in parentheses.

1. **A:** <u>Where is the backpack?</u>   (backpack)

   B: <u>It's next to the table.</u>

2. **A:** _____ (books)

   B: _____

3. **A:** _____ (cell phone)

   B: _____

4. **A:** _____ (pens)

   B: _____

5. **A:** _____ (purse)

   B: _____

6. **A:** _____ (sunglasses)

   B: _____

B Write two more questions and answers about the picture.

1. **A:** _____

   B: _____

2. **A:** _____

   B: _____

3 Where are you from?

1 Cities and countries

A Complete the chart with the languages and nationalities in the box.

☐ Arabic   ☐ Japanese
☐ Argentine   ☐ Korean
☑ Brazilian   ☑ Portuguese
☐ Canadian   ☐ South Korean
☐ Colombian   ☐ Spanish
☐ Egyptian   ☐ Spanish
☐ English   ☐ Turkish
☐ French   ☐ Turkish
☐ Japanese

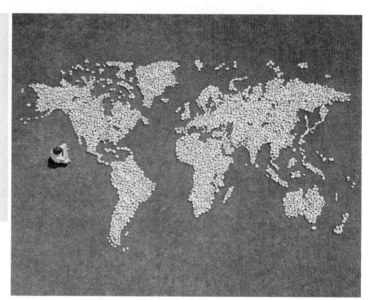

Countries	Nationalities	Languages
Brazil	Brazilian	Portuguese
Colombia		
South Korea		
Canada		
Turkey		
Argentina		
Japan		
Egypt		

B Where are these cities? Complete the sentences with the countries in part A.

1. Istanbul and Ankara _are in Turkey._
2. Bogotá _____
3. Tokyo _____
4. São Paulo and Rio de Janeiro _____
5. Seoul and Daejeon _____
6. Buenos Aires _____
7. Vancouver and Ottawa _____
8. Cairo _____

2 **Complete the conversations with** *am, 'm, are, 're, is,* **or** *'s.*

1. **A:** _____Are_____ you and your family from New Zealand?

   B: No, we _____ not.
   We _____ from Australia.

   A: Oh, so you _____ Australian.

   B: Yes, I _____ . I _____ from Melbourne.

2. **A:** _____ Brazil in Central America?

   B: No, it _____ not. It _____ in South America.

   A: Oh. _____ we from Brazil, Dad?

   B: Yes, we _____ . We _____ from Brazil originally, but we _____ here in the U.S. now.

3. **A:** _____ this your wallet?

   B: Yes, it _____ . Thanks.

   A: And _____ these your sunglasses?

   B: Yes, they _____ .

   A: Well, they _____ very nice sunglasses.

   B: Thank you!

4. **A:** _____ your English teacher from the U.S.?

   B: No, she _____ not.
   She _____ from Canada. Montreal, Canada.

   A: _____ English her first language?

   B: No, it _____ not. Her first language _____ French.

3 **Answer the questions.**

1. A: Are they from Colombia?

   B: No, they're not. They're from Brazil.

2. A: Is she from India?

   B: _____

3. A: Is she from Canada?

   B: _____

4. A: Are they in Mexico?

   B: _____

5. A: Is he in Bangkok?

   B: _____

6. A: Are they in Egypt?

   B: _____

4 Spell the numbers.

1. 14 _____fourteen_____   6. 102 _____

2. 40 _____   7. 11 _____

3. 60 _____   8. 30 _____

4. 13 _____   9. 18 _____

5. 27 _____   10. 80 _____

5 Complete the conversations with the correct responses.

1. **A:** Where are they from?

   B: _She's from the U.K., and he's from the U.S._

   • She's Emily Blunt, and he's John Krasinski.

   • She's from the U.K., and he's from the U.S.

2. **A:** Is your first language English?

   B: _____

   • No, it's Japan.

   • No, it's Japanese.

3. **A:** What are they like?

   B: _____

   • They're very serious.

   • They're in Hong Kong.

4. **A:** Who's that?

   B: _____

   • He's the new math teacher.

   • It's my new tablet.

5. **A:** Where are Rahul and his family?

   B: _____

   • They're in the U.S. now.

   • They're from Mumbai.

6. **A:** How old is he now?

   B: _____

   • It's twenty-eight.

   • He's twenty-eight.

7. **A:** What's Marrakech like?

   B: _____

   • It's in Morocco.

   • It's very interesting.

6 Descriptions

A Write sentences about the people in the pictures. Use the words in the box.

☐ funny	☐ serious	☐ talkative
☐ heavy	☐ short	☐ tall
☐ kind	☑ shy	☐ thin

1. Julia is _____ shy _____ .

2. Mark and Carlos are
_____ .

3. Brian is _____
and Owen is _____ .

4. Daniel is _____ .

5. Mariko is _____
and Ben is _____ .

6. Ginny is _____ .

7. Dr. Lopez is _____ .

B Answer the questions.

1. Is Ben tall? _Yes, he is._____

2. Is Ginny serious? _____

3. Is Owen thin? _____

4. Is Julia young? _____

5. Are Mark and Carlos male? _____

6. Is Dr. Lopez old? _____

7. Are you kind? _____

8. Are you shy? _____

7 Complete the conversations. Use the words in the boxes.

☐ her   ☐ not   ☑ what's
☐ is   ☐ she's   ☐ where

1. **A:** Annette, _____what's_____ your best friend like?
   B: _____ very nice. _____
   name is Valentina. I call her Tina.
   A: _____ is she from? _____
   she from Spain?
   B: No, she's _____ . She's from Italy.

☐ are   ☐ my   ☐ we're
☐ her   ☐ we   ☐ what's

2. **A:** Toshi, are you and Naomi from Japan?
   B: Yes, _____ are. _____ from
   Osaka.
   A: _____ your first language?
   B: _____ first language is Japanese,
   but Naomi's first language is English.
   _____ parents _____ from
   New York originally.

8 Answer the questions. Use your own information.

1. Where are you from?

   _____

2. What's your first language?

   _____

3. How are you today?

   _____

4. Where is your teacher from?

   _____

5. What is your teacher like?

   _____

6. What are you like?

   _____

4 Is this coat yours?

1 **Label the clothes. Use the words in the box.**

☐ belt	☐ high heels	☐ skirt	☐ T-shirt	☐ blouse
✓ jacket	☐ sneakers	☐ cap	☐ shorts	☐ socks

SPORTS CLUB

1. _____jacket_____

2. _____

3. _____

4. _____

5. _____

6. _____

7. _____

8. _____

9. _____

10. _____

2 What clothes don't belong? Check (✓) the things.

For work	For home	For cold weather	For warm weather
☐ shirt	☐ T-shirt	☐ boots	☐ swimsuit
✓ shorts	☐ shorts	☐ scarf	☐ T-shirt
☐ tie	☐ suit	☐ shorts	☐ boots
☐ belt	☐ dress	☐ pants	☐ sneakers
✓ swimsuit	☐ jeans	☐ sweater	☐ shorts
☐ shoes	☐ pajamas	☐ gloves	☐ sweater
☐ jacket	☐ coat	☐ T-shirt	☐ cap

3 What things in your classroom are these colors? Write sentences.

beige	brown	gray	light blue	pink	red	yellow
black	dark blue	green	orange	purple	white	

1. My desk is brown. _____ (brown)
2. Celia's bag is purple. _____ (purple)
3. _____ (gray)
4. _____ (white)
5. _____ (red)
6. _____ (green)
7. _____ (black)
8. _____
9. _____
10. _____

4 Whose clothes are these?

Max

Maya

Lisa

A Complete the conversations.

1. A: Whose <u>scarf is this</u> ?
   B: <u>It's Maya's</u> .

2. A: Whose _____ ?
   B: _____ .

3. A: Whose _____ ?
   B: _____ .

4. A: Whose _____ ?
   B: _____ .

5. A: Whose _____ ?
   B: _____ .

6. A: Whose _____ ?
   B: _____ .

B Complete the conversations with the correct words in parentheses.

1. A: _____Whose_____ (Whose / His) T-shirt is this? Is it Ayumi's?

   B: No, it's not _____ (her / hers). It's _____ (my / mine).

2. A: Are these _____ (your / yours) jeans?

   B: No, they aren't _____ (my / mine) jeans. Let's ask Mohammed. I think they're
   _____ (his / he's).

3. A: Are these Stephanie's and Jennifer's socks?

   B: No, they aren't _____ (their / theirs). They're _____ (your / yours).

   A: I don't think so. These socks are white, and _____ (my / mine) are blue.

5 **What season is it? How is the weather? Write two sentences about each picture.**

1. It's fall.

It's very windy.

2. _____

_____

3. _____

_____

4. _____

_____

5. _____

_____

6. _____

_____

6 Waiting for the bus

A Write sentences. Use the words in parentheses.

Steven   Carolina   Sung-min   Allison   Liz   Pablo

1. _Pablo is wearing a tie._ (tie)
2. _Steven and Carolina are wearing boots._ (boots)
3. _____ (T-shirt)
4. _____ (skirt)
5. _____ (dress)
6. _____ (sneakers)
7. _____ (scarf)
8. _____ (hats)

B Correct the false sentences.

1. Sung-min is wearing jeans.

   No, he isn't. / No, he's not. He's wearing shorts.

2. Liz and Pablo are wearing raincoats.

   _____

3. Carolina is wearing a skirt.

   _____

4. Allison is wearing pajamas.

   _____

5. Carolina and Liz are wearing T-shirts.

   _____

6. Steven and Pablo are wearing shorts.

   _____

7 Complete the sentences.

1. My name's Jamie. I'm wearing_____
a T-shirt and shorts. I _____
sneakers, too. It _____
raining, but I _____
a raincoat.

2. It's winter, so Maria _____
high heels – she _____
boots. She _____ a scarf,
but she _____ a hat.

3. It's very sunny today, so Richard and Meg
_____ sunglasses. It's
hot, so Richard _____
shorts and Meg _____
light pants. They _____
sweaters.

4. Ed _____ a suit.
He _____ a scarf,
but he _____ a tie.
He _____ shoes and
socks. It's very windy.

8 Complete these sentences with *and, but,* or *so.*

1. He's wearing jeans and sneakers, _____and_____ he's wearing a T-shirt.

2. It's very cold outside, _____ I'm not wearing a coat.

3. Her skirt is blue, _____ her blouse is blue, too.

4. It's raining, _____ I need an umbrella.

5. He's wearing an expensive suit, _____ he's wearing sneakers.

6. It's summer and it's very sunny, _____ it's hot.

1 Write each sentence a different way.

1. It's midnight.   It's twelve o'clock at night.
2. It's 7:00 A.M.   _____
3. It's 2:45 P.M.   _____
4. It's 9:20 A.M.   _____
5. It's 6:15 P.M.   _____
6. It's 11:00 P.M.   _____
7. It's 3:30 A.M.   _____
8. It's 12:00 P.M.   _____

2 What time is it in each city? Write the time in two different ways.

1. It's 10:00 A.M. in Seattle.
   It's ten o'clock in the morning.
2. _____
   _____
3. _____
   _____
4. _____
   _____
5. _____
   _____
6. _____
   _____

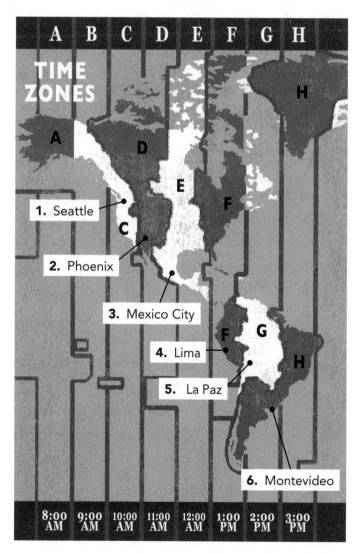

A B C D E F G H

TIME ZONES

A D E F H

1. Seattle
C
2. Phoenix
3. Mexico City
F G
4. Lima
5. La Paz
H
6. Montevideo

| 8:00 AM | 9:00 AM | 10:00 AM | 11:00 AM | 12:00 AM | 1:00 PM | 2:00 PM | 3:00 PM |

3 What time is it? Use the sentences in the box.

- ☑ It's a quarter after five.
- ☐ It's a quarter to two.
- ☐ It's four-thirty.
- ☐ It's nine-oh-three.
- ☐ It's ten after eight.
- ☐ It's twelve o'clock.

1. It's a quarter after five.   **2.** _____   **3.** _____

4. _____   **5.** _____   **6.** _____

4 Complete the sentences. Write each time a different way.

1. It's six in the morning. It's six _____A.M._____
2. It's 10:00 P.M. It's ten at _____ .
3. It's 5:15. It's five- _____ .
4. It's 7:00 P.M. It's seven in the _____ .
5. It's 4:30. It's four- _____ .
6. It's 8:00 A.M. It's eight in the _____ .
7. It's twelve P.M. It's _____ .
8. It's 2:00 P.M. It's two in the _____ .
9. It's twelve A.M. It's _____ .
10. It's 6:45. It's a _____ to seven.
11. It's 11:15. It's a quarter _____ eleven.

5 What are these people doing? Write sentences. Use the words in the box.

☐ call a friend	☑ make coffee	☐ take a walk
☐ drive	☐ ride a bike	☐ watch a movie
☐ have breakfast	☐ shop	☐ work

1. _He's making coffee._

2. _____

3. _____

4. _____

5. _____

6. _____

7. _____

8. _____

9. _____

6 Answer these questions.

1. Is Salma sleeping?

No, she's not. She's studying.

2. Are Richard and Laura playing tennis?

No, they're not. They're dancing.

3. Is Charles visiting friends?

_____

4. Is Jerry eating dinner?

_____

5. Are Mary and Jennifer checking their messages?

_____

6. Is Carol listening to music?

_____

7. Is Kevin driving?

_____

8. Are the friends watching a movie?

_____

7 **Write questions about these people. Use the words in parentheses.**
Then answer the questions.

1. **A:** _Is Min wearing jeans?_

   (Min / wear jeans)

   B: _No, she's not. She's wearing a dress._

2. **A:** _____

   (Bob / drink soda)

   B: _____

3. **A:** _____

   (Jason and Beth / watch a movie)

   B: _____

4. **A:** _____

   (Adriana / wear jeans)

   B: _____

5. **A:** _____

   (Amy and Gabriela / chat online)

   B: _____

6. **A:** _____

   (Daniel / talk to Adriana)

   B: _____

7. **A:** _____

   (Bob / wear shorts)

   B: _____

8. **A:** _____

   (Min / talk on the phone)

   B: _____

8 Write questions and answers. Use *What* + *doing* and the words in parentheses.

1. **A:** _What is Linda doing?_ (Linda)

   B: _She's checking her messages._ (check her messages)

2. **A:** _What are you and Akira doing?_ (you and Akira)

   B: _We're eating lunch._ (eat lunch)

3. **A:** _____ (Tom and Donna)

   B: _____ (visit friends)

4. **A:** _____ (Sandra)

   B: _____ (get up)

5. **A:** _____ (you and Isabella)

   B: _____ (ride bikes)

6. **A:** _____ (Diego and Patricia)

   B: _____ (work)

7. **A:** _____ (Tim)

   B: _____ (listen to music)

8. **A:** _____ (you)

   B: _____ (study English)

9. **A:** _____ (Sonya and Annie)

   B: _____ (have dinner)

10. **A:** _____ (I)

    B: _____ (finish this exercise)

9 What are you doing? What are your friends doing? Write sentences.

1. _____

_____

2. _____

_____

3. _____

_____

4. _____

_____

5. _____

_____

6. _____

_____

6 I ride my bike to school.

1 Family

A Angela is talking about her family. Complete the sentences with the words in the box.

- ☐ brother
- ☐ husband
- ☐ father
- ☐ sister
- ☑ parents
- ☐ daughters
- ☐ wife
- ☐ mother
- ☐ children
- ☐ son

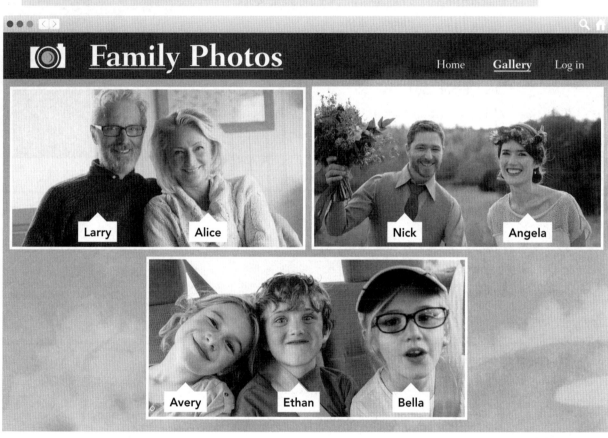

Family Photos   Home   **Gallery**   Log in

Larry   Alice

Nick   Angela

Avery   Ethan   Bella

1. Alice and Larry are my ___parents___ . Alice is my _____ , and Larry is my _____ .

2. Nick is my _____ . I'm his _____ .

3. Ethan, Avery, and Bella are our _____ . Avery and Bella are our _____ , and Ethan is our _____ . Avery is Bella's _____ , and Ethan is her _____ .

B Write four sentences about your family.

1. _____

2. _____

3. _____

4. _____

2 Complete the conversation with the correct words in parentheses.

Christine: So, do you live downtown, Sarah?

Sarah: Yes, I _____live_____ with my brother.
(live / lives)

He _____ an apartment near here.
(have / has)

Christine: Oh, so you _____ to work.
(walk / walks)

Sarah: Actually, I _____ walk to work in
(don't / doesn't)

the morning. I _____ the bus to work,
(take / takes)

and then I _____ home at night.
(walk / walks)

What about you?

Christine: Well, my husband and I _____ a house
(have / has)

in the suburbs now, so I _____ to work.
(drive / drives)

My husband doesn't _____ downtown.
(work / works)

He _____ in the suburbs near our house,
(work / works)

so he _____ to work by bus.
(go / goes)

3 Third-person singular –s endings

A Write the third-person singular forms of these verbs.

1. dance ___dances___
2. do ___does___
3. go _____
4. have _____

5. live _____
6. ride _____
7. sleep _____
8. study _____

9. take _____
10. use _____
11. walk _____
12. watch _____

B Practice the words in part A. Then add them to the chart.

s = /s/	s = /z/	(e)s = /ɪz/	irregular
_____	_____	___dances___	___does___
_____	_____	_____	_____
_____	_____	_____	_____

4 | True or false?

A Are these sentences true for you? Check (✓) True or False.

	True	False
1. I ride the bus to school.	☐	☐
2. I have a car.	☐	☐
3. I live in the suburbs.	☐	☐
4. I have brothers / a brother.	☐	☐
5. I do my homework at the library.	☐	☐
6. I do my homework alone.	☐	☐
7. I live in a house.	☐	☐
8. I have sisters / a sister.	☐	☐
9. I live with my parents.	☐	☐
10. I work in an office.	☐	☐

B Correct the false statements in part A.

I don't ride the bus to school. I ride my bike to school.

_____

_____

_____

_____

_____

_____

_____

_____

_____

_____

_____

_____

_____

_____

5 Write about Daniela's weekly schedule. Use the words in parentheses.

	Monday	Tuesday	Wednesday	Thursday	Friday
7:00 A.M.	get up ————————————————————————→				
8:00 A.M.	go to work ————————————————————→				
9:00 A.M.					
10:00 A.M.					
11:00 A.M.	have lunch ————————————————————→				
12:00 P.M.					
1:00 P.M.					
2:00 P.M.	take a walk ————————————————————→				
3:00 P.M.					
4:00 P.M.					
5:00 P.M.	finish work ————————————————————→				
6:00 P.M.	play basketball	go to class	eat dinner with my family	go to class	watch a movie

1. _She gets up at 7:00 every day._ (7:00)
2. _____ (8:00)
3. _____ (11:00)
4. _____ (2:00)
5. _____ (5:00)
6. _____ (6:00 / Mondays)
7. _____ (6:00 / Tuesdays and Thursdays)
8. _____ (6:00 / Fridays)

6 Write something you do and something you don't do on each day.
Use the phrases in the box or your own information.

check email	exercise	have dinner late	sleep late
drive a car	get up early	play video games	talk on the phone
eat breakfast	go to school	see my friends	watch a movie

1. Monday _I get up early on Mondays. I don't sleep late on Mondays._
2. Tuesday _____
3. Wednesday _____
4. Thursday _____
5. Friday _____
6. Saturday _____
7. Sunday _____

7 Complete these conversations with *at*, *in*, or *on*. (If you don't need a preposition, write Ø.)

1. A: Do you go to bed __Ø__ late __on__ weekends?

B: Yes, I do. I go to bed _____ midnight. But I go to bed _____ early _____ weekdays.

2. A: Do you study _____ the afternoon?

B: No, I study _____ the morning _____ weekends, and I study _____ the evening _____ Mondays and Wednesdays.

3. A: What time do you get up _____ the morning _____ weekdays?

B: I get up _____ 6:00 _____ every day.

4. A: Do you have English class _____ the morning?

B: No, I have English _____ 3:30 _____ the afternoon _____ Tuesdays and Thursdays. _____ Mondays, Wednesdays, and Fridays, our class is _____ 5:00.

8 Write questions to complete the conversations.

1. A: *Do you live alone?*

B: No, I don't live alone. I live with my mom and dad.

2. A: _____

B: Yes, my family and I watch television in the afternoon.

3. A: _____

B: Yes, I get up early on Fridays.

A: _____

B: I get up at 5:30.

4. A: _____

B: No, my sister doesn't drive to work.

A: _____

B: No, she doesn't take the bus. She takes the train.

5. A: _____

B: No, my dad doesn't work on weekends.

A: _____

B: He works on weekdays.

6. A: _____

B: Yes, my mom works in the city. She's a restaurant manager.

A: _____

B: No, she doesn't use public transportation. She drives to work.

7. A: _____

B: Yes, we have a big lunch on Sundays.

A: _____

B: We have lunch at 1:00.

9 Write each sentence a different way. Use the sentences in the box.

☐ He goes to work before noon.
☐ I don't work far from here.
☑ Kimberly is Dan's wife.

☐ She doesn't get up early on Sundays.
☐ We don't live in the suburbs.
☐ We take the bus, the train, or the subway.

1. Dan is Kimberly's husband.

Kimberly is Dan's wife.

2. We have an apartment in the city.

_____

3. We use public transportation.

_____

4. He goes to work in the morning.

_____

5. My office is near here.

_____

6. She sleeps late on Sundays.

_____

10 Answer the questions about your schedule.

1. What do you do on weekdays?

_____

2. What do you do on weekends?

_____

3. What do you do on Friday nights?

_____

4. What do you do on Sunday mornings?

_____

Does it have a view?

1 | Label the parts of the house.

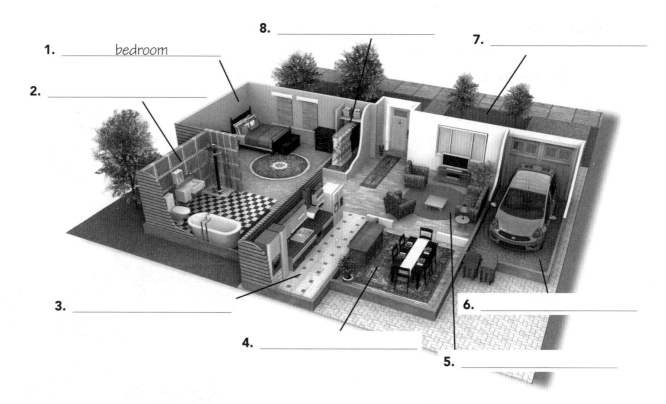

1. _____bedroom_____

2. _____

3. _____

4. _____

5. _____

6. _____

7. _____

8. _____

2 | Complete the conversation. Use the sentences in the box.

☐ No, I don't. I live with my sisters.   ☐ Yes, it has three bedrooms.

☑ No, I live in an apartment.   ☐ Yes, it has a great view of the city.

Ji-hye: Do you live in a house, Fernanda?

Fernanda: _No, I live in an apartment._

Ji-hye: Well, is it very big?

Fernanda: _____

Ji-hye: Does it have a view?

Fernanda: _____

Ji-hye: Oh, that's great! And do you live alone?

Fernanda: _____

3 Complete the conversation with the correct words in parentheses.

Al: _____Do_____ you _____ near here, Brandon?
(Do / Does)   (live / lives)

Brandon: Yes, I _____ . My wife and I _____ on Main Street.
(do / does)   (live / lives)

Al: Oh, do you _____ in an apartment?
(live / lives)

Brandon: No, we _____ . We _____ a house.
(don't / doesn't)   (have / has)

Al: Oh, great! _____ you _____ children?
(Do / Does)   (have / has)

Brandon: No, we _____ .
(don't / doesn't)

But my mother _____ with us.
(live / lives)

Al: Really? Does she do a lot of work at home?

Brandon: Yes, she _____ .
(do / does)

In fact, she _____ dinner every night!
(cook / cooks)

Al: You're lucky! I _____ alone,
(live / lives)

and I _____ my own dinner.
(cook / cooks)

4 Answer these questions with your information. Use short answers.

1. Do you live in a house?   Yes, I do. / No, I don't.
2. Do you have a garage?   _____
3. Do you live with your family?   _____
4. Does your city or town have a park?   _____
5. Does your teacher have a car?   _____
6. Do you and your classmates speak English? _____
7. Do you and your classmates study together? _____
8. Does your classroom have a view?   _____
9. Does your school have a lobby?   _____
10. Does your city or town have a subway?   _____

5 | What furniture do they have?

A Answer the questions about the pictures.

1. A: Do they have a rug?

   B: _Yes, they do._

2. A: Do they need a table?

   B: _____

3. A: Do they have chairs?

   B: _____

4. A: Do they need a dresser?

   B: _____

5. A: Do they have a mirror?

   B: _____

6. A: Do they have curtains?

   B: _____

7. A: Does he have a bookcase?

   B: _____

8. A: Does he need curtains?

   B: _____

9. A: Does he need a sofa?

   B: _____

10. A: Does he have a chair?

   B: _____

11. A: Does he have a lamp?

   B: _____

12. A: Does he need pictures?

   B: _____

B What furniture do you have? What furniture do you need? Write four sentences.

1. _____

_____

2. _____

_____

3. _____

_____

4. _____

_____

6 Complete the description with 's, are, or aren't.

In Martin's apartment, there's _____ a big living room. There _____ two bedrooms and two bathrooms. There _____ no elevator, but there _____ stairs. He has a lot of books, so there _____ bookcases in the living room and bedrooms. There _____ any chairs in the kitchen, but there _____ a big table with chairs in the dining room. There _____ no coffee maker in the kitchen, but there _____ a microwave oven. There _____ two televisions in Martin's apartment – there _____ one television in the living room, and there _____ one television in the bedroom.

7 Answer these questions with information about your home. Use the phrases in the box.

there are no . . .	there isn't a . . .
there are some . . .	there's a . . .
there aren't any . . .	there's no . . .

1. Does your kitchen have a microwave?

   Yes, there's a microwave in my kitchen.

   No, there isn't a microwave. / No, there's no microwave.

2. Does your kitchen have a stove?

   _____

3. Do you have a sofa in your living room?

   _____

4. Do you have bookcases in your living room?

   _____

5. Does your bathroom have a clock?

   _____

6. Do you have pictures in your bedroom?

   _____

7. Does your bedroom have a closet?

   _____

8 What's wrong with this house?

A Write sentences about the house. Use *there* and the words in parentheses.

1. <u>There is no stove in the kitchen. / There isn't a stove in the kitchen.</u> (stove / kitchen)
2. _____ (chairs / dining room)
3. _____ (stove / living room)
4. _____ (refrigerator / bedroom)
5. _____ (bed / bedroom)
6. _____ (armchairs / bathroom)
7. _____ (bed / kitchen)
8. _____ (bookcases / living room)

B Write four more sentences about the house.

1. _____
2. _____
3. _____
4. _____

9 Choose the correct responses.

1. A: My apartment has a view of the park.

    B: _You're lucky._

- Guess what!
- You're lucky.

2. A: Do you need living room furniture?

    B: _____

- Yes, I do. I need a sofa and a coffee table.
- No, I don't. I need a sofa and a coffee table.

3. A: I really need a new desk.

    B: _____

- So let's go shopping this weekend.
- That's great!

4. A: Do you have chairs in your kitchen?

    B: _____

- Yes, I do. I need six chairs.
- Yes, I do. I have six chairs.

10 Draw a picture of your home. Then write a description. Use the questions in the box for ideas.

Do you live in a house or an apartment?   What rooms does your home have?
What furniture do you have?   Who lives with you?

_____

_____

_____

_____

8 Where do you work?

1 Match these jobs with the correct pictures.

1. lawyer ___c___

2. photographer _____

3. bellhop _____

4. police officer _____

5. pilot _____

6. nurse _____

7. server _____

8. salesperson _____

9. cashier _____

10. front desk clerk _____

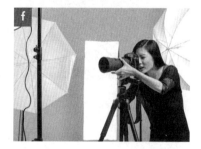

2 **What do these people do? Write three sentences about each person. Use the phrases in the box and your own ideas.**

handle food	help people	wear a uniform	work inside
handle money	sit / stand all day	work hard	work outside

1. _She's a doctor._
   She helps people.
   She works in a hospital.

2. _____

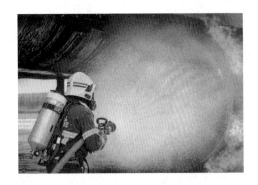

3. _____

4. _____

5. _____

6. _____

3 **Complete the questions in these conversations.**

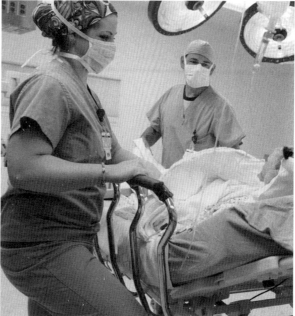

1. A: Where _does your sister work_ ?

B: My sister? She works in a restaurant.

A: What _does she do_ ?

B: She works in the kitchen. She's a chef.

2. A: What _____ ?

B: Victoria and Jon are nurses. And they work together, too.

A: Where _____ ?

B: At Springfield Hospital.

3. A: Where _____ ?

B: My daughter works in an office.

A: What _____ ?

B: She's an accountant.

4. A: What _____ ?

B: Don and I? We're software engineers.

A: How _____ ?

B: We like it a lot!

4 Complete the conversations.

1. **A:** _____Do_____ you _____have_____ a job?

   B: Yes, I _____ .

   A: Oh, what _____ you _____ ?

   B: I _____ a graphic designer.

   A: Where _____ you _____ ?

   B: I _____ at home.

   A: Oh, wow! How _____ you _____ your job?

   B: I really _____ it. It's a great job!

   A: What time _____ you start work?

   B: I _____ work at 8:00 A.M., and I _____ at 3:00 P.M.

2. **A:** My brother _____ a new job.

   B: Really? Where _____ he _____ ?

   A: He _____ at the Town Center Mall.

   B: What _____ he _____ there?

   A: He _____ a security guard.

   B: How _____ he _____ his job?

   A: Oh, I guess he _____ it.

   B: What time _____ he _____ work?

   A: He _____ work at 10:00 A.M., and he _____ at 6:00 P.M.

5 Exciting or boring?

A Match the adjectives.

1. _d_ exciting
2. _____ easy
3. _____ relaxing
4. _____ safe

a. not stressful
b. not difficult
c. not dangerous
d. not boring

B Write each sentence two different ways.

1. An actor's job is exciting.
   An actor has an exciting job.
   An actor doesn't have a boring job.

2. A security guard has a boring job.
   _____
   _____

3. Paul's job is dangerous.
   _____
   _____

4. A front desk clerk's job is stressful.
   _____
   _____

5. Amanda has a small apartment.
   _____
   _____

6. Cristina's house is big.
   _____
   _____

7. Brenda has a talkative brother.
   _____
   _____

8. My job is easy.
   _____
   _____

6 Write sentences with your opinion about each job.

athlete

mechanic

artist

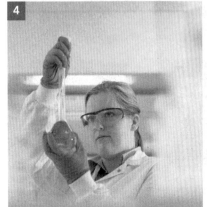

scientist

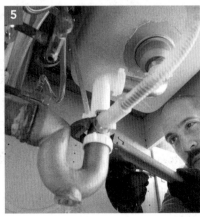

plumber

reporter

1. <u>An athlete has an exciting job. / An athlete's job isn't boring.</u>

2. _____

3. _____

4. _____

5. _____

6. _____

7 Imagine you have a dream job. Write a description. Use the questions in the box for ideas.

What's the job?	What do you do, exactly?
Where do you work?	What's the job like? (Is it dangerous, relaxing, or . . . ?)

_____

_____

_____

_____

I always eat breakfast.

1 **Write the names of the foods.**

Fruit

1. _____blueberries_____
2. _____
3. _____
4. _____

Vegetables

5. _____
6. _____
7. _____
8. _____

Grains

9. _____
10. _____
11. _____
12. _____

Dairy

13. _____
14. _____

Fats and oils

15. _____
16. _____

Meat and other proteins

17. _____
18. _____
19. _____
20. _____

2 **Complete the sentences with the articles _a_ or _an_. If you don't need an article, write Ø.**

1. This is _____a_____ tomato.   **2.** This is _____ yogurt.   **3.** This is _____ potato.

4. This is _____ egg.   **5.** This is _____ onion.   **6.** This is _____ rice.

3 **What foods do you like? What foods don't you like? Write sentences.**

1. fruit

I like bananas, oranges, and apples. I don't like lemons.

2. drinks

_____

3. vegetables

_____

4. meat and other proteins

_____

5. dairy

_____

6. grains

_____

4 **Complete the conversations with *some* or *any*.**

1. **A:** What do you eat for lunch?

   B: Well, I usually have ____*some*____ noodles in broth.

   A: That sounds good. Do you have _____ vegetables?

   B: No, I don't eat _____ vegetables for lunch.

   A: Really? Do you have anything else?

   B: Well, I usually have _____ fruit – grapes or strawberries, but I don't eat _____ dessert.

   A: Do you drink anything with your lunch?

   B: I always have _____ water and coffee. I don't put _____ milk in my coffee, but I like _____ sugar in it.

2. **A:** What do you want for dinner?

   B: Let's make _____ chicken soup.

   A: Good idea. Do we have _____ chicken?

   B: Yes, we have _____ chicken, but we don't have _____ vegetables. Let's get _____ celery and onions.

   A: OK. Do we need _____ pasta for the soup?

   B: Yes, let's get _____ pasta. Oh, and _____ garlic, too.

   A: Great. We have _____ salt and pepper, so we don't need _____ spices.

   B: Yeah, but let's get _____ bread. And _____ crackers, too.

5 **What do you need to make these foods? What don't you need? Write sentences.**

1. meatloaf

   You need some beef, crackers, eggs, and onions. You don't need any oranges.

2. a vegetable salad

3. spaghetti

4. a fish sandwich

5. a fruit salad

6. your favorite food

6 Food habits

A Put the adverbs in the correct places.

1. In Japan, people have fish for breakfast. (sometimes)

 <u>In Japan, people sometimes have fish for breakfast.</u>

2. In Canada, people have salad for breakfast. (hardly ever)

_____

3. Some people in South Korea eat pickled vegetables for breakfast. (always)

_____

4. Americans put cream in their coffee. (often)

_____

5. Brazilians make drinks with fruit. (often)

_____

6. In England, people put milk in their tea. (usually)

_____

7. Some people in Mexico eat pasta. (never)

_____

8. In China, people put sugar in their tea. (hardly ever)

_____

B Rewrite the sentences in part A. Use your own information.

1. In Japan, people sometimes have fish for breakfast.

 <u>I hardly ever have fish for breakfast. /</u>
 <u>I sometimes have cereal for breakfast.</u>

2. _____

_____

3. _____

_____

4. _____

_____

5. _____

_____

6. _____

_____

7. _____

_____

8. _____

_____

7 How often do you have these things for lunch? Write sentences. Use the adverbs in the box.

always	hardly ever	never	often	sometimes	usually

1. cheese _I hardly ever have cheese for lunch._
2. pasta _____
3. coffee _____
4. eggs _____
5. beef _____
6. rice _____
7. beans _____
8. salad _____

8 Answer the questions with your own information.

1. What's your favorite restaurant?

   _____

2. What do you usually have for dinner?

   _____

3. Do you ever cook?

   _____

4. What's your favorite kind of food?

   _____

5. What's your favorite snack?

   _____

10 What sports do you like?

1 Sports

A Match these sports with the correct pictures.

1. hockey __b__

2. basketball _____

3. bike riding _____

4. swimming _____

5. baseball _____

6. ice-skating _____

7. hiking _____

8. soccer _____

9. tennis _____

10. football _____

B Which sports in part A follow *go*? Which sports follow *play*? Complete the chart.

go		play	
_____ _____		_____hockey_____ _____	
_____ _____		_____ _____	

2 **Complete the conversation. Use the questions in the box.**

- ☐ Does your husband go snowboarding, too?
- ☑ What do you do on the weekends?
- ☐ What do you like to do in the summer?
- ☐ Who do you practice with?
- ☐ What sports do you like?

Katie: _What do you do on the weekends?_

Isabela: I like to play sports.

Katie: Really? _____

Isabela: Well, I love to go snowboarding.

Katie: _____

Isabela: No, he doesn't like cold weather. He likes to play basketball.

Katie: _____

Isabela: I like to play tennis when the weather is warm.

Katie: _____

Isabela: I practice with my sister. She loves tennis, too.

3 **Unscramble the questions. Then answer with your own information.**

1. you   do   like   volleyball

Do you like volleyball?

Yes, I do. / No, I don't.

2. sports   what   do   watch   you

_____

_____

3. you   play   sports   what   do

_____

_____

4. swimming   do   you   how   often   go

_____

_____

5. do   with   who   sports   you   play

_____

_____

4 Write questions and answers about these people.

Maddie

Doug

1. _Can Maddie run a marathon?_

   Yes, she can.

2. _____

   _____

Mariana

Felipe and Ken

3. _____

   _____

4. _____

   _____

George

Ana and Debbie

5. _____

   _____

6. _____

   _____

5 Write sentences about these people. Use *can*, *can't*, and *but*.

1. <u>He can tell good jokes,</u>
<u>but he can't play golf.</u>

2. _____

3. _____

4. _____

6 Choose the correct responses.

1. A: Do you like to play soccer?

   B: <u>No, I don't.</u>

- Yes, I can.
- No, I don't.

2. A: Who do you go bike riding with?

   B: _____

- I do.
- My friends from school.

3. A: Who can play the piano?

   B: _____

- Marco can.
- Yes, he can.

4. A: Where do you go hiking?

   B: _____

- In summer.
- In the mountains.

7 Can or can't?

A Can you do these things? Check (✓) *can* or *can't*.

	can	can't
1. sing	☐	☐
2. ice-skate	☐	☐
3. build a website	☐	☐
4. drive a car	☐	☐
5. play tennis	☐	☐
6. take good photos	☐	☐
7. speak Japanese	☐	☐
8. swim	☐	☐
9. tell good jokes	☐	☐
10. play baseball	☐	☐

B Write sentences about the things in part A.

1. I can sing really well.

2. I can't ice-skate at all.

3. _____

4. _____

5. _____

6. _____

7. _____

8. _____

9. _____

10. _____

8 **Write each sentence a different way. Use the sentences in the box.**

☐ He can play sports well. ☐ I love it.
☐ He can't dance at all. ☐ She has many talents.
☑ I hardly ever go hiking. ☐ She tells good jokes.

1. I don't go hiking very often.
   I hardly ever go hiking.

2. He's a great athlete.
   _____

3. She has a lot of abilities.
   _____

4. I really like it.
   _____

5. He's a terrible dancer.
   _____

6. She's very funny.
   _____

9 **Answer these questions with short answers. Use your own information.**

1. Can you fix a computer? _____
2. Can you speak Spanish? _____
3. Can you act? _____
4. Are you good at sports? _____
5. Are you a good student? _____
6. Do you like your English class? _____
7. Can you play a musical instrument? _____
8. Do you ever go swimming? _____
9. Do you ever play soccer? _____
10. Can you draw very well? _____

10 **What can your friends and family do? What can't they do? Write sentences.**

1. _____
2. _____
3. _____
4. _____

11 I'm going to have a party.

1 Months and dates

A Put the months in the box in time order.

☐ April	✓ January	☐ May
☐ August	☐ July	☐ November
☐ December	☐ June	☐ October
☐ February	☐ March	☐ September

1. _____January_____
2. _____
3. _____
4. _____

5. _____
6. _____
7. _____
8. _____

9. _____
10. _____
11. _____
12. _____

B When are the seasons in your country? Write the months for each season.

Spring

Summer

Fall

Winter

C Write each date a different way.

1. January 11th   _January eleventh_
2. March 15th   _____
3. November 1st   _____
4. August 16th   _____

5. July 24th   _____
6. May 10th   _____
7. February 2nd   _____
8. December 27th   _____

2 It's January first. How old are these people going to be on their next birthdays?
Write sentences.

	Lucas	Liz	Ruth and Sharon	You
Age now	16	32	68	_____
Birthday	April 12th	October 6th	September 21st	_____

1. Lucas is going to be seventeen on April twelfth. _____

2. _____

3. _____

4. _____

3 Read Tom's calendar. Write sentences about his plans. Use the words
in parentheses.

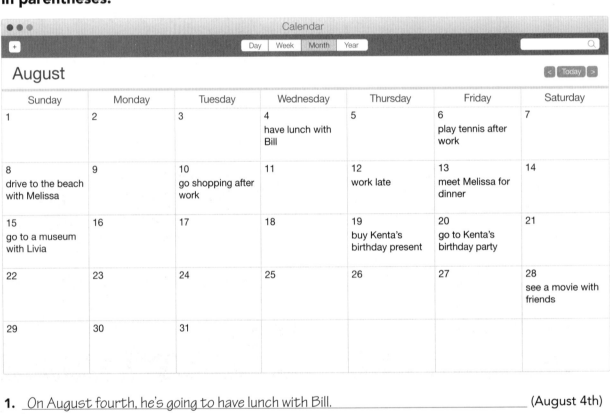

1. On August fourth, he's going to have lunch with Bill. _____ (August 4th)

2. _____ (August 6th)

3. _____ (August 8th)

4. _____ (August 10th)

5. _____ (August 12th)

6. _____ (August 13th)

7. _____ (August 15th)

8. _____ (August 19th)

9. _____ (August 20th)

10. _____ (August 28th)

4 Complete these sentences. Use the correct form of *be going to* and the verbs in parentheses.

1. This ___is going to be___ (be) a very busy weekend.

2. On Friday, my friend Joe and I _____ (see) a movie. After the movie, we _____ (eat) dinner at our favorite Mexican restaurant.

3. On Saturday morning, my parents _____ (visit). They _____ (drive) into the city, and we _____ (go) to the art museum. I think my mother _____ (love) it, but my father _____ (not like) it. Later, we _____ (watch) a baseball game on TV. My parents _____ (go) home after dinner.

4. On Sunday, I _____ (get up) early. Then I _____ (take) a walk. On Sunday afternoon, I _____ (do) yoga. In the evening, my friend Eve and I _____ (study) together.

5 Complete these conversations. Write questions with *be going to.*

1. **Eric:** _What are you going to do this weekend?_

    Alex: This weekend? I'm going to go to the city with my son.

    Eric: That's nice. _____
    _____

    Alex: We're going to stay at my sister's apartment. She lives there.

    Eric: Really? _____
    _____

    Alex: I think we're going to go to a museum.

    Eric: _____
    _____

    Alex: No, my sister isn't going to go with us. She's going to go bike riding.

2. **Scott:** I'm going to have a birthday party for Ben next Saturday. Can you come?

    Emily: Sure. _____
    _____

    Scott: It's going to be at my house. Do you have the address?

    Emily: Yes, I do. And _____
    _____

    Scott: It's going to start at seven o'clock.

    Emily: _____
    _____

    Scott: No, Bob isn't going to be there.

    Emily: That's too bad. _____
    _____

    Scott: No, I'm not going to bake a cake. I can't bake! I'm going to buy one.

    Emily: OK. Sounds good. See you on Saturday.

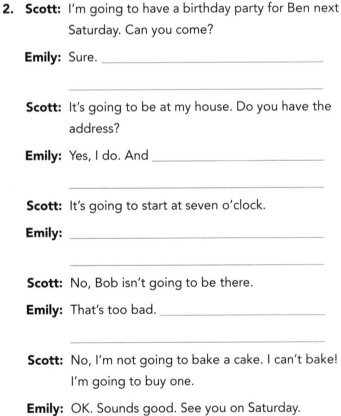

6 Next weekend

A What are these people going to do next weekend? Write sentences.

1. <u>They're going to go</u>
<u>bike riding.</u>

2. _____
_____

3. _____
_____

4. _____
_____

5. _____
_____

6. _____
_____

7. _____
_____

8. _____
_____

9. _____
_____

B What are you going to do next weekend? How about your family and friends? Write sentences.

1. _____

2. _____

3. _____

4. _____

7 Are you going to do anything special on these holidays or special occasions? Write sentences. Use the phrases in the box or your own information.

dance	go to a parade	sing songs
eat special food	go to a restaurant	stay home
give gifts	have a party	stay out late
go on a picnic	play games	watch fireworks
go out with friends	play music	wear special clothes

1. Your next birthday

I'm not going to have a party. I'm going to go to a restaurant with my friends, but we're not going to stay out late.

2. Your best friend's birthday

_____

_____

_____

3. New Year's Eve

_____

_____

_____

4. New Year's Day

_____

_____

_____

5. Valentine's Day

_____

_____

_____

6. The last day of class

_____

_____

_____

1 Label the parts of the body. Use the words in the box.

☐ arm	☐ leg
☐ ear	☐ mouth
☐ elbow	☐ neck
☑ eye	☐ nose
☐ fingers	☐ shoulder
☐ foot	☐ stomach
☐ hair	☐ teeth
☐ hand	☐ toes

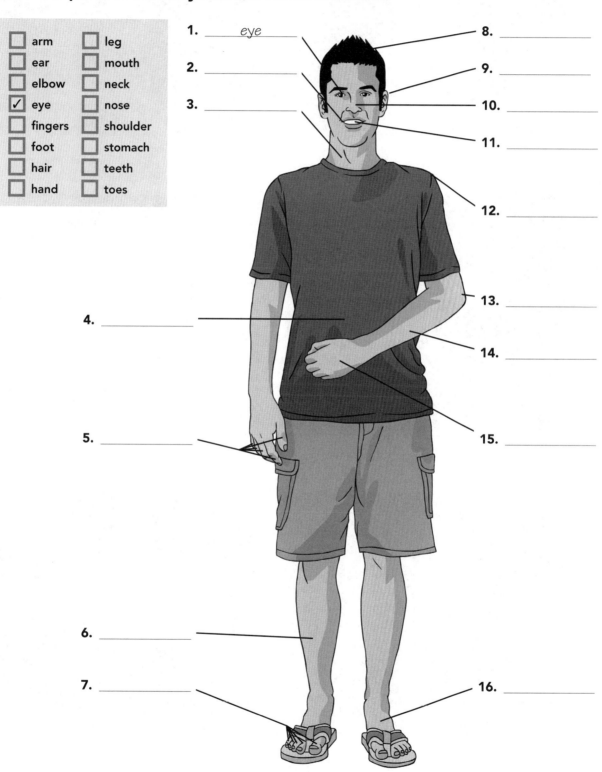

1. _eye_
2. _____
3. _____
4. _____
5. _____
6. _____
7. _____
8. _____
9. _____
10. _____
11. _____
12. _____
13. _____
14. _____
15. _____
16. _____

2 What's wrong with these people? Write sentences.

1. <u>He has a toothache.</u>

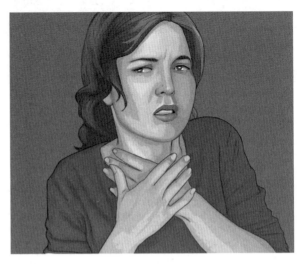

2. _____

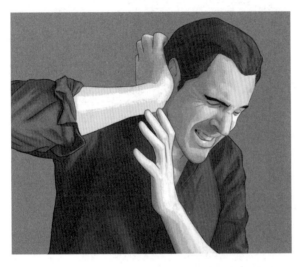

3. _____

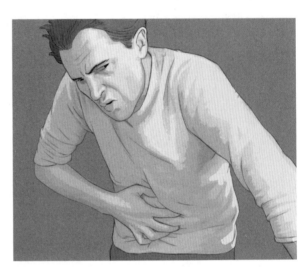

4. _____

5. _____

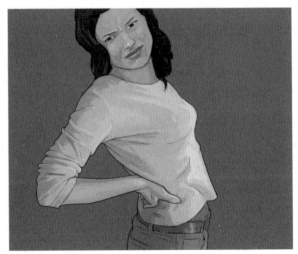

6. _____

Complete the conversations. Use the questions and sentences in the box.

☐	Great. See you later.	☐	OK. Get some rest.
☐	How do you feel today?	☐	So, are you going to go to the meeting this afternoon?
✓	I'm fine, thanks. How about you?	☐	That's too bad. Are you going to see a doctor?
☐	I'm glad to hear that.	☐	What's wrong?

Tuesday morning

1. **Jake:** Hi, Camila. How are you?

    Camila: _I'm fine, thanks. How about you?_

    Jake: Not so good. Actually, I feel really awful.

    Camila: _____

    _____

    Jake: I think I have the flu.

    Camila: _____

    _____

    Jake: No, I'm going to go home now.

    Camila: _____

    _____

    Jake: OK. Thanks.

Thursday morning

2. **Camila:** _____

    _____

    Jake: I feel much better.

    Camila: _____

    _____

    Jake: Thanks.

    Camila: _____

    _____

    Jake: Yes, I am.

    Camila: _____

    _____

Tuesday morning

Thursday morning

4 Complete the sentences with the correct medications.

1. His nose is very congested. He needs some
   _____ nasal spray _____ .

2. I have a horrible cold, so I'm going to buy
   some _____ .

3. Your eyes look red and tired. Get some
   _____ .

4. Alan has a stomachache, so he's going to get
   some _____ .

5. I have a terrible headache. I need some
   _____ .

6. Mandy's cough sounds awful. I'm going to
   give her some _____ .

5 Write each sentence a different way. Use the sentences in the box.

☐ My head feels terrible.	✔ I'm not happy.
☐ I have a stomachache.	☐ I'm sorry to hear that.
☐ What's wrong?	☐ I'm very tired.
☐ I'm glad to hear that.	☐ I have a sore throat.

1. I feel sad.
   I'm not happy.

2. What's the matter?
   _____

3. I'm exhausted.
   _____

4. That's too bad.
   _____

5. That's good.
   _____

6. I have a headache.
   _____

7. My stomach hurts.
   _____

8. My throat is sore.
   _____

6 Give these people advice. Use the phrases in the box.

☐ drink some water	☐ have a hot drink
☐ go home early	☐ lift heavy things
☑ go outside	☐ stay up late
☐ go to the grocery store	☐ work too hard

1. _Don't go outside._   **2.** _____

3. _____   **4.** _____

5. _____   **6.** _____

7. _____   **8.** _____

7 Write two pieces of advice for each problem.

1. I have a sore throat.   _Don't go to work today. Drink some chamomile tea._
2. I have a toothache. _____
3. I have a cough. _____
4. I have a cold. _____
5. I have a stomachache. _____
6. I have a headache. _____
7. I have the flu. _____
8. I have a fever. _____

8 Health survey

A How healthy and happy are you?
Complete the survey.

How often do you . . . ?

	Often	Sometimes	Hardly ever	Never
get a headache	☐	☐	☐	☐
get an earache	☐	☐	☐	☐
get a cold	☐	☐	☐	☐
get the flu	☐	☐	☐	☐
get a stomachache	☐	☐	☐	☐
stay up late	☐	☐	☐	☐
feel sleepy	☐	☐	☐	☐
get a fever	☐	☐	☐	☐

B Write four sentences about your health. Use the information from the survey in part A.

Examples:

I sometimes stay up late, but I hardly ever feel sleepy.

I hardly ever get a cold or the flu.

1. _____
2. _____
3. _____
4. _____

13 How do I get there?

1 Places

A Complete these sentences with the correct places. Write one letter on each line.

1. I work at a <u>b</u> <u>o</u> <u>o</u> <u>k</u> <u>s</u> <u>t</u> <u>o</u> <u>r</u> <u>e</u> . I love books, so it's a great job.

2. I'm going to go to the ____ ____ ____ ____ . I need a new debit card.

3. My car is almost out of gasoline. Is there a ____ ____ ____
____ ____ ____ ____ ____ ____ ____ near here?

4. Are you going to the ____ ____ ____ ____   ____ ____ ____ ____ ____ ____ ?
I need some stamps.

5. On Sundays, I buy food for my family at the
____ ____ ____ ____ ____ ____ ____ ____ ____ ____ ____ .

6. We're going to have an espresso at the ____ ____ ____ ____ ____ ____
____ ____ ____ ____ before class.

7. Anita is going to get some medicine at the ____ ____ ____ ____ ____ ____ ____ ____ ____ ____ .

8. My son is going to school next week. We're going to the
____ ____ ____ ____ ____ ____ ____ ____   ____ ____ ____ ____ ____
downtown to buy him a backpack.

B Match the pictures to the places in part A.

2 Look at the map. Complete the sentences with the prepositions in the box.

- [ ] across from
- [ ] behind
- [ ] between
- [ ] next to
- [✓] on
- [ ] on the corner of

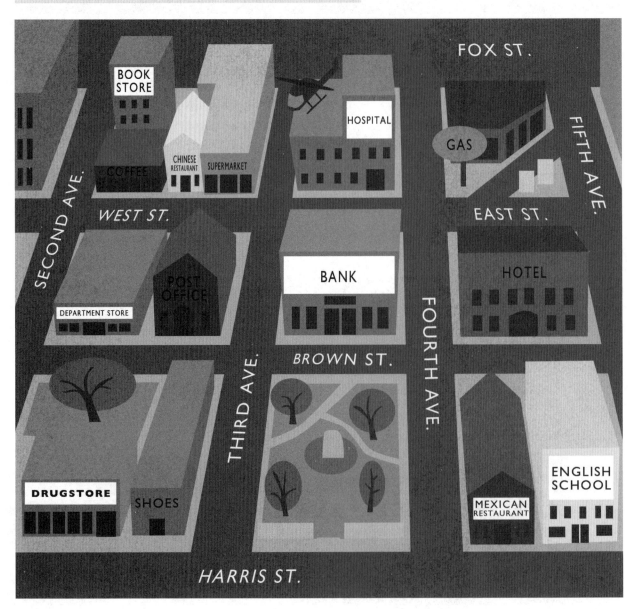

1. The department store is _____on_____ Brown Street.
2. The hospital is _____ the bank.
3. The bookstore is _____ Fox Street and Second Avenue.
4. The Chinese restaurant is on West Street, _____ the coffee shop and the supermarket.
5. The shoe store is _____ the drugstore.
6. The Mexican restaurant is _____ the park.

3 Where is it?

A Look at the map in Exercise 2 again. Where is each place? Write two sentences.

1. post office   _The post office is on the corner of Brown Street_
                and Third Avenue. It's next to the department store.

2. supermarket _____

3. English school _____

4. gas station _____

5. coffee shop _____

6. hotel _____

7. drugstore _____

8. bank _____

B Where is your school? Draw a map. Then write two sentences.

4 Complete the conversation. Use the sentences and questions in the box.

☑ Excuse me. Can you help me?   ☐ Thanks a lot.
☐ Is there a restroom around here?   ☐ Where on West Street?
☐ Next to the Chinese restaurant?

Tom: _Excuse me. Can you help me?_

Woman: Sure.

Tom: _____

Woman: Yes, there is. It's in the supermarket on West Street.

Tom: _____

Woman: It's on the corner of West Street and Third Avenue.

Tom: _____

Woman: Yes, that's right. It's right next to the Chinese restaurant.

Tom: _____

Woman: You're welcome.

5 Complete the sentences with the opposites.

1. The post office isn't on the right. It's on the _____left_____ .
2. The Empire State Building is far from here, but Central Park is _____ here. You can walk there.
3. Don't walk down Columbus Avenue. Walk _____ Columbus Avenue.
4. The New London Hotel isn't in front of the bank. It's _____ it.
5. Don't turn left on Sixteenth Street. Turn _____ .

6 **Look at the map. Give these people directions.**
Use the phrases and sentences in the box.

It's on the left/right.	Walk down/Go down . . . Street/Avenue.
Turn left on . . . Street/Avenue.	Walk to . . . Street/Avenue.
Turn right on . . . Street/Avenue.	Walk up/Go up . . . Street/Avenue.

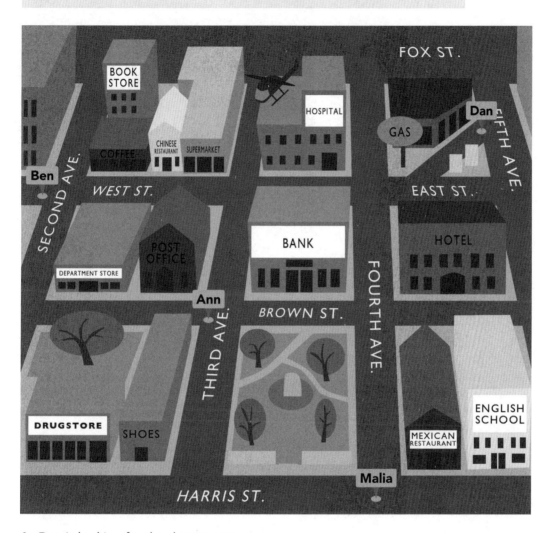

1. Dan is looking for the department store.

 Walk down Fifth Avenue. Turn right on Brown Street.

 Walk to Second Avenue. It's on the right.

2. Malia is looking for the Chinese restaurant.

 _____

 _____

3. Ben is looking for the Mexican restaurant.

 _____

 _____

4. Ann is looking for the bookstore.

 _____

 _____

7 **Imagine you're going to have a party. Complete the invitation. Then draw a map and write directions to the party from your school.**

MAP TO THE PARTY

PARTY

DATE: _____

TIME: _____

PLACE: _____

DIRECTIONS TO THE PARTY

Start at the school. Then _____

_____

_____

_____

14 I had a good time.

Last Saturday

A What did these people do last Saturday? Write sentences.

1	2	3	4
visit relatives	**answer email**	**exercise**	**clean the house**
5	6	7	8
do the laundry	**study**	**wash the car**	**go grocery shopping**

1. _They visited relatives._   5. _____
2. _____   6. _____
3. _____   7. _____
4. _____   8. _____

B What did you do last Saturday? Write three sentences.

1. _____
2. _____
3. _____

2 **Kim and Alisha are sending text messages. Complete the sentences. Use the simple past form of the verbs in parentheses.**

Messages

Alisha

How was your weekend?

Kim

It was really busy. I ___worked___ (work) on Friday, then I _____ (invite) friends over after work. I _____ (cook) dinner for them. We _____ (listen) to music and _____ (talk) about work, but they _____ (not stay) very late.

Alisha

What did you do on Saturday and Sunday?

Kim

I _____ (get up) early on Saturday because I _____ (play) basketball with Angela. Then I _____ (visit) relatives. We _____ (walk) downtown and _____ (eat) dinner. Oh, and we _____ (see) a movie. On Sunday, I _____ (study) for my math test with my friends. I _____ (do) laundry on Sunday afternoon, too.

Alisha

Wow! That was a busy weekend! I _____ (not do) much this weekend. I _____ (answer) email on Friday night and I _____ (watch) TV, too. On Saturday, I _____ (not get up) early. I _____ (clean) the house and I _____ (go) grocery shopping. I _____ (not do) anything on Sunday!

3 Claudia and Hiro did different things last weekend. Write sentences about them.

Claudia

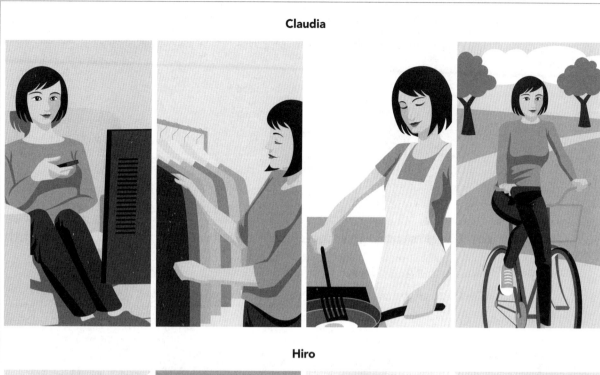

Hiro

1. watch TV   <u>Claudia watched TV. Hiro didn't watch TV.</u>

2. go to a museum   _____

3. ride a bicycle   _____

4. cook   _____

5. study   _____

6. shop   _____

7. play tennis   _____

4 Complete the chart.

Present	Past	Present	Past
buy	_____bought_____	go	_____
come	_____	_____	had
_____	did	read	_____
eat	_____	ride	_____
_____	felt	_____	saw
_____	met	sit	_____

5 Complete the conversation. Use the simple past forms of the verbs in parentheses.

Aaron: So, Beth, _____did_____ you
_____have_____ (have) a good summer?

Beth: Well, I _____ (have) an interesting
summer. My sister and her family
_____ (come) to visit for two weeks.

Aaron: That's nice.

Beth: Yes and no. My sister _____ (not feel)
well, so she _____ (sit) on the sofa
and _____ (watch) TV. She hardly ever
_____ (get up).

Aaron: Oh, well. _____ her husband and kids
_____ (have) a good time?

Beth: I think so. They _____ (play) volleyball
and _____ (ride) their bikes every day.

Aaron: _____ you _____ (go out) to
any restaurants?

Beth: No, I _____ (cook) breakfast,
lunch, and dinner every day.
They _____ (eat) a lot of food, but
they _____ (not wash) any dishes.

Aaron: That's too bad. _____ you _____ (relax) at all last summer?

Beth: Yes. My sister and her family finally _____ (go) home, and then
I _____ (relax). I just _____ (read) some books and
_____ (listen) to music.

6 Unscramble the questions about last summer. Then answer with your own information.

Last summer, . . . ?

1. did any books you read good

A: _Did you read any good books?_

B: _Yes, I did. I read three great books. / No, I didn't. I read one boring book._

2. go interesting anywhere you did

A: _____

B: _____

3. any take did you pictures

A: _____

B: _____

4. buy you did anything interesting

A: _____

B: _____

5. did eat you foods any new

A: _____

B: _____

6. games did you any play

A: _____

B: _____

7. you did sports play any

A: _____

B: _____

8. you did interesting meet any people

A: _____

B: _____

9. any see you did movies good

A: _____

B: _____

7 Summer activities

A The Johnson family did many fun activities last summer. Write sentences about them.

1. _They rode horses._

2. _____

3. _____

4. _____

5. _____

6. _____

7. _____

8. _____

B Write sentences about your activities last summer.

1. _____

2. _____

3. _____

4. _____

1 **Complete the conversation. Use the sentences in the box.**

☐ I was sixteen.	☐ No, it wasn't. I loved it!
☑ No, I wasn't. I was born in Europe.	☐ No, I'm from Belgium.
☐ We came here for my father's job.	☐ We moved here in 2009.
☐ I was born in Brussels.	☐ Yes, they were. We were all born there.

Jason: Were you born here in the U.S., Marie?

Marie: _No, I wasn't. I was born in Europe._

Jason: Oh, were you born in France?

Marie: _____

Jason: Really? What city were you born in?

Marie: _____

Jason: Were your parents born in Brussels, too?

Marie: _____

Jason: And why did you come to the U.S.?

Marie: _____

Jason: So when did you move here?

Marie: _____

Jason: Really? How old were you then?

Marie: _____

Jason: Was it scary?

Marie: _____

2 Complete these conversations with *was*, *wasn't*, *were*, or *weren't*.

1. **Sandra:** _____Were_____ you born in the U.S., Ivan?

   Ivan: Yes, I _____ . My brother and I _____ born here in Miami.

   Sandra: I _____ born here, too. What about your parents? _____ they born here?

   Ivan: Well, my father _____ . He _____ born in Cuba, but my mother _____ born in the U.S. – in Detroit.

   Sandra: Detroit? Really? My parents _____ born in Detroit, too!

2. **Kristin:** I called you on Saturday, but you _____ home.

   Jennifer: No, I _____ . I _____ at the beach all weekend.

   Kristin: That's nice. How _____ the weather there?

   Jennifer: It _____ beautiful.

   Kristin: _____ your parents there?

   Jennifer: No, they _____ . I _____ with my sister. It _____ great!

3. **Mindy:** _____ you in college last year, Alan?

   Alan: No, I _____ . I graduated from college two years ago.

   Mindy: So where _____ you last year?

   Alan: I _____ in Japan.

   Mindy: Oh! _____ you in Tokyo?

   Alan: No, I _____ . I _____ in Osaka. I had a job there.

   Mindy: What _____ the job?

   Alan: I _____ an English teacher.

3 **Write four sentences about each person.**

Marie Curie, scientist
(1867–1934)
- born in Poland
- won Nobel Prizes in 1903 and 1911

Gabriel García Márquez, author (1927–2014)
- born in Colombia
- wrote *One Hundred Years of Solitude*, 1967

Maya Angelou, author (1928–2014)
- born in the U.S.
- wrote *I Know Why the Caged Bird Sings*, 1969

Pat Morita, actor
(1932–2005)
- born in the U.S.
- was in the movie *The Karate Kid*, 1984

Grace Kelly, actress
(1929–1982)
- born in the U.S.
- married Prince Rainier III of Monaco, 1956

Salvador Dalí, artist
(1904–1989)
- born in Spain
- painted *The Persistence of Memory*, 1931

1. Marie Curie was a scientist. She was born in 1867 in Poland.
   She won Nobel Prizes in 1903 and 1911. She died in 1934.

2. _____

3. _____

4. _____

5. _____

6. _____

4 Complete these questions. Use the words in the box.

☐ How ☐ How old ☑ What ☐ When ☐ Where ☐ Who ☐ Why

1. **A:** _____What_____ was your favorite subject in high school?

   B: It was art.

2. **A:** _____ was your favorite teacher?

   B: My art teacher, Mrs. Heintz.

3. **A:** _____ did you graduate from high school?

   B: In 2006.

4. **A:** _____ did you go to college?

   B: I went to Duke University.

5. **A:** _____ did you study physics?

   B: Because I wanted to become an astronaut!

6. **A:** _____ were your professors in college?

   B: They were great.

7. **A:** _____ were you when you graduated?

   B: I was 22 years old.

5 Write whether each sentence is *true* or *false*. Correct the false sentences.

1. Students usually go to middle school before elementary school.

   False. Students usually go to middle school after elementary school. /

   Students usually go to elementary school before middle school.

2. Students often study in the library.

   _____

3. Students never eat lunch in the cafeteria.

   _____

4. Physical education classes are almost always in an auditorium.

   _____

5. Students usually study history and science in high school.

   _____

6 Unscramble the questions about your elementary school days. Then answer with your own information.

1. was your of school how first day

  A: _How was your first day of school?_

  B: _____

2. your was teacher who favorite

  A: _____

  B: _____

3. favorite was your what class

  A: _____

  B: _____

4. your who best were friends

  A: _____

  B: _____

5. spend did your where you free time

  A: _____

  B: _____

6. leave did when you elementary school

  A: _____

  B: _____

7 Childhood memories

A Complete the questions with *did*, *was*, or *were*. Then answer the questions. Use short answers.

1. **A:** _____Were_____ you born here?

   B: _Yes, I was. / No, I wasn't._

2. **A:** _____ you grow up in a big city?

   B: _____

3. **A:** _____ you play sports?

   B: _____

4. **A:** _____ your home near your school?

   B: _____

5. **A:** _____ you ride a bus to school?

   B: _____

6. **A:** _____ you a good student?

   B: _____

7. **A:** _____ your teachers nice?

   B: _____

8. **A:** _____ you have a lot of friends?

   B: _____

9. **A:** _____ your grandparents live near you?

   B: _____

10. **A:** _____ both your parents work?

    B: _____

B Write sentences about your childhood.

1. _____

   _____

2. _____

   _____

3. _____

   _____

4. _____

   _____

5. _____

   _____

6. _____

   _____

16 Can I take a message?

1 **Make a phone conversation. Use the sentences and questions in the box.**

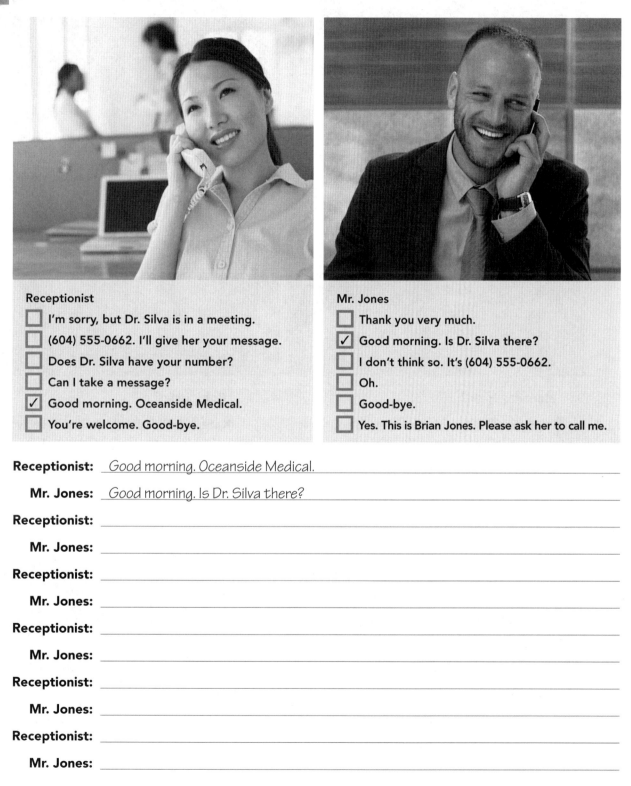

Receptionist
- ☐ I'm sorry, but Dr. Silva is in a meeting.
- ☐ (604) 555-0662. I'll give her your message.
- ☐ Does Dr. Silva have your number?
- ☐ Can I take a message?
- ☑ Good morning. Oceanside Medical.
- ☐ You're welcome. Good-bye.

Mr. Jones
- ☐ Thank you very much.
- ☑ Good morning. Is Dr. Silva there?
- ☐ I don't think so. It's (604) 555-0662.
- ☐ Oh.
- ☐ Good-bye.
- ☐ Yes. This is Brian Jones. Please ask her to call me.

Receptionist: *Good morning. Oceanside Medical.*

Mr. Jones: *Good morning. Is Dr. Silva there?*

Receptionist: _____

Mr. Jones: _____

Receptionist: _____

Mr. Jones: _____

Receptionist: _____

Mr. Jones: _____

Receptionist: _____

Mr. Jones: _____

Receptionist: _____

Mr. Jones: _____

2 **Kate called her friends yesterday. Where were they? Complete the conversations. Use the words in the box.**

☐ bed	☐ hospital	☐ library	☑ mall	☐ vacation	☐ work

1. **Sally:** Hello?

    Kate: Hello, Sally? It's Kate.

    Sally: Oh, hi, Kate. Listen. I can't talk right now. I'm _at the mall_ . Call me later?

2. **Jay:** Hello?

    Kate: Hey, Jay. It's –

    Jay: Kate. Sorry, can you call me in the morning? I'm _____ .

3. **Marcela:** Hello?

    Kate: Hi, Marcela. It's Kate. Do you want to see a movie tonight?

    Marcela: I'd love to, but I can't. I'm _____ with my parents.

4. **Bob:** Hello?

    Kate: Hi, Bob. It's Kate. You know, you sound terrible. Are you OK?

    Bob: Not really. I'm _____ . I broke my leg!

5. **Angie:** Hello?

    Kate: Hello, Angie? It's Kate. Why are you whispering? Where are you?

    Angie: Oh, I'm _____ .

6. **Pedro:** Hello?

    Kate: Hey, Pedro. Do you have a minute?

    Pedro: Not really. I'm _____ . Call me tonight.

3 Unscramble the sentences.

1. with   night   I   him   studied   last   .

   I studied with him last night.

2. you   help   I   can   ?

   _____

3. her   the   gave   they   book   .

   _____

4. remember   you   me   do   ?

   _____

5. his   I   call   missed   yesterday   .

   _____

6. weekend   last   we   them   visited   .

   _____

4 Heidi is checking her voice-mail messages. Complete the messages with the correct pronouns.

Ann's message

Hello, Miss Anderson. This is Ann Lopez. _____I_____
work at First City Bank. _____ left your
wallet here this morning. Please call _____
at (808) 555-1247. I'd like to give it back to
_____ before we close today.

Jim's message

Hey, Heidi. It's Jim. I'm sorry _____
missed your call yesterday. Listen, my friends and I
are going to go out for coffee tomorrow morning.
_____ 're meeting at my house at 9:00.
Would you like to join _____ ? Give
_____ a call!

Sarah's message

Hi, Heidi. It's Sarah. Did you see Marco today?
_____ 's having a birthday party on Friday.
Do you want to go with _____ ? I'm
going to buy _____ a present later. Call
_____ ! Thanks!

5 Complete the phone conversation. Use the words in the box.

☐ at   ☐ call   ☐ does   ☐ her   ☐ please
☐ but   ☑ can   ☐ have   ☐ in   ☐ this

Allison: Hello?

Evan: Hello. _____Can_____ I speak to
Roberta, _____ ?

Allison: I'm sorry, _____ she's
_____ a meeting. Can I give
_____ a message?

Evan: Yes. _____ is Evan Martin.
Please ask her to _____ me.
I'm _____ work.

Allison: Does she _____ your
number?

Evan: Yes, she _____ .

6 Complete the excuses. Use your own ideas.

1. A: Can you drive me to class this evening?
   B: I'm sorry, but I have to _____babysit_____ .

2. A: Do you want to see a movie with me this weekend?
   B: I'd like to, but I need to _____ .

3. A: Can you walk my dog on Sunday?
   B: I'm sorry, but I can't. I have to _____ .

4. A: Can you help me with my homework tonight?
   B: I'm sorry, but I can't. I have to _____ .

5. A: Would you like to play tennis on Saturday?
   B: I'd like to, but I need to _____ .

6. A: Can you go to the mall this weekend?
   B: I'm sorry, but I have to _____ .

7 **Imagine your friends invite you to do these things. Accept or refuse their invitations as indicated. Use the phrases and sentences in the box.**

Accepting	Refusing and making excuses
I'd love to.	I'm sorry, but I can't. I have to / need to / want to . . .
I'd like to.	I'd like to, but I have to / need to / want to . . .

1. **A:** Do you want to play soccer with us this afternoon?

   B: (refuse) _I'd like to, but I have to work._

2. **A:** Do you want to have dinner with me tomorrow?

   B: (refuse) _____

   _____

3. **A:** Do you want to study at my house after class?

   B: (accept) _____

4. **A:** Do you want to go swimming with me on Saturday morning?

   B: (accept) _____

5. **A:** Do you want to go hiking with me this weekend?

   B: (refuse) _____

   _____

8 **Complete each sentence with *like to*, *love to*, or *want to*.**

1. **A:** Would you _____like to_____ go to Bill's party on Thursday night?

   B: I'd _____ go, but I have to study. I have a test on Friday.

2. **A:** Do you _____ play tennis after work?

   B: I'd _____ , but I have to work late.

3. **A:** Would you _____ have dinner at our house?

   B: Yes, I'd _____ !

4. **A:** Do you _____ visit the science museum tomorrow?

   B: I'd _____ go, but I already have plans.

5. **A:** Would you _____ go to the movies tonight?

   B: Yes, but I don't _____ see *Horror House 3*. I don't like scary movies!

6. **A:** Do you _____ leave a message?

   B: Yes, please tell Dr. O'Brien that I'd _____ speak with her about our meeting.

9 **Answer the questions. Write sentences with *like to*, *want to*, and *need to*.**

1. Where are two places you want to visit?

I want to visit Seoul, South Korea.

I want to visit Rio de Janeiro, Brazil.

2. What are two things you like to do often?

_____

_____

3. What are two things you need to do this week?

_____

_____

4. Who are two famous people you want to meet?

_____

_____

5. What are two foods you like to eat?

_____

_____

6. What are two things you want to do this year?

_____

_____

7. What are two things you like to do after class?

_____

_____

8. Where are two places you like to go on weekends?

_____

_____